The
Medieval Warrior

✤

The
Medieval Warrior

PAUL LACROIX

AND

WALTER CLIFFORD MELLER

FEATURING THE ILLUSTRATIONS OF

JOHN BATCHELOR

INTRODUCTION BY

WILLIAM YENNE

BCL PRESS
NEW YORK

Published by BCL Press/Book Creation,LLC,
New York, by arrangement with O.G. Publishing Corp.
© 2002 O.G. Publishing Corp.

Produced by AGS BookWorks
PO Box 460313
San Francisco, CA 94146
agsbookworks.com

Design and text © 2002 American Graphic Systems, Inc.
Illustrations, except as otherwise noted, are © Collection of William Yenne.

ISBN 0-9710070-5-5
Printed and bound in China

Designed by Bill Yenne with design assistance from Azia Yenne.
Proofreading by Joan B. Hayes. Captioning by Bill Yenne.

All illustrations are from the private collection of William Yenne
(and are provided exclusively for this publication
by special permission), with the following exceptions:

© John Batchelor: 2, 29, 34, 43, 54, 65, 66-67, 68, 71,
75, 78, 80, 103, 106-107, 114-115, covers.

The Dore Library:
57, 95, 96, 129, 141, 143, 145, 146, 153, 155, 160.

Dover: 1, 4, 45, 50

IMSI: 23 (top), 30, 31, 52, 53, 69 (both), 70 (both), 72 (bottom),
73, 76, 77, 81, 82, 84 (bottom), 105, 108, 112, 118 (bottom), 120
(bottom), 123 (top), 124, 126 (bottom), 125 (top), 140.

Western Museum of Ethnography, European Special Collections:
10 (both), 49, 74, 91 (top), 117, 128, 139, 150,
151 (bottom), 154 (bottom), 156, 157.

The illustrations above and on page one are medieval Celtic insignias.
The illustration on page two of an early — fifteenth — century
German knight is by John Batchelor.

Table of Contents

INTRODUCTION 6

THE WORLD OF THE
    MEDIEVAL WARRIOR 8
    A Bloody World 8
    The Early Medieval Warlords 11
    The Origin and Organization of
        Feudalism 15
    Feudalism in France 16
    Feudalism in Italy 19
    Feudalism in the North 20
    Feudalism in England 21
    The Cruel Aspects of Feudalism 22
    The Decline of Feudalism 23

A KNIGHT'S LIFE 28
    A Portrait of the Knight 30
    The Birth of a Knight 30
    The Child Knight 31
    Training for Knighthood 35
    Preparing the Youth for Knighthood 36
    The Esquire 37
    Growing into Knighthood 38
    Classes of Esquires 39
    Alternative Paths to Knighthood 40
    The Calendar of Investiture 42
    Confession 42
    Conferring Knighthood 44
    The Vigil and Bath 45
    Forms of Investiture 46
    Ecclesiastical Knighting 47
    L'Ordene de Chevalerie 48
    The Vows of Knighthood 49
    Failing to Achieve Knighthood 49
    The First Act by the New Knight 51
    Punishment and Degradation 51
    The Code of the Knight 52
    The Virtue of Gallantry 53
    Pursuit of Good 53
    A Knight's Garments 55
    The Knight's Finery 55
    Wearing Their Lady's Colors 55
    The Privileges of Knighthood 56

THE DEATH OF A KNIGHT 58
    Warlords on Their Deathbeds 58
    Penance by Proxy 60
    Funeral Preparations 61
    Coffins and Burial Rituals 62

MEDIEVAL ARMS AND ARMOR 64
    The Sword 64
    Helmets and Body Armor 67
    Archers 73
    The Crossbow 74
    Superseding the Crossbow 74
    Advancements in Weapons 74
    Infantry Arms and Armor 76
    The Medieval Warhorse 78
    Horse Armor 83
    Draft Horses 83

THE MEDIEVAL ART OF WAR 84
    Medieval Warriors and Their Art 84
    Wars Against the Huns
        and the Rise of the Goths 87
    Feudal Warfare 88
    Insignia 91
    Order Within the Ranks 92
    Free-Lancers 92
    Enlistment 92
    Banners 93
    Ways of Acquiring a Banner 94
    Demanding a Banner 94
    Attacking Fortifications 94

TOURNAMENTS AND JOUSTS 98
    What Were Tournaments? 100
    Proclaiming a Tournament 102
    Preparing for a Tournament 102
    The Laws of Chivalry Regarding
        the Tournament 104
    The Night Before 104
    The Tournament 105
    The Tournament Lance 105
    Cheering at the Tournament 106
    Pas D'Armes and Jousts 109
    The Joust 109
    The Ladies' Day 110
    In Lieu of Battle 111
    For the Ladies 111
    Weapons of the Joust 111
    The Scale and Violence of
        Tournaments 112
    A Tournament on Magdalene's Day 113
    The Duel 115

THE MYSTIQUE OF CHIVALRY 118
    When Chivalry Was in Flower 120
    The Origins of Chivalry 122
    In Service of the Ideal Woman 122
    The Nature of Chivalry 123
    Chivalry During the Collapse
        of Feudalism 124
    Chivalry During the Crusades 125

WOMEN IN THE WORLD OF THE
    MEDIEVAL WARRIOR 126
    Courts of Love 126
    Damsels in the Service of the Warrior 128
    Women Warriors 128

THE MEDIEVAL WARRIOR AT
    HOME 130
    The Medieval Hall and Table 130
    Self-Sufficiency 133
    At Home in the Castle 133
    Splendor in the Castle 134
    The Household of Gaston, Count of Foix 134
    The Chapel and Churches 135
    The Hunt 136
    The Dogs 137
    Falconry 137
    Indoor Amusements: Chess and Dice 138
    Ladies and Chess 138

THE CRUSADES 140
    Pilgrimages 142
    The First Crusade 142
    Leaders of the Crusade 144
    The Second and Third Crusades 147
    The Fourth and "Children's" Crusades 148
    The Fifth Crusade 148
    The Sixth and Seventh Crusades 149
    The Failure of the Crusades 149
    Military Orders 150
    The Results of the Crusades 151

EPILOGUE: THE DECLINE OF
    MEDIEVAL SOCIETY 154
    The Evolution of Late-Medieval Armies 156
    French Standing Armies 157
    Nostalgia for the Old Days 157

INDEX 158

Introduction

BY WILLIAM YENNE

THE MIDDLE AGES were the epoch of the warrior. It was an era of almost constant warfare punctuated by the grand adventure of the Crusades, in which the medieval Christian warriors of Europe met the medieval Moslem warriors of the East. Indeed, they met not only in battle but also in the realm of ideas, and this, in turn, enriched the complexity of chivalry and the code of conduct of the warrior.

The Middle Ages span the years, roughly from the rise of Charlemagne in the late eighth century to the flowering of the Renaissance at the beginning of the sixteenth century. Those years were an era in Western civilization when a political force — such as was represented in earlier times by the Roman Empire — did not exist.

There did exist, however, a unifying force. This was the complex code of knighthood that prevailed in England, France, Germany, Italy, and beyond. Knighthood and chivalry governed all of medieval society, not just the knights themselves. These complex ideals affected not only the daily lives of the medieval warriors but the lives of all those around them.

This book is adapted from the nineteenth-and early-twentieth century scholarship of Paul LaCroix and Walter Clifford Meller, two of the most highly regarded students of medieval warriorhood who ever penned a treatise. In the nineteenth century, few historians studied the military life of the Middle Ages in more detail than Paul LaCroix. His work relied on original source material — much of it lost since he worked with it — in which he

examined not only the armaments and tactics of the Middle Ages but the culture of the medieval military classes as well. Meller is without peer for his insightful studies of chivalry. He examines the knights and warriors, as well as the doctrine of chivalry, and how this system of ethical ideals developed among the knights. He shows how chivalry was born within feudal society, combining military virtues with those of Christianity.

LaCroix and Meller give us a rare view of the medieval warrior, a truly distinguished character in the history of our civilization. The rules by which he bound himself created a unique individual. He swore not to avoid the perilous nor to turn out of his way for fear of meeting powerful enemies, or from any dread of monsters, savage beasts, or spirits. He committed himself to defending the honor of a lady, and to dying rather than desert her or suffer her to be offended. He swore allegiance to the code of chivalry, a system of honor and duty by which the medieval European knight sought to distinguish himself from other warriors of the Middle Ages.

Derived from the French *cheval* and the Latin *caballus*, chivalry had three aspects: the military, the social, and the religious. As Meller points out, in the military sense, chivalry was the heavy cavalry of the Middle Ages which constituted the chief and most effective warrior force. From a social point of view, knighthood was a great honor reserved for the warrior class. Knighthood was not hereditary, though only the sons of a knight were eligible for its ranks. In boyhood, they were sent to the court of a

Above: Medieval warriors embarking, under their banners, for the crusades.

noble, where they were trained in the use of horses and weapons, and were taught lessons of courtesy. From the thirteenth century, the candidates, after they had attained the rank of squire, were allowed to take part in battles.

In this book, we present a detailed look at the medieval warrior in combat, at home and in that unique military game, the tournament.

As we see in the writings of LaCroix and Meller, the tournament becomes a microcosm of medieval warriorhood, in terms of the arms and armor as well as the devotion to chivalry and the honor of women.

The tournament, indeed, was looked upon as a veritable military school, for by these voluntary and regulated combats a warrior exercised himself and trained himself for that offensive and defensive strife which entirely filled the life of the medieval warrior.

Here, too, he learned that subtlety and "finesse" in fighting which made the knights so victorious in other lands, for it was not so much brute force as a dexterity in wielding his arms that made those arms bring him victory.

Despite the style and sophistication implicit in chivalry and

Above: Medieval warriors and a lady.

knighthood, the world of the medieval warrior was a harsh one. At home, security required a great stone fortress or castle, which was usually cold and drafty — not to mention expensive to staff. Between the castles and the surrounding towns, the medieval countryside was a dangerous place ruled by outlaws and brigands, against whom only a fully armed and armored knight was safe.

In battle, which was an isolated moment of activity in dirty, tiring campaigns lasting months or years, the warrior faced opponents wielding cruel weapons such as rusty battle axes and boiling oil poured from the tops of parapets.

The Middle Ages were a distant and different time, but one that excites the imagination. Paul LaCroix and Walter Clifford Meller have done a masterful job of capturing this world of the medieval warrior. In presenting their work, we have retained their colorful prose style, which is itself a charming artifact of a past era.

This, then, is the story of the the knights and their world, the battles fought, the times in which they lived, and the codes of conduct that made the medieval warriors unique in the history of the world.

The World of the Medieval Warrior

URING THE MIDDLE AGES, Europe was a feudal society, with a strict caste system. The kings and feudal lords were at the top, with the clergy at their right hand. The knights and warriors were next in line, with the common people arranged beneath and the poor, landless serfs and vassals at the bottom.

In Europe, feudalism had long been gradually developing among the Franks and related peoples who recaptured Roman Gaul from the Romans. Their great leader, Clovis, shared dominion over this territory among his comrades in arms, for it had been won at the price of their blood while fighting under his orders. From the day when, by his miraculous baptism after the victory at Tolbiac, he became a Christian, there simultaneously sprang into existence a theocratic and a martial aristocracy that was to define medieval warriorhood in Europe and beyond.

A Bloody World

In Thuringia and Saxony, Ireland and Norway, the ancient Celtic and Teutonic societies that were thought of as "barbarian" by Roman society resisted longer than elsewhere the growing influence of Christianity. They exhibit their

ABOVE: A "BARBARIAN" WARRIOR.

semi-paganism in certain passages of *The Ring of the Nibelung*, the German epic poem of the thirteenth century (popularized in the nineteenth century by Richard Wagner's operatic cycle), in which ancient Teutonic mythology and symbolism are still clear and distinct.

Between the seventh and the eleventh centuries the traces of these origins still strongly showed themselves among the Franks, whose bravery consisted in spilling their blood, in fearing nothing, and in sparing no one.

This thirst for blood was not unknown in the sunny south of Europe, specifically in Italy and the South of France. However, here, people's dispositions were amiable and gentle, and as far back as the eleventh century chivalric gallantry was regulated by fixed laws, and gave birth to a learned and refined school of poetry. From Provence, this spirit of gallantry and poetry made its way into Italy and Sicily, where the barbarous Teutonic knights had been so frequently turned into ridicule. Eventually, little by little, German chivalry was affected by these southern influences.

In Great Britain, where the actual has always overshadowed the ideal, chivalry remained cold and aristocratic. Meanwhile, it was passionately worshiped by the Spaniards, those noble descendants of the

ABOVE: CLOVIS, KING OF THE FRANKS, AND A VANQUISHED ENEMY.

Goths and Iberians, whose struggle with the Arabs was one long tournament that lasted for more than seven centuries.

In religious countries, chivalry assumed monastic characteristics. Among nations of a festive and lively disposition, it verged on the voluptuous and licentious. Alphonso X, King of Leon and Castile, forced his subjects to submit to monkish regulations and prescribed the shape of their clothes, as well as the manner in which they were to spend their time.

In Provence, chivalry regarded unlawful lore with an indulgent eye, and made a jest of marriage. Chivalry was, in fact, a fraternal association, or, rather, an enthusiastic compact between men of feeling and courage, delicacy and devotion; such, at least, was the noble aim it had in view, and which it constantly strove to attain. However praiseworthy its motives and intentions, chivalry was not favorably regarded by everybody.

In its feudal aspect it was displeasing to sovereigns, who constantly endeavored to create beside it, and sometimes above it, a nobility of the sword, an individual and personal rank that could not be handed down from father to son.

Frederick Barbarossa knighted peasants who had displayed personal bravery on the field of battle. As for the Church, it contented itself with warning the medieval warriors against too bellicose a spirit, and with imbuing them as far as possible with the sentiments of Christian charity. In fact, knights were frequently considered to be a species of Levite. "There was," says *L'Ordene de Chevalerie,* "a great resemblance between the duties of a knight and those of a priest." Thence the reason that the priest was "the hero of the faith," and the knight "the pontiff of true honor." Thence the name of ordene, or ordination, given to the investiture of knighthood.

In the sixteenth century, the Spanish knight Don Ignatio (Ignatius) de Loyola, who became so famous as the founder of the Order of the Jesuits, made himself a knight of

ABOVE AND BELOW: CRUCIFIXION AND EPIPHANY IN TWELFTH-CENTURY FRENCH STAINED GLASS.

the Virgin and solemnized his entrance into God's service. According to medieval custom, this meant keeping the *veillée des armes.* This was the night watch kept over his armor by the candidate for admission to the order of knighthood before the sacred image of the mother of Christ.

The Church has never forbidden legitimate wars, although it seeks to maintain peace and has a horror of bloodshed, and thus good King St. Louis never shrank on the field of battle from driving his sword up to the very hilt into his enemy's heart. The Church, while approving of the noble character, as well as the enthusiasm of chivalry, always endeavored to restrain its more romantic and warlike tendencies. Its pacific and charitable spirit is expressed in the solemn blessing on the sword of a knight, which we take from the "pontifical."

"Most holy Lord," said the officiating prelate, "omnipotent Father, eternal God, who alone ordains and disposes all things; who, to restrain the malice of the wicked and to protect justice, hast, by a wise arrangement, permitted the use of the sword to men upon this earth, and willed the institution of the military order for the protection of thy people. Grant strength and courage for the defense of the faith and justice; grant him an increase of faith, hope, and charity. Inspire him with thy fear and love; give him humility, perseverance, obedience, and patience; make his disposition in everything such that he may wound no person unjustly either with this sword or with any other, but that he may use it to defend all that is just and all that is right."

The bishop gave the naked sword to the new knight, saying, "Receive this blade in the name of the Father, of the Son, and of the Holy Ghost, and use it for your own defense and for that of God's Holy Church, and for the confusion of the enemies of the cross of Christ and of the Christian faith. And — as far as human frailty permits it — wound no one unjustly with it."

The new-made knight then rose, brandished the sword, wiped it on his left arm, and replaced it in its scabbard.

The prelate then gave him the kiss of peace, saying, "Peace be with thee." With the naked sword in his right hand, he struck the knight gently thrice across the shoulders, saying, "Be thou a peaceable, brave, and faithful warrior." Then, the other knights present put on his spurs, while the bishop said, "Valiant warrior, thou who surpasses in beauty the children of men, gird thyself with thy sword upon thy thigh."

The Early Medieval Warlords

Clovis (whose German and Celtic names were Chlodwig and Chlodowech) was the son of Childeric, who became king of the Salic Franks. In 492 or 493, Clovis, who was master of Gaul from the Loire to the frontiers of the Rhineland Kingdom of Cologne, married Clotilda, the niece of Gondebaud, King of the Burgundians. The popular epic of the Franks has transformed the story of this marriage into a veritable nuptial poem, the analysis of which will be found in the article on Clotilda. Clotilda, who was a Catholic, and very pious, won the consent of Clovis to the baptism of their son, and then urged that he himself embrace the Catholic faith. He deliberated for a long time. Finally, during a battle against the Alemanni — which has been called the Battle of Tolbiac (Zulpich) — seeing his troops on the point of yielding, he invoked the aid of Clotilda's God, and promised to become a Christian if only victory should be granted him. He conquered and, true to his word, was baptized at Rheims by St. Remigius, bishop of that city, with his sister Albofledis and three thousand of his warriors at the same time embracing Christianity. Gregory of Tours, in his ecclesiastical history of the Franks, has described this event, which took place amid great pomp at Christmas, 496.

In the simultaneous double origin of feudalism, there might already have been perceived the hidden cause of the future inevitable antagonism between the modern influence of the Cross and the material power of the sword. Conspiracies, bloodthirsty executions, continual revolts, diverse plots, in which were concerned at one time the king's companions at arms, at another the principal clergy; ecclesiastical censures, ceaselessly threatening these blind and savage tyrants, who, while bending to the reproof, at the same time panted for revenge; uncurbed ambitions, terrible hatred, the continued strife of opposing races; on one side the Gallo-Romanic and its heir, the Gothic, on the other the "barbarous" Germanic and Slavonian, more or less Christianized. All these were the endless signs by which the coming reign of feudalism, at each successive stage of modern civilization, marked its advent.

In the centuries after the collapse of the Roman Empire, in A.D. 476, fragments of the former whole became individual power centers ruled by notable individual mon-

ABOVE: THE BAPTISM OF CLOVIS AFTER THE VICTORY AT TOLBIAC (ZULPICH).

archs whose names are now legendary. Theodoric the Great ruled the Ostragothic Kingdom of Italy, Clovis presided over the Franks in what is now France, Justinian the Great reigned in Byzantium over the former Eastern Roman Empire, and King Arthur held court at Camelot in Britain.

However, when Europe lost the unity of the Roman Empire and became a patchwork of squabbling kingdoms, it took a step backward culturally. Thus began the Middle Ages — or, as they were once described, the Dark Ages.

Except for Spain, which was ruled by the Islamic Moors, Europe was fragmented politically but unified religiously by the common bond of Christianity. While the home of the Christian popes in Rome remained the spiritual center of Europe, the Franks in northern Europe emerged as the strongest military and secular power. By the end of

ABOVE: THE EMPEROR CHARLEMAGNE.

the eighth century, their most powerful leader was the 26-year-old Charlemagne (the French word for Charles the Great), who lived from A.D. 742 to 814 and is now considered to be one of the greatest rulers in European history. His greatest opposition was from the Italian king Desiderius, who wanted Pope Adrian I to crown the underage children of Charlemagne's predecessor as monarchs of segments of the kingdom of the Franks.

After Charlemagne defeated Desiderius, he consolidated most of the states of northern Italy under Frankish control. Charlemagne then went to Rome to meet with the pope and found that their long-range strategies were quite compatible. Charlemagne's goal was to become head of an

empire on the scale of the old Roman Empire, and Adrian I wanted one dominant, unified, political force to rule Europe that would ally itself with the Church and could serve to protect and expand Christendom the way the Moorish armies were spreading Islam.

With the spiritual and political blessing of the pope, Charlemagne added much of Denmark, Germany, and Central Europe to an empire that already included France and most of Italy. He also recaptured part of Spain from the Moors. On Christmas Day in A.D. 800, while he was attending Mass in Rome, Charlemagne unexpectedly found himself being crowned "Emperor of the Romans" by Adrian's successor, Pope Leo III. The Western Roman Empire, which had not existed for 325 years, was back in business, this time as the *Holy Roman Empire* (though it was not yet *officially* known as such). Although he was not recognized by the emperor of the Eastern Roman Empire until A.D. 812, Charlemagne quickly won the respect of most of the peoples of his empire, enabling Europe to once again experience the *Pax Romana* of a unified and basically peaceful environment. Because of this, Charlemagne's rule can be said to have been a moment of sunshine in the midst of the darkness of the Dark Ages.

In 814, Charlemagne's empire was inherited by his intended successor, Louis the Pious (Louis the Debonair). However, after Louis died in 840, infighting among his sons caused the empire to collapse into pieces. This void was filled by the Catholic Church itself, which began to assert increasing political, as well as spiritual, power.

Europe, however, had begun to sink back into the Dark Ages. The disunity that preceded Charlemagne's brilliant rule had returned. Both Italy and France were a morass of warring factions, but among the Germans a new leader emerged. Henry I, known as "The Fowler," was a forceful leader who consolidated the German states, leaving to his son and successor, Otto I, a formidable power base. Otto I sought to bring unity to the lands that had once comprised Charlemagne's vast empire. Again, as had been with Charlemagne, Otto's authority sprang from the pope's desire for a strong northern Europe that would restore order in Italy. Pope John XII was at war with the Italian king Berengar and offered Otto the crown and title of Holy Roman Emperor if he would defeat Berengar and unite the peninsula. This accomplished, Otto I was crowned on February 2, A.D. 962.

The idea of a Holy Roman Empire had been born with Charlemagne, and now it was reborn with Otto I. Charlemagne's empire survived his death by only 27 years. The Holy Roman Empire would survive Otto's death by more than eight centuries. The Holy Roman Empire essentially consisted of the present territory of Germany, Austria, Italy, the Czech Republic, and some adjacent territory. It would continue to wield might and power until the fifteenth century, and it would survive in name until 1806. As was intended, the Holy Roman Empire brought political as well as spiritual union to the heart of Europe by bringing many diverse peoples together. In the centuries that followed, all the superpowers that appeared were outside the Holy Roman Empire. These were England, France, and Spain. However, the autonomy that remained in individual kingdoms prevented the emergence of a true power center within the Holy Roman Empire.

Master of France, Germany, and Italy, and protector of the Church, Charlemagne had enjoyed all the prerogatives of the Western emperors. On two occasions, he delivered the Holy See from its enemies, and in Germany as well as Italy, he placed his sword at the service of the Christian faith.

Pope Adrian bestowed upon Charlemagne the dignity of patronage. In the year 800, Adrian's successor, Pope Leo III, placed the imperial crown upon his head. This might have been seen as being better than in the days of the Roman and Greek Emperors — the spectacle of the Church protected by the head of the state, to whom the seignorial aristocracy paid feudal obedience, and who controlled with an iron hand their tendencies to schism.

ABOVE: THE CORONATION OF CHARLEMAGNE BY POPE LEO III AT ST. PETER'S IN ROME ON DECEMBER 25, 800.

ABOVE: THIS FIFTEENTH-CENTURY ALLEGORY FOR ECCLESIASTICAL PREEMINENCE OVER HERESY ALSO SUGGESTS THE STRATA OF FEUDAL SOCIETY.

The Origin and Organization of Feudalism

The political system, for which a barbarous legal code had been inaugurated for the benefit of the lords, was entirely opposed to the system sanctioned by Roman law. It was the desire of the lords that a seignior, the owner of the land and of the men who cultivated it, should possess the right of "infeudalising," that is to say, of ceding, as an inferior freehold, a certain portion of his own estate, abandoning in so doing to the concessionaire or vassal not only the rights of the soil but the sovereignty over those who occupied it. For a vassal to forfeit his rights, he must first have failed to fulfill the engagements he undertook when he received the investiture of the fief. The cession of lands and the rights attached to it, which were the foundation of a dawning feudalism, remained for more than a century in that state of oscillation which precedes a stable equilibrium.

Feudalism, which was gathering strength, and which already knew its own power, never retrograded. It sometimes halted and was at rest, but it was only waiting on a more propitious season to continue its path. Charlemagne's successors were, in fact, neither the kings of France nor the emperors of Germany, but the feudal lords, the great landowners. Their power waxed all the greater from the fact that, in 853, an edict of Charles the Bald ordered the reconstruction of the medieval manors, the repair of their fortifications, and the construction of new ones, so as to arrest the devastating invasions by the Normans, the Moslem Arabs (Saracens), the Hungarians, and the Danes. Thus, Europe became dotted with fortresses, behind which both nobles and villains found a refuge against the new flood of barbarians. There was soon scarcely a stream, a mountain pass, or an important road which was left undefended, either by military posts or strong walls.

The invaders, formerly rendered so bold and indomitable by the fear they had succeeded in inspiring, now ceased their raids, or, at most, ventured no farther than the shores on which they had disembarked. Little by little, a sense of security returned to the inhabitants, and the welfare of the civilized world was assured. A service of this importance, rendered by the nobles and seigniors to society at large, naturally gave them legitimate claims to the fealty of society at large, and natural guardianship of the frontiers which they protected from the common enemy.

Toward the tenth century, every noble who desired to obtain from another noble, richer or more powerful than himself, a portion of land to be held as a fief, and who consented thus to become his vassal, personally declared in the chief's presence, that for the future, he wished to be his faithful, devoted servant and his defender until death. With his sword girded to his side and his spurs on his heels, he solemnly swore this on the Holy Writ. In the subsequent ceremony of homage, the vassal, bareheaded, knelt on one knee and, placing his hands within those of his seignior, swore fealty to him and undertook to follow him to war (as seen in the illustration at left), an obligation not necessarily entailed by a simple act of homage. Thereafter, the seignior ceded to him the land or the feudal domain, by investiture or by seizing in a ceremony often accompanied by the giving of a symbolic sign, such as a clod of earth, a little stick, or a stone, according to the custom of the soil. The investiture of kingdoms was conferred with the sword, that of provinces with a standard.

The reciprocal obligations of the vassal and his suzerain were numerous, moral, and sometimes material. The vassal was bound to loyally preserve the secrets confided to him by his suzerain (note the illustration at the left), to prevent and frustrate any treachery on the part of his enemies, to defend him at the risk of his own life, to resign his own horse on the battlefield should his lord have lost his, to go as a prisoner in his stead, to cause his honor to be respected, and to assist him with his advice. At the simple request of the suzerain, the vassal was bound to follow him to the field, either alone or accompanied by a specified number of armed men, according to the importance of the fief. The duration of this military service varied, in like manner, in proportion

SEALS COMMEMORATING ACTS OF FAITH AND HOMAGE FROM THE THIRTEENTH CENTURY, SHOWING THE ARCHBISHOP OF ARLES AND RAIMOND DE MONTDRAGON (ABOVE); AND THE SEAL OF GERARD DE SAINT-AMAND FROM 1199 (BELOW).

to the fief, from 20 to 60 days — a period that did not admit of very distant expeditions. The feudal seignior stood in place of the sovereign, and, being invested with executive authority, had necessarily, in order to exercise it, recourse to the latent force distributed among his vassals, and he naturally did so in accordance with his own convenience.

Vassals of the same suzerain, residing in the same territory, and possessing fiefs of a similar value, were identified as *pares*, or equals. Suzerains of every rank, the king included, had their pairs, and all could claim the privilege of being tried by these pairs in the presence of his immediate seignior. If the seignior refused to act justly, and the vassal considered himself unrighteously condemned, he had the right of making an appeal in default of justice to the suzerain of his own seignior. Another right of appeal, that of arms, prevailed also in feudal society. The nobles, as a rule, preferred to carry out their own justice rather than await from others a slow and uncertain decision. This was the cause of there being so many small wars and so many desperate and bloody struggles between different seigniorships.

Might made right. Custom, nevertheless, to some extent regulated the formalities that preceded these internecine conflicts, so that the seignior or the vassal who was to be attacked might be forearmed and might put himself upon his guard. Further, to remedy as much as possible the calamities ensuing from these perpetual contentions, the Church had the power of suspending and preventing them, under pain of excommunication, from sunset on Wednesday to sunrise on Monday during the festivals of Lent and Advent, and at all periods of high religious solemnity. This was the Peace or the Truce of God. The seigniors possessed no right of uniform justice.

Feudalism in France

In France, a superior, a middle, and an inferior judicial court were recognized. The first alone possessed the power of life and death. The more considerable fiefs had usually attached to them the right to exercise the highest justice, but there were exceptions to this rule. A vassal, for instance, might sometimes appeal against

ABOVE: FRENCH LADIES OF THE NOBILITY.

this highest justice, while a seignior, who was entitled to exercise only the inferior justiciary rights, might inflict death on all robbers caught in flagrante delicto on his lands. The privilege of coining money, always a sure index of sovereignty, together with the exclusion of all foreign jurisdiction and all external authority from the area of each fief, also constituted two important prerogatives. Finally, the fief, with its privileges, always remained intact. It passed invariably to the eldest of the family, on the sole condition of his paying homage to the suzerain. Most of the churches and abbeys, such as those of Saint-Denis, Saint-Martin des Champs, and Saint-Germain des Prés (see illustration on page 18), which proudly reared their towers and spires opposite the Louvre of the kings of France, exercised on their own account all the feudal rights which they had acquired by reason of the territorial possessions as well as by the concessions lavishly ceded to them by their sovereigns.

The archbishops, the bishops, and the abbots thus became temporal lords, and were consequently forced to have vassals for military service and to keep up a court of justice. In this case, bishops enjoyed the temporal rank of count-spiritual with political authority. This twofold power made the prelate the suzerain of all the seigniors in his diocese. Toward the end of the tenth century, the feudal ecclesiastics, by reason of the permission granted to laymen to bequeath their property to the Church, as well as of the strictness of the laws which forbade the alienation of ecclesiastical property, possessed a fifth part of all French and English soil, and nearly a third of Germany; while the last surviving Carolingian could claim only the town of Laon, where he resided, to such an extent had his predecessors despoiled themselves of their lands in favor of their great vassals, who still, however, recognized him as their suzerain.

In the eleventh century, Europe was divided into a multitude of fiefs, each having its own mode of life, its own laws, its own customs, and its ecclesiastical or lay head, who was as independent as he well could be. Around these, but under certain conditions of dependence and subordination, was developed the much more numerous class of freedmen. Gradually, manual labor and the efforts of a growing intelligence led to the political existence of the bour-geois, those worthy representatives of the laboring portion of society. The part which was taken by the latter was not always of a passive character. As early as the year 987, the villains of Normandy rebelled and leagued themselves against their feudal lords, claiming the right of fishing and of the chase, and the privilege of having an administration and a magistracy of their own. It was thus that the innate power of the people revealed itself: The towns and the boroughs were peopled with inhabitants who held their homes in tenure from the seigniors — who were the proprietors of the soil — under certain servile obligations as to the payment of taxes.

As soon as the establishment of the hierarchy of fiefs had put an end to discord and anarchy, the germs of the Great Revolu-tion — destined to restore civil liberty to the heirs of the countless inhabitants whom the misfortunes of Gaul and the tyranny of the emperors had reduced to servitude — began to show themselves. It was in this wise that the communal movement originated, and the town of Le Mans is generally credited with being the first to set the example of having, through the agency of the working classes, conspired against the seignior. We find in the annals of Metz, about the year 1098, record of the election for life of a *maître-échevin* (high-sheriff), named Millon, in place of one, by the name of Hennolu-Bertin, who had been elected for one year, but who, doubtless, was not the first in his office. We find a sher-iff's council, identified as the council of the 12, enjoying functions at once magisterial, administrative, and military.

ABOVE: THE FEUDAL CASTLE OF PIERREFONDS IN FRANCE.

Metz possessed at the same time, by the side of their communal organization, a count by the name of Gerald, who was succeeded in 1063 by another count named Folmar. It had also a bishop, rich, powerful, firm, full of learning, named Adalberon, a favorite both with the pope and with the emperor, influential enough to obtain anything, but never asking anything but what was just. It was, therefore, under the protection of the sword of the count and of the crozier of the bishop that the munici-pal liberties of Metz began to grow. Liberties became, with-in a single century, so developed and powerful that Bertram, another bishop of Saxon origin, undertook the task of restricting them, and endeavored to regulate them by a charter which restored to the Church its electoral, but not its governmental, influence.

This first communal organization, a type similar to many other municipalities in France and Germany, was inaugurated without bloodshed. But this was not the case everywhere. At Cambrai, for instance, the commune was established only after a century of open warfare between the

inhabitants and the bishop, their suzerain. At Laon — the medieval feudal city where the nobility and the burgesses engaged in various brigandage, where the bishop, who was a famous warrior and huntsman, was in the habit of sharing with the dignitaries of his cathedral and with the aristocracy of the town the fruit of his exactions — the commune inaugurated itself with the blood of its bishop, who was assassinated in the midst of an insurrection.

The towns of Amiens, Beauvais, Noyon, Saint-Quentin, Sens, Soissons, and Vézelay, underwent nearly the same vicissitudes that Cambrai and Laon had experienced, and finally attained, after similar trials, a similar position. Perhaps Cambrai, of all the French communes, was the most exacting toward the feudal power that it was trampling underfoot. No vassal had ever claimed or obtained more in the exercise of his feudal rights (see opposite, top).

The inauguration of the communal system had taken place without a struggle, and almost without opposition, as a useful and necessary reform at Metz, at Rheims, in a few midland towns, such as Bourges, Moulin, Lyons and Perigeux, and in most of the southern French cities, such as Arles, Aigues-Mortes, Marseilles, Narbonne, Cahors, Carcassonne, Nîmes, and Bordeaux. This was explained by the fact that this independent action of the people had been prepared by the system adopted by the Franks, who allowed no difference to exist between the condition of the conquerors and that of the conquered.

The rights they might enjoy and the duties they were to perform had been equally shared among all the freedmen of the monarchy without any distinction, as was nationality. The Franks would have feared, had they acted differently, that they were reserving for the sovereign the possibility of using the oppressed nations as a weapon to overcome the conquerors themselves, and that in this way they might be leaving a loophole through which the monarchy might degenerate into despotism.

The name "Ville-neuve," which is so often found repeated in the charters and deeds of the Middle Ages — as, for example, Ville-neuve-l'Es-

ABOVE: THE ABBEY OF SAINT-GERMAIN DES PRÉS AS VIEWED FROM THE EAST IN 1361.
A: THE ROAD LEADING TO THE RIVER SEINE. B: ST. PETER'S CHAPEL. C: THE CLOSE.
D: A ROAD TO PRÉ-AUX-CLERES. E: THE BREACH. F: THE MOAT. G: THE PAPAL GATE.
H: THE CLOISTER. I: THE REFECTORY. K: THE DORMITORY. L: THE CHURCH.
M: THE CHAPEL OF THE VIRGIN. N: A ROAD TO PRE-AUX-CLERES. O: RUE DES OISEAUX.
P: THE GREAT GATE OF THE MONASTERY. Q: THE ROAD TO THE RIVER. R: THE WALL NEAR
THE MOAT. S: LE TAVERNE DU CHAPEAU ROUGE (THE RED HAT INN). T: THE PILLORY.

tang, Ville-neuve-Saint-George, Ville-neuve-le-Roi, Ville-neuve-les-Avignon, and so forth — is evidence of what was an ordinary event in the twelfth century; namely, the creation of a free town, enfranchised from its birth, and subject to some small and insignificant payments to the seignior. The inhabitants, just yesterday serfs or villains, were now proprietors of portions of the soil, which they might dispose of or bequeath, either by gift or testamentary disposition, under the immediate protection of their nominal seignior.

Some medieval towns of the royal domains of France, such as Paris, Orléans, Meaux, Senlis, and others, were each governed by a provost, who was the officer and lieutenant of the king, their seignior, and they further enjoyed certain special liberties and privileges. These cities do not seem to have preserved the least trace of Roman institutions. An exception was the company of the Nantes Parisiennes, who are thought of as the true founders of the medieval municipality of Paris.

In 1137, Louis VII, at the suggestion of his minister Suger, forbade his provost and officers to annoy the burgesses in any manner whatsoever, and fixed the amount of their taxation himself. Ten years later, the same sovereign abolished the right of mortmain, repressed the abuses of the fiscal taxes, instituted a judicial system, and greatly encouraged commerce. It was not as king, but as seignior suzerain, that Louis VII acted in this manner.

The French bourgeoisie was, at this time, of recent origin. It had sprung from a triumphant villainage, and was beginning to form a new branch, from which was to issue, a few centuries later, the third estate.

Legal jurisdiction, the right of coinage, and feudal privileges of which the royal suzerain had always been very jealous, were favors it then, but seldom, enjoyed. Philip-Augustus understood better than his predecessors the interests of the royal power, for he graciously granted 78 communal charters. He was rewarded by the effectual assistance the communal levies afforded him at the Battle of Bouvines (1214), when

ABOVE: THOMAS AND JOAN, COUNT AND COUNTESS OF SAVOY, GRANT A CHARTER OF PEACE BETWEEN HAINAUT AND CAMBRAI TO THE CITY OF CAMBRAI (1240).

he was fortunate enough to overthrow the coalition that foreign feudalism had formed with his rebellious great vassals. He forced the latter to return to their duty, and one of them, the Count of Flanders, remained 12 years a prisoner in the principal tower of the Louvre. Philip-Augustus had not shrunk from granting a legal constitution to the bourgeoisie of Paris and the principal towns in opposition to the feudal nobility.

Feudalism in Italy

Beyond the Alps, particularly in Lombardy, under the fostering action of liberal institutions, commerce and manufactures developed themselves, particularly in Milan, Pavia, Verona, and Florence. They developed to a still higher degree in coastal cities, specifically Venice and Genoa.

In these rich and prosperous cities the seignorial nobility and the Church reigned side by side, enjoying a nearly equal and parallel influence. When feudalism attempted to absorb them by its inflexible despotism, the manufacturing and the commercial classes selected as their leaders a few of the more prominent artisans and some of the most respected of the clergy, allied themselves with the lesser rural nobles, and, with the assistance of the latter's vassals, succeeded in repulsing its crushing yoke. This, however, was not accomplished without tremendous struggles, nor without painful trials and heavy sacrifices.

Feudalism in the North

In the Low Countries, which had always so highly exalted the sentiment of local patriotism, the struggle of the villains against the nobles, whether lay or ecclesiastic, differed but little from the struggle of the towns in the north of France against the seigniors. However, it assumed larger proportions in accordance with the immense resources of every kind which they had at their disposal. The feudal lord had his drawbridge, his battlements, and his men-at-arms cased in iron. However, his rebellious vassal could boast, in addition to the narrow and winding streets of his stronghold and the number of his fellow combatants, many well-made weapons which he himself had manufactured. When feudalism, in order to crush what it then identified as the populace, summoned to its banner hordes of adventurers recruited from all parts of the world, it was encountered by undisciplined levies of armed mechanics and artisans, who went forth from Gent, Brugge, and Liege, and not infrequently returned victorious. Beyond the Meuse, the Moselle, and the Rhine, feudalism flourished. Lofty fortresses, surrounded by a triple moat, everywhere cast their shadows athwart the land, though the towns enjoyed a full share of municipal liberty, and were not infrequently the disinterested spectators of the terrible struggles that the feudal nobility carried on among themselves.

Nowhere did feudalism display more arrogance or barbarity than in Germany, which resembled some vast camp to which the nobles flocked to meet face-to-face in desperate combat.

When it came to pass that the industrial and populous towns of Germany cried out for municipal liberties similar to those enjoyed by the towns of France, Italy, and the Low Countries, the emperor hastened to grant and confirm their desires. He did more. He gave them the right of immedi-

ABOVE: A FLEMISH DUKE.

ate appeal against the princes of the empire — that is to say, any towns situated in the territory of any prince were responsible not to the latter but directly and immediately to the emperor himself, who thus laid for himself the foundations of strong natural supports in the very heart of the larger fiefs.

The towns of Germany, already rich and flourishing, increased their commerce and their wealth, thanks to the new position they thus acquired. The Emperor Henry V greatly assisted this pacific revolution by granting privileges to the lower class of citizens and to the artisans, who up to that time had, according to the spirit of the Roman law, lived apart from the freedmen and remained at the lowest degree of the social scale. He relieved them, in particular, from the bondage of a custom by virtue of which the seignior at their deaths became entitled to all their personal property, or, at least, enjoyed the power of claiming everything worth having which they had left behind.

In many towns, Henry V deprived the bishop of his temporal authority, and formed the burgesses into companies or guilds according to the nature of their manual occupation, a custom that was immediately imitated and adopted in other commercial countries. The bourgeoisie, organized in this manner into distinct groups, soon elected councils among themselves, the members of which, under the rule of senators, *prud'hommes, bonshommes, échevins,* and others, began by assisting the representative of the imperial authority, whether duke, count, judge, or bishop. They ended by exercising a special and independent authority of their own, not over the vassals but over citizens and commoners. It will be asked, What then, was the commune which had established itself with more or less effort and sacrifice in the principal parts of Europe? Further, as the commune had succeeded in one way or another in establishing itself, what privileges or immunities remained to the feudal lord, whether clerical or lay?

Gilbert de Nogent, the open adversary of communal institutions, will perhaps give the best answer to these inquiries: "Those who pay taxes now pay only once a year the rent they owe to their seignior. If they commit some misdemeanor, they have at the most to pay a fine, the amount of which is legally fixed. As for the money that was wont to be levied from the serfs, they are now quite exempt from them." Gilbert de Nogent might have indicated other victories obtained by the bourgeois, victories that were still more important in their moral influence, and which sooner or later were destined to change the face of society. The more intelligent seigniors who better understood their own personal interest, as well as the logical results of a paternal administration, attempted to favor the instinctive movement of the rural populations, who, to shield themselves from the tyranny, the exactions, and the bad treatment of their feudal masters, were in the habit of seeking shelter and protection from some lord more humane or political than the rest. The rural population sought those who once (on the faith of a communal charter) settled beside the ramparts of some seignorial manor, around some loopholed church, or in the shade of some fortified monastery. The seignior was, in these cases, the gainer of so many able-bodied men, either artisans or agriculturists, but soldiers in ease of need. And he was the gainer, moreover, in matters of revenue and influence.

It can easily be understood that in those times many charters were drawn up similar to the following, which is worth quoting as a type: "I, Henry, Count of Troyes, make known to all present and to come, that I have established the undermentioned rules for the inhabitants of my new town (in the neighborhood of Pont-sur-Seine) between the bridges Pugny. Every man inhabiting the said town shall pay every year 12 deniers and a measure of oats as the price of his dwelling, and if he desires to hold a portion of land or meadow, he must pay four deniers yearly for every acre. The houses, vines, and fields may be sold or alienated at the pleasure of the holder. The men who reside in the said town shall go neither to an army in the field, nor shall they join any expedition unless I myself am at their head. I hereby allow them, moreover, to have six aldermen to administer the ordinary business of the town and to assist my provost in his duties. I have decreed that no seignior, be he knight or other, should be allowed to withdraw from the town any of the men inhabitants for any reason

ABOVE: A FLEMISH LADY.

whatsoever, unless such be his own men, or unless he owe the seignior any arrears of taxes. Given at Provence, in the year of the Incarnation, 1175."

Feudalism in England

The communal movement, a natural development of the legal rights introduced by the Franks, was scarcely felt in England. Already, long before the Norman Conquest, under the Anglo-Saxon rule, many busy towns, wealthy and populous, such as Canterbury, London, Oxford, and York, took a share in public affairs, a limited share, it is true, but one sufficient for their well-being and prosperity. The victorious invasion of William of Normandy, so fatal to the whole country, was still more so to the large towns, which were compelled to behold their own material ruin, the sequestration and confiscation of their property, the dispersion and enslavement of their inhabitants, their agriculturists, and their farmers. Unable any longer to invoke the protection of an easy-natured sovereign, they were forced to bow their heads beneath the sway of strangers, lucky adventurers, bold, exacting, despotic, and cruel men, believing in no faith and obeying no law, the very dregs of French feudalism.

King Henry I (1068–1135), the third son of William the Conqueror, after many bloody struggles, in which his barons were not found wanting in fealty to him, granted them many important liberties. The Magna Carta of 1215 is usually, but erroneously, considered the fundamental origin of English liberties, but I believe they really dated from a prior period. In 1132, Henry I released the burgesses of London from the lamentable state of degradation in which they had existed since the Conquest in 1066. In the reign of Henry II (1154–1182) — who was an administrative and judicial reformer — many towns acquired the right to purchase the freehold of the soil they occupied, and to free themselves from several special taxes by paying a fixed sum to the feudal lord. This occurred in England as well as in the parts of Scotland and Ireland which he had conquered.

Thereafter arose that haughty bourgeoisie, with which the barons had soon to reckon, a class which John Lackland favored proportionately as he dreaded the continual rebellions of the feudal seigniors. Twice was Prince Louis, the son of Philip-Augustus, summoned by the Anglo-Norman barons to cross the channel with an army to force England's King John to fulfill the clauses of the Magna Carta which he had granted to his subject lords in 1215. On the other hand, the towns and communes, grown rich and powerful, thanks to the privileges which had been granted to them, as well as to the intelligent activity of their manufactures, forced the nobles to respect them. The latter no longer attempted to compel assistance, but solicited it, often even humbly, so that the communes and the landed aristocracy held an equal position in the feudal hierarchy.

The title of noble and baron, bestowed on the lending citizens of London and the Cinque Ports, raised the middle class to a higher position. Indeed, to enable it, already powerful by its wealth and by its alliances, to become a political body, it only needed the privilege of sending representatives to parliament. This privilege was granted in 1264 to the principal towns of the kingdom. In France, at about the same period, the industrial and trading bourgeoisie had seats in the privy council of St. Louis (1214–1270), and, advancing in letters and science, it gradually obtained possession of all the chairs at the university. As early as the reign (1270–1285) of Philip the Bold, the bourgeoisie occupied all the higher positions in the judicature, and hence it assumed a place in the great bailiwicks and parliaments, from which the feudal nobility did not condescend to oust it. Later, it was enabled to offer a successful resistance to the abuse of power on the part of this same nobility, whose authority steadily diminished.

A decline in the wealth of the nobility dated from the First Crusade (1097–1099), when they encumbered their estates to pay the expenses of distant expeditions, which they undertook almost entirely at their own cost. When they wished to recover possession of the properties which they had handed over to some

third party, they found them loaded with fresh debts, which had been contracted during their absence, and producing but nominal revenues for want of hands to cultivate the soil. They then were obliged to sell a portion of the property, and that at a great loss.

The Cruel Aspects of Feudalism

Feudalism had been a confederacy of little sovereigns, of small despots, unequal among themselves and possessing and owing, each toward the other, rights and duties, yet invested in their own domains, over their own immediate subjects, with absolute, arbitrary power. This is what feudalism really was, and this is what distinguishes it from every other aristocratic form and every other kind of government. From the tenth to the thirteenth century, liberty, equality, and peace were all wanting. To the inhabitants of a feudal estate, their sovereigns — however petty they were — were at their very doors. Not one of them was too obscure for his notice, nor too far removed from his power — and that power of their retainers was often of the most savage kind.

The historian Peter of Val-de-Cernay writes: "Bernard of Cahuzac, a petty lord of Perigord, spends his life in looting and destroying churches, in attacking pilgrims, in oppressing the widow and the poor. It pleases him especially to mutilate the innocent. In a single monastery, that of the Black Monks of Sarlat, 150 men and women were found, whose hands and feet had been cut off, or whose eyes had been put out by him. His wife, as cruel as he, aided in his deeds. She took pleasure in torturing these poor women herself. She had their breasts slit, or their nails torn out so that they would not be able to work."

Foucaud, a knight and a comrade of Simon de Montfort, angered even the warriors by his cruelties. Every prisoner who did not have the means of paying 100 sous as ransom was condemned to death. He enclosed his prisoners in subterranean dungeons and let them die of starvation. Sometimes he had them brought forth half-dead and thrown into cesspools before his own eyes. It was said that on one of his first expeditions he returned with two captives, a father and son, and that he forced the father to hang his own son.

Giraud, a troubadour who wrote at the beginning of the thirteenth century, deplored these habits of pillage, unworthy of men of the sword, writing: "I used to see the barons in beautiful armor following tournaments, and I heard those who had given the best blow spoken of for many a day. Now honor lies in stealing cattle, sheep, and oxen, or pillaging churches and travelers. Oh, he upon the knight who drives off sheep and pillages churches and travelers, and then appears before a lady."

The Decline of Feudalism

The massacre of more than 6,000 chevaliers at Courtrai in 1302, by the Flemish militia, was a heavy blow to the pride of the generous, but reckless, nobility of France. It was humiliating to these lords to find that the villains knew how to wield the arms which they had been in the habit of making for others. They saw that they possessed the courage and skill needed to win battles, and that, hereafter, they must be reckoned upon as a force able to take the field, as well as formidable when engaged in street riots.

In Germany, the fall of the Hohenstaufen family, formerly dukes of Swabia and Franconia, favored the enfranchisement of towns. All the cities in these two principalities, hitherto subject to the mediated lords, reverted to the emperor, who, without any real power over them, left them free to establish the franchise and immunities of a republic. In order to increase their populations, they followed the example of the sovereigns and feudal lords of France and Lombardy in regard to the formation of new towns, and establishing around their walls, as feudalism had done outside its dungeons, fields of refuge. These were occupied by a host of strangers who received the designation of Pfahlburger — citizens of the palisades, or faubourgians, originally sheltered and protected by a wooden barrier.

These receded in proportion as the number of inhabitants increased, and according as their trade developed. Many serfs deserted the neighboring fiefs to seek in these free towns the independence, position, success, and all the advantages which they could not enjoy under the feudal regime. Their lords demanded their extradition by virtue of their feudal rights, accompanying the demand with threats, which were sometimes effectual. However, the free towns, not less interested in keeping the fugitive than the latter was in remaining with them, endeavored to gain time and to favor his retreat until after the expiration of 365 days, when the right of the lord to his vassal ceased.

The imperial towns — which, from the twelfth to the fourteenth century, after having freed themselves from the fetters of feudalism, had risen to such a height of independence that the emperor himself had but a nominal supremacy over them. The towns were Ratisbon, in Bavaria; Augsburg and Ulm in Swabia; Nuremberg, Spiers, Worms, and Frankfurt-am-Main in Franconia; Magdeburg in Saxony; as well as Hamburg, Bremen, and Lübeck in the Hanseatic League. There were also Aix-la-Chapelle (Aachen), Bonn, Cologne (Koln), Coblenz, Mainz, Strasbourg, and Metz in the Rhineland and Lotharingian provinces. These were the towns in which the middle classes were, for the most part, supreme. They formed vast emporiums, teeming with the products of the north, the south, and the east. They were looked upon as the storehouses and arsenals of Europe.

Feudalism, unable to produce anything for itself, was always replenishing from these depots the resources necessary for equipping and feeding its armies. From them came the arms and the engines of warfare, as well as the special workmen, the crossbowmen, the carpenters, the founders, and the artillery units, who composed the personnel of the artillery at this period.

If the free towns had arrived at a common understanding, and formed a pacific league between themselves, they would have presented a serious obstacle to the struggles of the suzerain lords. However, their distance from each other, especially those in the center of Germany, prevented them from coming to such an arrangement. Nor could they, as in England, form an alliance with the feudal nobility, nor, as in France, make common cause with the suzerain.

As the emperor left them to act independently, they were obliged to organize their own defense, to contract alliances with some powerful neighbor, and weaken those enemies by dividing those whom they deemed stronger than themselves. Thus, these free towns never constituted a homogeneous body. They were isolated and spread over a vast extent of territory, being brought together only by feelings of interest and sympathy, but without any mutual tie or political cohesion.

The lord with whom they were at war today would enter their service and pay the next, with the title of soldarien. At times, a single town would have as many as 300 of these allies, who were always followed by a swarm of marauders, and who spread desolation throughout the land. The lords who were without fortune represented the petty feudalism of the country districts, finding in the service of these towns a means for keeping up their state and paying their followers. The lords passed from one town to the other, and enlisted only under the standard of a sovereign prince for want of better employment, for the latter did not, as a rule, pay so well as these free towns.

From the eleventh to the fourteenth century, the position of the bishop, in point of political influence, did not improve in these free or republican towns, either in England, France, or Germany. Suzerain lord by moral authority, he was so only to a very limited degree in respect to his temporal power. He exercised justice only over his vassals, or at most over the members of the secular and inferior clergy, for the canons, the incumbents, and even the deacons, enjoying as they did special immunities, would have appealed, in the event of a dispute or of censure, to their metropolitan archbishop, or even to Rome.

As the nobility could always claim to be judged by their peers, there was rarely any infraction of this feudal principle, and then only where some diocesan bishop or metropolitan was powerful enough to substitute his own will for the customary right. In nearly all the episcopal towns, the judgment of the prelate or of his delegates was delivered from the square in front of the cathedral or from the doorway of some exterior and adjacent chapel. This practice, maintained during the first centuries of the Church's existence, ceased when another form of justice, namely civil justice, took its place.

The mint of the prelate was established there. However, so wide was the disagreement between the ecclesiastical and the civil authorities, and so sustained the struggle between the feudal and the middle-class interests, that it often happened that the episcopal money was not accepted as current coin, even in the town where the bishop was spiritually supreme, nor in the territory annexed to the free town and enjoying equal prerogatives.

As the highest representatives of feudalism, the Holy Roman Emperor and the kings of France and England possessed in every large city — notably in the cities identified as imperial or royal — an official delegate, called burgrave, count, or viscount. Originally at the head of the army, the

magistracy, and the finances, he gradually lost his prerogatives till, in the thirteenth century, he was scarcely more than a mere dignitary, with neither power nor credit.

Many bishops, authorized by the lay sovereign, took the title of count, without, however, adding in any material degree to their influence. Besides, whatever may have been the nature and extent of the functions of a count, it does not appear that the free towns paid any more heed to this official than to the preeminence of the bishop in all that appertained to the administration and government of the commune. In many places, especially in Italy and upon the banks of the Moselle and the Rhine, the bourgeoisie possessed councils invested both with the judicial and executive power, also a senate and a parliament, which was summoned by the ringing of a bell. To this, the lords inhabiting the adjacent castles were admitted, but only as ordinary citizens; without, however, losing any of their nominal privileges.

Though feudalism possessed nearly the same generic type in all European countries, it presented here and there varying shades of nationality, due to the dissimilarity of race, the habits of the people, the different modes in which it had been introduced, and the diverse phases of its struggle and growth. The illustrious house of Franconia, alarmed at the incessant progress of high German feudalism, and anxious to check it, created, in the midst of the duchies by which it was threatened, a number of immediate lordships, owing fealty only to the emperor, and having a hereditary right over the fiefs of medieval society.

This step met with an obstinate resistance from the great vassals who possessed this hereditary right, which the elected monarch did not enjoy of himself. On the other hand, the palatine lords, agents of the emperor, empowered to represent him in the great fiefs or in his domains, and the burgraves of the towns, impatient to free themselves from the imperial suzerainty, displayed at the same time the insubordination which the lords had practiced in the Carolingian epoch, and endeavored to establish for themselves an independence transmissible to their heirs.

While this movement was going on, the pope was lowering the status of the empire. Innocent II compelled the Emperor Lothair II to receive in fee from him Tuscany, the Duchy of Spoleto, the Marches of Ancona, Bologna, Parma, and Placenta, forming part of the legacy bequeathed to the Holy See by the Countess Matilda.

From this flagrant humiliation, submitted to by Conrad of Hohenstaufen, the successor of Lothair, and haughtily

ud it phelippe descendy treser
cellent et tres redoubte price
Charle par la grace de dieu

ABOVE: A FIFTEENTH-CENTURY MINIATURE DEPICTING CHARLES, THE DUKE OF BURGUNDY, WITH HIS COUNCILORS AND BARONS.

rejected by Henry the Haughty when he refused to render feudal homage to the pope, arose the celebrated quarrel of the Guelphs and the Ghibellines, which, from the banks of the Rhine, spread beyond the Alps, and implanted itself in the very heart of Italy.

Henry the Haughty, chief of the Guelphs, independent and royal, was proscribed and stripped of his duchies, while Conrad, chief of the Ghibellines, inaugurated the brilliant dynasty of the Hohenstaufens. Thirty years of bitter warfare led to the treaty of Constance, which brought to a definite close the struggle of the feudal empire against the popular independence of the cities of Italy. During this time, the alliance of the papacy with the national party was cemented, seconded by the efforts of petty feudalism,

The pope had recovered the freeholds left him by the Countess Matilda. The towns preserved their regal prerogatives, entire liberty to raise armies, surround themselves with walls, exercise criminal and civil jurisdiction, and form confederations with other towns, and so forth.

The emperor was left with no other privileges than those of confirming, through his ambassadors, the consular elections, and of appointing in each town a judge of appeal in his name. It was in vain that the Emperor Henry VI endeavored to reestablish high feudalism; he died in 1099 while trying, and Pope Innocent III, who considered himself the natural defender of all the rights and the supreme judge in all the monarchies in Europe, resisted every effort made by Henry VI.

Several Crusades, moreover, which occurred during this period, created a modification in the warlike sentiments of the feudal nobility, until the independence of Italy rose triumphant from the tomb which opened for the Emperor Frederick II on December 13, 1250. Influential to this was the policy of the illustrious pontiff who had occupied the chair of St. Peter, and the efforts of the Italian free towns, in turn backed up by the petty feudal nobility.

In England, John Lackland had, by the Magna Carta of 1215, promised the clergy to respect the liberties of the Church, and notably the freedom of election; to the feudal lords he had promised to observe the feudal conditions of release, of ward, and of marriage; to the bourgeois, that no new tax should be levied without the consent of the common council; and to all his subjects he accorded the habeas corpus — that is to say, the liberty of the person, with trial by jury, and by constituting the court of common pleas at a certain fixed place.

A second charter, called the Forest Charter, mitigated the extreme severity of the penalties for infraction of the laws appertaining to the chase. It guaranteed the whole of the liberties which had been extracted from him by creating a tribunal of 25 barons, entrusted with the function of seeing that this charter was carried out, and, further, of keeping watch over the action of the crown. This was submitting the government to a regular course of discipline. Just as the feudal nobility had been kept under and oppressed by the sovereign power, so was the latter now hedged in, thwarted, and hampered in its despotic tendencies.

In France, St. Louis, following in the footsteps of Philip-Augustus, labored to suppress the abuses of the feudal regime; he compelled his barons to choose between the fiefs which they held from him and those which they had received from the kings of England; he rooted out the old feudal stocks, and created a new feudalism. It was not less valiant but more moral than the old, and never lost sight of the formidable opposition which the old nobility had ventured to set up against the Queen-Regent, Blanche of Castile, when it declared that the young King Louis should not be consecrated until the suzerain aristocracy was restored to the plenitude of its privileges.

After Louis IX, French feudalism, transformed by the saint-king, was neither less haughty, less trivial, nor less insolent than before, but it was more favorable to the crown and less hostile to the Church. It formed a brilliant array of medieval culture, full of enthusiasm and impetuosity, commencing a battle well, always winning it at the very beginning of the action, but losing it afterward for want of being supported by a national body of infantry, whose help it despised. It made up a body of cavalry admirably adapted for tournaments and feats of arms but incapable of carrying on a regular warfare, or even of ensuring success in a great battle. The victories of Mons-en-Puelle, under Philip IV, and of Cassel, under Philip of Valois (1328), increased to the utmost the blind confidence of the French nobility, and brought about, by absolutely identical means, the disasters of Crécy, Poitiers, and Agincourt in 1346, 1356, and 1415, respectively.

From the events which took place during the space of a century, from the accession to the imperial throne of the Emperor Louis V (1313) to the Peace of Bretigny (1360), it was made manifest that the destinies of the feudal world rested henceforth upon France and England, those two rival powers, both of which were acquisitive and inflexible. The emperor and the pope occupied but the second place in this latest evolution of feudalism. Rome, compelled to bend toward France, gave the latter a considerable preponderance, and the force of equilibrium must inevitably bring together the King of England and the Emperor of Germany.

The French royalty, despite the vicissitudes caused by an incessant struggle against the English, despite the ravages of the plague, which had depopulated two-thirds of the kingdom, despite its financial burdens and the precarious position of the monarchy, continued its work of assimilation and feudal incorporation. The suzerainty attaching to the great fiefs gradually fell under the jurisdiction of the sovereign, while, upon the right bank of the Rhine, the great barons remained almost as omnipotent as ever they had been.

There existed in Germany at that time two kinds of leagues between the nobility, the one offensive and the other defensive: that of the Gauerbinate or Gauerbschaften, by virtue of which the petty nobility formed family pacts for transmitting their fiefs by indirect line when the direct line should fail, and for reconstructing or repairing their castles out of a common fund; and that of the Teutonic Hanseatic League, the league of the prince-archbishops and electors with 60 towns upon the Rhine.

Rudolf of Hapsburg, a monarch as resolute as he was able, put a stop to proceedings which were full of danger to the imperial authority, compelled his vassals to do him homage, and razed to the ground 70 fortresses whose feudal brigandage 35 had scattered desolation and ruin. However, after his death, the usurpation of the suzerain lords began afresh, and the Bulle d'Or, which was the basis of public right in Germany, confirmed the downfall of the imperial power (1378).

In France, on the other hand, as each convocation of the States-General was attended with the creation or levying of some new tax, the third estate attempted to exact all the more from royalty in proportion as it gratified the latter's pecuniary demands, claiming to have a voice in the question

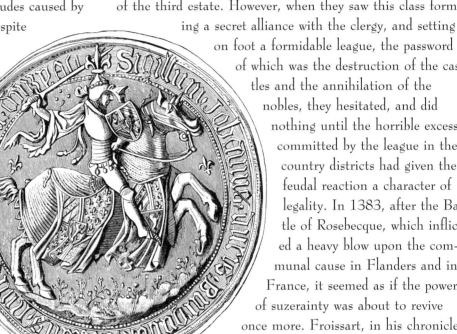

ABOVE: THE SEAL OF JEAN SANS PEUR
(1371–1419), THE DUKE OF BURGUNDY,
AND THE BARON OF DONZY.

of peace or war, to direct the financial affairs of the kingdom, to be convoked every year, and to share, with the two other orders, the weight of the charges the profit of which ought to be shared by all.

The feudal nobility resisted the exorbitant pretensions of the third estate. However, when they saw this class forming a secret alliance with the clergy, and setting on foot a formidable league, the password of which was the destruction of the castles and the annihilation of the nobles, they hesitated, and did nothing until the horrible excesses committed by the league in the country districts had given the feudal reaction a character of legality. In 1383, after the Battle of Rosebecque, which inflicted a heavy blow upon the communal cause in Flanders and in France, it seemed as if the power of suzerainty was about to revive once more. Froissart, in his chronicles, rejoiced at this fact, because he believed that social order was threatened with utter ruin. But French chivalry succumbed in its turn at Agincourt in 1415 beneath the onslaught of the English archers.

This was the final condemnation of feudal armies, as well as of the system which these armies represented, and which they had failed to sustain. French feudalism had already ceased to be anything more than a storehouse of traditions which were still held in respect, and of old customs which had fallen into disuse among the medieval nobility. In England, Scotland, and Ireland, high feudalism was rapidly in the course of decay before Henry VIII dealt it its deathblow.

In Germany, feudalism struggled for existence during the reign of Maximilian. In France it was crushed by Louis XI with the help of the third estate. Beyond the Alps, in Italy, its existence was prolonged for a short period, partly under a clerical disguise, partly by the hired help of the condottieri, and, in some places, by the support of the urban democracy — that is, the industrial and trading part of the population. Everywhere, however, it disappeared with the Middle Ages, of which, both in its acts and in its first principles, it bore the ineffaceable imprint.

A Knight's Life

THE SECRET OF KNIGHTHOOD'S STRENGTH lay in its human elements, its regard for life, and its infinite tenderness, with sympathies so wide it could not restrict itself to the narrow circle of caste. Throughout medieval history, the man who had won his spurs, by fair conduct on the field, might wear them. The gentleman without fortune might command barons in war and be called brother by his king. To be brave, loyal, and generous established a claim to the title deeds which were good throughout Europe. It was a life that was sung of by every wandering minstrel.

During the Middle Ages, France, England, and northern Europe covered a landscape of vast tracts of primeval forest, wild and unenclosed moors and commons, and marshes and mires. The towns were surrounded by walls and towers, and the narrow streets of picturesque gabled timber houses were divided by spaces of gardens and grove, above which rose numerous steeples of churches and abbeys, full of artistic wealth.

The narrow lanes were full of merchants and buyers, while the many sign-boards over the booths and merchandise gave color to the scene. Fairs, of course, played a great part in medieval commerce. The principal

ABOVE: A MOUNTED WARRIOR IN CHAIN MAIL.

French fairs were, for example, those which were held at Falaise in Champagne and at Saint-Denis, near Paris.

The villages consisted of a group of cottages, often mere hovels, scattered round a wide green, with a village cross in the middle. In England, close to the villages was the moated manor house. This was occupied by the lord of the manor, or by his bailiff, or seneschal, and was often held from overlords. When this overlord was the king, the manor was said to be held "in capite."

The castles of the knights varied considerably, but, for the most part, they took on the characteristics of a prison with their frowning dungeons, their impassable moats, their embattled walls, and their jealously guarded portals suggestive of war and rapine. Their interiors, by nineteenth or twentieth-century standards of comfort, were cold and churlish. Through narrow loopholes and unglazed windows — for oiled paper or horn, or wooden shutters alone were then used—the winter blasts blew. The mailed foot of the medieval warrior and the silken slipper of the chatelaine reposed upon the undressed flagstones, whose coldness was somewhat relieved by a covering of straw or green herbs.

The household ate together, with the exception that the knight and his lady sat "above the salt," or, if of the noblesse, on

Above: An Italian knight of the late fifteenth century.

a dais above the floor. To counteract the bareness of the walls and to give some protection against incessant draughts, hangings of silken velvet embroidered with gold were suspended against them. Gold and silver plate ornamented the sideboard, which varied in the number of its shelves according to the rank of the owner. In times of peace, the knight and his lady were decked out in rich furs, silks, and velvets obtained either by private purchase or at one of the great fairs.

A Portrait of the Knight

Except in the case of a few descriptions found in the old chroniclers and poets, the beauty of damsels or young squires is of a fair or blond type. In the "Chansons" nearly all the heroes are fair, although an exception to this rule is mentioned in *The Ballad of Ogier*. The ideal lad of both mothers and ladies was one perfectly proportioned and graceful, slender, lively, with regular features and having locks as yellow as gold, and these curled, frizzed and plaited, and his eyes beautiful like a falcon's of a gray, changeful hue. (Of course, the ideal *damsel* of both mothers and lads was one perfectly proportioned and graceful, slender, lively, with regular features and having locks as yellow as gold, and these curled, frizzed and plaited, and eyes beautiful like a falcon's of a gray, changeful hue.)

The eyes of the squire should be large and dashed somewhat with his proud spirit, and yet not displeasing. *The Ballad of Ogier* notes that "His nose should be straight and slender with a laughing mouth; and perhaps above it, there should be the down of early manhood. As to his body — his chest and shoulders, they should be broad and strong — *gros par les costes, grailes par le baldrer*. His arms should be full of muscle and sinew in order to give a ready blow, while his hands should be kept white and his fingers tapering, and his legs should be long and shaped well for the saddle."

If such a description appears effeminate, remember that it was a picture of only one side of a young esquire's character and life. If the frizzled hair, the clear complexion, and golden tresses were the means of

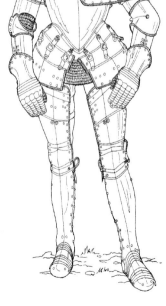

Above: An English Knight.

furthering "courtesy" as it was then called, which embraced all we know now of graceful dalliance on a lady's whims and smiles, there was always underlying it the sterner one of military training. Beneath were aspirations for what every noble lad so earnestly looked forward to as the consummation of his years of training: a knight's spurs, and a knight's career.

Such a youth, reared up in his father's or a neighboring lord's house, gained a vocation for chivalry without effort. Everything combined to foster it.

The esquire was nurtured on the conversation of his elders, and their tales at the end of the banquets, as well as on the reading of the old stories of Charlemagne or Arthur and his knights and the paintings and tapestries on the old walls depicting fights of warriors in a bygone age. With every breath he drew, the young esquire drew in the spirit of the chivalrous life. Indeed, he had two choices, the helmet or the tonsure, and he generally preferred the former.

The Birth of a Knight

Into a world of lights and shadows, much good and much evil, in one of these gray weather-beaten old castles in France or England, with its tiny town or village of retainers nestling at its foot, was born the heir of future knighthood. His was to be a warlike, yet a religious, vocation, sworn to fidelity to the Holy Church, and the champion of the widow and the fatherless; fitly he was the outcome of the bridal night when the nuptial bed had been blessed by some aged lord or grandfather.

In those days of constant warfare, whether between conflicting countries or the petty feuds hardly ever ceasing between neighboring barons and knights, the birth of a male child was a valuable asset, both in a knight's family and for the lord's banner under whom he might ultimately serve.

Battles in those days, it is true, even the more important ones, measured by modern ones caused very little loss of life, and those who were slain were chiefly archers, men-at-arms, and camp followers. The others of a higher class, such as the knights and squires of high degree, were nearly always held for ransom. Still, a certain number of them in these constant little battles fell, and it was therefore requisite to look for children to be born to fill up these gaps, The vassals also saw in the birth of a male child a future protector and the fief remaining in the possession of those under whom they were accustomed to serve. If instead of a son, a daughter was born, they must expect — no other issue forthcoming — that the overlord would one day take her into his wardship and bestow her hand and lands on some alien knight.

King Edward I gave 50 marks for news of the birth of his granddaughter Margaret de Bohun in 1303, but appears to have reduced the sum to 10 for her sister Alianora the next year. The birth of his grandson Edward Monthermer in 1304 found him more generously disposed to the extent of 40 marks. Edward II was more lavish; he settled 80 pounds per annum on John Launge for news of the birth of his eldest son.

If, and when, a male child was born, the news would be brought to the impatient father pacing up and down the great rush-strewn hall, littered with hounds and the implements of the chase. "It is a son!" one cries. *"Par le foi que vos doi, un damoiseau est né,"* exclaims the Duchess Parise in the ballad that bears her name. When the father hears it, rejoicing already, he thinks of the valiant future of his little boy. *"Dans quinz ans mon fils sera chevalier,"* thus the old knight Fromont whispers in *The Ballad of Garins le Loherains*. The announcer of the event, too, looks forward. *"Il est né, le seigneur dont vous tiendrez vos terres, il est ne celui qui vous donnera les riches fourrures, le vair et le gris, les belles armes et les chevaux de prix."* So again, in the medieval Breton ballad of *The Clerk of Rohan* (1241), the knight about to go crusading looks forward to his newborn child to do likewise someday.

Immediately after birth, this much desired child was bathed — the father often superintending it — and as his son was placed in the water, it reminded him of that bath that he as a candidate for knighthood had once long ago entered. Then the infant was swaddled in many folds, his tiny arms bound close to his side, while his feet were held together by ligatures of linen. In the same fashion, the ancient Romans bound up the limbs of a newborn child. Indeed, the medieval

ABOVE: AN ENGLISH KNIGHT.

miniatures of such a child are exactly similar to the fresco of an infant so swaddled found at Pompeii. *"Quand les dames l'auront molt bien emmaillotee,"* we are told in *The Ballad of the Knight of the Swan*. So Quicherat in his *History of Costume* confirms this custom as being the outcome of the ancient Romans. *"Tous les enfants ont les bras enfermés dans leur maillot. Chez les Romains, les enfants étaient emmaillotés exactement de la meme façon."*

Tradition records that the first morsel of solid food was put into the baby boy's mouth on the point of his father's sword, that he might be a valiant warrior and die on the field of battle. However, before he was allowed to take any nourishment, it was often the custom that baptism must first take place. This rite of baptism was, in the age of chivalry, perhaps more highly thought of than ever before or since, for until the infant was immersed in the font, it was an evil thing — when it was lifted from it, it was not only a Christian but had, in its heart, the makings of a Christian knight.

During the thirteenth and fourteenth centuries, custom varied as to the number of sponsors at a child's baptism. At one period, one alone was thought best, to signify the Unity of God; three at another to represent the blessed Trinity, so it is laid down in the Council of Salisbury in 1217, Treves (Trier) in 1227, and Worcester in 1240. The Council of Trent (1545 to 1563) at last decided that two sponsors only should be appointed, thus ending differences, but doing away with the mystical number of one or three.

The Child Knight

Sometimes after baptism, the child's warlike destiny was prefigured. Thus, after the second son of Charles V of France was baptized in 1371, the Constable du Guesclin, his godparent, placed his bare sword in the naked infant's hands (*nudo tradidit ensem nudum*), so also the Duchess of Burgundy's infant, in 1393, was immediately after baptism admitted a knight of the Golden Fleece.

The day when the knight's lady was able to leave her chamber and repair to the nearest church, to offer her thanks and gifts, was made a great day of rejoicing.

She was accompanied by a great throng of relatives and friends, and, after hearing Mass, she made her appointed offerings. St. Elizabeth of Hungary is said to have offered a lamb and wax taper, but this seems the only instance in medieval chroniclers of departing from the usual gifts of gold or silver or wax for the many altars. Before setting forth to the church, she was gorgeously clothed in her chamber, often in an overdress of ermine and a mantle over it of gray fur, ornamented with tufts of sable. During this robing, a carol suitable to the occasion was frequently sung.

Back at the castle, troubadours and jugglers congregated with the guests and sang and played until the day declined. At the end of the long feasting, a herald stood forth and announced a tournament to be held as a suitable termination for a brave knight's hospitality on behalf of a young life born to one day enter the lists of chivalry himself.

Before leaving the castle, the guests universally left gifts for the newborn child. The godfather frequently gave his in gold or silver, and the godmother left furred robes, frocks, and shoes. These gifts were often afterward distributed to the poor.

All this time, the child was not left alone. Immediately at his birth, a "foster mother" was waiting to give him nourishment, for the knightly ladies hardly ever suckled their own children. Because few high-born mothers suckled or attended to their children themselves, the nurse was a very important person. Some of their names are still on record as regards the English princes. The nurse of Henry III was named Helen of Winchester and was the wife of William Dun. She was in receipt of a pension as late as 1237. The nurse of Edward II was Alice de Lethegrew, and the wardship of Geoffrey de Scotland was granted to her in 1284. Edward III's nurse was Margaret de Daventie, and judging from his grants to her and his foster sister Hawise, he seems to have been much attached to them. Richard II was one of the two medieval kings who were nursed by French women. His nurse bore the intriguing name of Mundina Danes, Danos or Denys from Aquitaine. Henry IV was nursed by an Irish woman, Margaret Taaf of Dublin. Highest in rank of royal nurses was Anne de Caux, the French nurse of

ABOVE: A KNIGHT'S MOTHER, IN ERMINE.

Edward IV. His brother Richard III conferred on her a pension of 20 pounds per annum.

During the Middle Ages, children in their early years were peculiarly under the influence of the fairies. These were believed to haunt the fountains and woods outside the castle, often appearing to favored mortals in lovely guise and to enter the sleeping chambers of the children within the castle. Sometimes they were accused of substituting one of their own elfin people for the lusty little heir; sometimes, in a more pleasant humor, they were credited with endowing him with gifts of wisdom and strength. It was customary in some places to leave towels and clean water by the fire after the child of the house had been bathed, for the fairy mother to use for her own elfin child.

To guard the crib, many spells were used and cradle songs sung. But not alone were these fairy guardians round the child, or later the young page or squire, but they were woven into the life of the knights themselves. Thus, in *The Ballad of Partenopeus de Blois*, the fairy "Melior," after sleeping with the nephew of Clovis, to prove to him the sincerity of her love and kisses, professes her faith in Christianity. The truth is that, at this period, the frontier line between the two beliefs—the magical and the Christian, the spells of fairy enchantment and the intervention of the saints — was hard to delineate.

The nurse of the sleeping infant, as well as the knight, his father, as often as not tried to placate the fairy folk, as they did the saints, to ward off trouble, recommending themselves to whichever invisible being they thought at the moment most efficacious for this purpose.

In the castle, the child found every day the game of chess, beloved of his knightly father, being played, in which, at a very early age, he was instructed. At the age of seven, the child was removed from his nursery and from the care of females, and generally from his home. He was placed in the household of some powerful lord or knight, where he was to learn the whole discipline of his future profession, and imbibe its emulous and enthusiastic spirit. The law which enforced leaving children in the hands of women until the age of seven was originally decreed by the Emperor Julian, and was incorporated into the laws of medieval France.

This custom was an inestimable advantage to the poorest nobility, who otherwise could hardly have given their sons the accomplishments of their station. The latter, thus placed in the center of all that could awaken their imagination in the creed of chivalry, gathered indelible impressions to last through their lives, and a thirst to join in those rude but glorious tournaments and battles which they daily saw their lord and his squires ride forth from the castle gate to join in. The dress of these children was a tunic cut off at the knee and usually bare legs if not with long stockings. In some cases leg bands wound round. A short mantle was fastened on the shoulder with a gold brooch or clasp. The cap set close to the head was usually of leather, in winter trimmed round with fur. The hair was cut to the poll straight across the forehead.

ABOVE: A CHILD IS TAKEN AWAY FROM HIS MOTHER TO BE TRAINED AS A KNIGHT.

At the early age of seven, under the chief huntsman or falconer, they were taught the rudiments of the hunt. In the gentler art of falconry they received the four first rules: how to fly a hawk; how to feed it in its mews; how to call it back when it was on the wing, and how to retain it when it had returned. So the boy Huon de Bordeaux says, "I know now how to 'mew' the sparrow-hawk; how to chase the wild boar and stag; and how to blow on the horn when I have killed the beast; and how to give the quarry to the hunting dogs."

So intense was the love of the chase, even in lads, that when an old chronicler wished to describe the thirst for future glory in the youthful Godfrey de Bouillon, he made him say, "I long for a battle against the infidel more than the possession of gold or silver, or of the love of a girl, or the flight of my falcon." So, too, in the *Enfance Vivien* the hero is offered a fine horse, as a youth, and he

ABOVE: A YOUNG FALCONER.

replies, "Nay, I care not for a horse but for two dogs and a falcon." We need hardly remind the reader that in the immortal combat of Roland and Oliver under the walls of Vienne, the whole quarrel was about a hawk. Thomas a Becket nearly lost his life as a boy for the sake of his hawk when he plunged into a mill race in the Thames where it had fallen, to save it. For these noble boys, another pastime in the open air was to venture on the destrier, the knight's great warhorse. They clung on the great croup and made the unwieldy horse gallop round the castle yard (*"et quand ils en ont si bien galopent destrier"*).

At the age of seven began the knightly boys' so-called education in letters, or what may be called the scant portion of it then in vogue, for the children of knights. The colleges under ecclesiastical patronage and the monastic schools were frequented only by those in the lower ranks of society, such as the citizen and, in some few cases, the villain, and most of their scholars were destined for the church or the law.

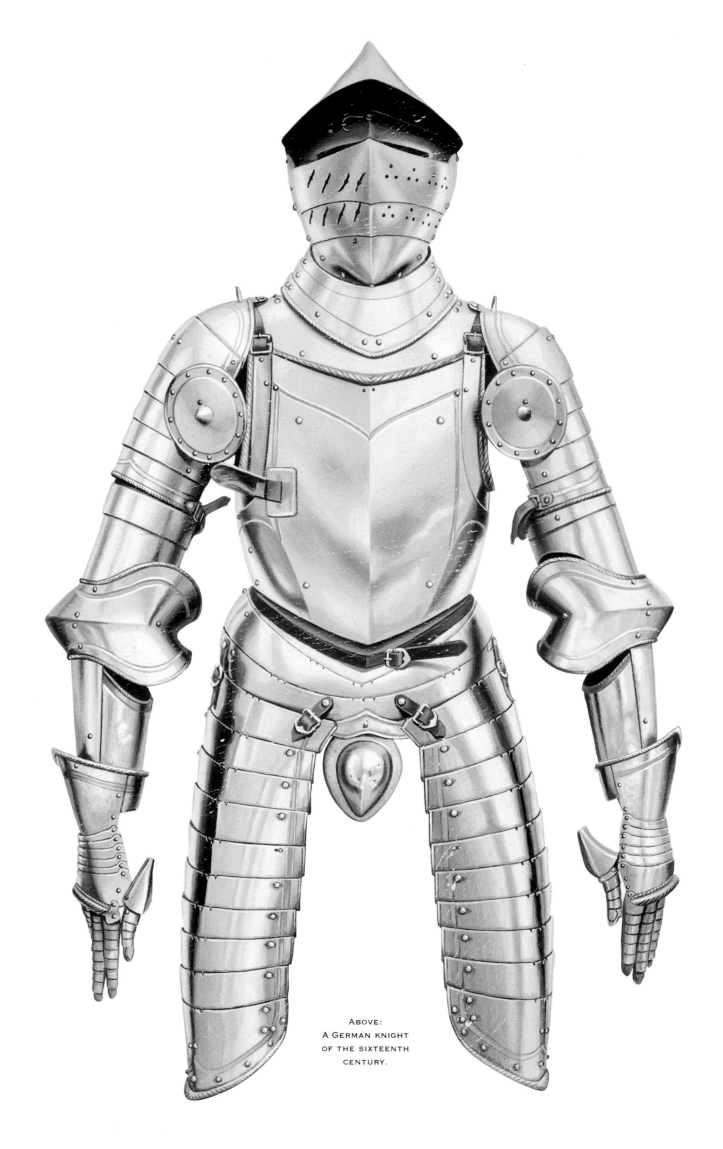

ABOVE:
A GERMAN KNIGHT
OF THE SIXTEENTH
CENTURY.

That villains attended these schools is apparent from the fact that a petition was addressed to Richard II demanding that they be restrained from sending their children to school because the ambition to rise in life by becoming a "clerk" was taking many workers from the land. The request was refused.

The education of a knight's or lord's children was conducted by the private chaplain. In some households, particularly if the owner was fond of music, there was attached to the private chapel a number of singers, priests, and officials. In the smallest castle, there was always the oratory and a chaplain to serve it.

In the poems of Eustache Deschamps, the latter knew everything of his lord's intimate affairs. So "honor," says one, "all the clergy, and speak to them with reverence, but no more." Again, "Attend every day at Mass but carry no news to the monastery."

The scion of knighthood, as a rule, was well instructed in his religion, even though his secular knowledge was spare. When Doon, in the ballad of his name, was lost in the forest, the little boy hid himself in the hole of an oak and is depicted as making the sign of the cross. After his prayers, we are told that he felt no fear though he was a lost child and away from his mother.

In *The Ballad of the Seven Wise Men,* we are told of a chaplain who rebuked in his pupils a love of excessive eating, teaching them courtesy and good manners and never quitting the side of such until they went to bed.

Though the Duke de Nevers, in *The Ballad of Gaufrey,* was able to boast that he could speak in French, German, Italian, Spanish, and Norman, the object in training these noble boys was not a proficiency in letters — that was left to the bourgeoisie and the clergy. The focus was on his future career as a knight, and to be brave in the field, to endure hardness, and to be expert at the mimic war of the chase. This is what every old knight who trained the boys — and even the chaplain who, with his brother ecclesiastics of that age, loved the chase — had in view. One knight said, "I swear by God's body, I would rather that my son should hang than study letters. For it becomes the sons of gentlemen to bear the horn nicely, and to hunt skillfully and elegantly, to carry and train a hawk. But the study of letters should be left to the sons of rustics."

Sometimes, it seems, so great was their ardor to arm themselves like their elders, that they were pacified by giving a religious significance to these arms they so wanted, and to the armor, which, even as boys, they could don. Thus, so bent on the chase were some of these noble lads in the Middle Ages that, to humor their tastes and yet impress them with religion, a chaplain of King John of France wrote, at the king's desire, a book on the subject for his son, Philip, the Duke of Burgundy, in 1359.

In a passage in this book, the chaplain compares the weapons used by a boy to his spiritual armor: "Steel plates shalt thou have of humility, So that through thy side, Pride cannot wound thee, To the heart, that nothing shall touch, If patience be the shield.

"The plates must be well clamped, Into the well-closed buckles, And take thou heed that in the shield, There be no flaw (want of virtue), Of Reason thou shalt make the bassinet, Thou shalt carry no lance, For fear that thou art yet too young."

The title bestowed on these boyish sons of the knights was that of "page." The duties of these pages were those found generally in domestic service about the person of their lord and lady. They accompanied them to the chase, in their journeying, in their visits to neighboring castles, in their walks, and often carried messages.

The chief lessons inculcated were love due to God, and love due to the ladies, with the ladies charging themselves to teach the boys their catechism and also the art of love.

In defense of the latter, there is no doubt that in the earliest ages of chivalry this love inculcated was pure and platonic, and possibly prevented youths from falling into regrettable disorders.

The wave of ardent and often nonplatonic love from Provence had not yet penetrated into the northern castles of France or England. As practice is better than precept, a boy was bidden to choose one of the fairest and most

TRAINING FOR KNIGHTHOOD

Led by the instinct of imitation peculiar to the young, the pages habitually played at doing everything they saw done by the knights. They practiced wielding the lance and the sword.

They played at combats, attacks, and duels among themselves. Excited by emulation, they coveted the honor of being considered brave, hoping that if they attained their wish, it would lead to their being attached to the service of some person of mark, or to their being promoted to the rank of esquire — a necessary step toward knighthood itself.

virtuous ladies about the court or castle he served in, and to look on her as his sovereign lady. To her he was to confide all his thoughts and actions, and she, in return, looked after his welfare and upbringing.

The constant companionship engendered by the castle walls promoted among the boys thrown together many close and enduring friendships, which were helped by their having a similar object in view: to become one day a valiant knight in the service of their present lord or future king. A knight offered no reward for the gratuitous reception of a brother knight's lads into his entourage as a page or a squire.

On the contrary, because it was from such a brave knight that the boys imbibed their first lessons in chivalry, and, in his person and bravery, saw the standard of knightly virtue, they rendered him the greatest obedience during their education, and ever afterward, when their days of instruction were over, tendered it to him by following his banner to the wars of their own free will.

At the age of 14, a boy was considered of an age to be admitted as an esquire. Such boys were allowed a greater intimacy with their lord and his lady than they had enjoyed as pages. Religion stepped in, and a certain religious service, not so elaborate or so solemn as that used in conferring the higher grade of knighthood, was held.

The future squire was presented to the priest before the altar by his parents, both holding blessed tapers in their hands, which afterward they presented as gifts to the Church. After certain prayers and blessings upon a sword and belt, which was henceforth to be his own, it was girded on the youthful squire's side. It is probable that this simple ceremony was used when raising a page to an esquire, and not, as some writers on the subject seem to have thought, when conferring knighthood.

The strict upbringing and education of the young esquire in the castle was not without its parallel in the monastic schools. Indeed, this fact strengthened the resemblance that the medieval writers sought to establish between chivalry and religion.

Each bishop thus congregated around him in the monastery "a bevy of youths emulous for the priesthood. These had daily and particular duties, often menial and personal to the lord-abbot or bishop. A strict code of morals, and of exercises, were laid down for them, and they were presided over, as the youthful esquires in the castle, by those older and more learned in their vocation."

Preparing the Youth for Knighthood

The son of a noble, or even of a commoner, intended for the ranks of knighthood, was at the age of seven taken away from the care of the women. However, they never allowed him to reach that age without instilling in him such sentiments of right that would govern his conduct during the rest of his life. He was then entrusted to the men, of whom he became not only the pupil but the servitor; for, says *Ordene de Chevalerie*, "It is proper that he should learn to obey before he governs; for otherwise he would not appreciate the nobility of his rank when he became a knight."

Moreover, the chivalric code, which distrusted the prejudices and weaknesses of paternal affection, required "every knight to place his son in the service of some other knight."

These youthful novices, particularly if they belonged to a noble and honorable family, always found plenty of princely courts, seignorial households, manors, and castles to receive them, which were, so to speak, the public schools of medieval society. There existed, besides, hospitals founded and maintained by wealthy and generous nobles, in the same manner as are the colleges of the University of Paris. And these hospitals were governed by old knights without family or fortune, who considered it no shame to retire to a pension in the shape of a house with board rather than a paid salary. This would be a kind of school of chivalry for the benefit of the youths, who promised at some future time to prove a credit to the institution. These youths, called pages, performed under their masters and mistresses the most humble and the most domestic functions: They followed them in their travels and to the chase. They formed part of their suites on occasions of ceremony. They wrote their letters and carried their messages. They waited on them at meals, carved their dishes, and poured out their drinks.

In the eyes even of those nobles who were most jealous of their birth and of their name, this temporary and casual servitude had nothing in it of either a humiliating or a degrading character, and its only effect was to knit still closer the ties of respect, obedience, and sympathy which bound a youth to his adopted parents, the aspirant for knighthood to his master and teacher. The latter by no means neglected the moral and religious education of the neophyte. The first lessons which were given him taught him not only to love God but to respect women. Lessons were given as soon as the young page had acquired sufficient experience to direct his own movements in the intricacies of chivalric life.

The Esquire

When the young men abandoned the position of pages in order to be made esquires, an event that never took place before their fourteenth year, their change of social condition was celebrated by a religious ceremony. The Church established this ceremony to consecrate their knightly vocation, and as a means of hallowing the use of the arms they were hereafter destined to carry. Standing at the altar and surrounded by his nearest relations, the youthful novice received the consecrated sword from the hands of the priest, promising always to wield it in the interests of religion and honor.

A higher position in the household of his lord or lady was then assigned to the new esquire. He was admitted to their private gatherings and took part in all assemblies and state ceremonies. It was now his duty to superintend the reception — that is to say, to regulate the laws of etiquette relating to the foreign nobles who visited his master's court. A passage from the history of Boucicaut, a marshal of France during the reign of Charles VI, will give an idea of the laborious and arduous existence of the young esquire who aspired to become a worthy knight: "Now cased in armor, he would practice leaping on to the back of a horse. Anon, to accustom himself to become long-winded and enduring, he would walk and run long distances on foot, or he would practice striking numerous and forcible blows with a battleaxe or mallet."

In order to accustom himself to the weight of his armor, he would turn somersaults while clad in a complete suit of mail, with the exception of his helmet, or would dance vigorously in a shirt of steel; he would place one hand on the saddlebow of a tall charger, and the other on his neck, and vault over him. He would climb up between two perpendicular walls that stood four or five feet asunder by the mere pressure of his arms and legs, and would thus reach the top, even if it was as high as a tower, without resting in either the ascent or the descent. When he was at home, he would practice

ABOVE: MEDIEVAL ESQUIRES.

with the other young esquires at lance-throwing and other warlike exercises, and this continually.

Besides all this, it was necessary for an esquire who wished to fulfill his duties properly to possess a number of physical qualities, great versatility of talent and capability, and a zeal that never flagged. At court, as in the larger seignorial households, there were various classes or categories of esquires who performed totally distinct duties, which in less important households were all entrusted to the same individual.

The first in importance was the body esquire, or the esquire of honor. Then the chamber esquire, or chamberlain. The carving esquire, the stable esquire, the cup-bearing esquire, and so forth — all separate personages, whose names sufficiently indicate their duties. It is scarcely necessary to remark that esquires, besides the domestic services expected from them within their master's house, had especially to give proof of their vigilance and skill in the duties of the stable — duties as a historian aptly observes, which were, of necessity, noble, since the military aristocracy never fought but on horseback. It was the duty of all esquires to break in their master's chargers and to teach the younger esquires the routine of the stable.

The duty of attending to the arms and armor devolved upon another class of esquires. We may add that, as each seignorial castle was also a species of fortress, most of the esquires, in addition to their other tasks, were required to perform certain military duties analogous to those practiced in a regular stronghold, such as rounds, sentry duty, watches, and so forth. When a lord mounted his horse, his esquires shared among them the honor of assisting him; some held his stirrup, while others carried various parts of his armor, such as the armlets, the helmet, the shield, the gauntlets, and so forth.

As soon as the knight had decided to mount his charger, his squires proceeded to arm him; that is to say, they firmly fastened together all the different pieces of his armor on his body, with straps attached to metal buckles for the purpose. It may be well conceived that no slight care was required to properly adjust such a cumbrous and complicated steel or iron casing. An esquire's neglect, indeed, frequently caused his master's death.

When a single combat took place, the esquires, drawn up behind their lord, remained for a few moments inactive spectators of the struggle. Watching the slightest movement and the smallest signals of their master, they stood ready to assist him in an indirect, but efficacious, manner if he attained any advantage, without actually becoming aggressors themselves, in order to assure his victory. If the knight were hurled from his steed, they helped him to remount, brought him a fresh horse, and warded off the blows that were aimed at him. If he were wounded and placed *hors de combat,* they did their utmost, at the risk of their own lives, to carry him off before he was slain outright. And, it was to his esquires that a successful knight confided the care of the prisoners he had taken on the battlefield.

The esquires, short of actually fighting themselves, a thing forbidden by the code of chivalry, were expected to display the greatest zeal, the greatest skill, and the greatest courage, and, consequently, had it very materially in their power to contribute to their master's success. A long novitiate and the consciousness of an aptitude for a military career were not always, however, sufficient to enable an esquire to attain the rank of knight.

He was frequently obliged, in the intermediate rank of pursuivant-at-arms, to travel through foreign countries, either as the acknowledged envoy of some prince or noble, or merely in the character of an ordinary traveler, and to be present at chivalric games and tournaments, without actually taking part in them himself. He thus acquired, by constant interaction with distinguished soldiers and high-born ladies, a thorough technical knowledge of the military calling and an intimate acquaintance with all the elegant refinements of courtesy.

In this way, pursuivants-at-arms went everywhere, one day being ceremoniously received at the court of a powerful noble, the next being simply entertained in the lowly manor of a poor gentleman. Wherever they might be, they acted honorably both in word and in deed, observing scrupulously the precepts both of honor and of virtue, showing themselves to be noble, brave, and devoted, and seeking every opportunity to prove themselves worthy of being ranked with the noble knights whose deeds and names were the theme of constant and universal praise.

Chance alone was not allowed to direct their wanderings and adventurous steps. They eagerly sought the most renowned princely and seignorial courts, at which they were certain to meet with medieval society's loftiest traditions. They thought themselves fortunate indeed when they were able to make their obeisance to some hero famous for his deeds in arms, or to elicit a smile from some lady celebrated for her beauty and her worth. While the most perfect respect and courtesy to ladies were the first duties instilled in each youthful aspirant, it must be owned that the education received by the ladies was one calculated to make them in every way worthy of such homage.

When the esquire, who was left undergoing his laborious novitiate, had at last performed all its numerous requirements, the investiture of knighthood was conferred upon him — a symbolic ceremony, as indeed were all the ceremonies that made up a chivalric ordination, but one of a more serious and solemn character than the rest.

Growing into Knighthood

It was probably during their apprenticeship as pages or esquires that many of those beautiful and lifelong friendships were contracted between knightly souls. Knights who felt a sufficiently strong sentiment toward each other engaged, under the most solemn vows, in a bond of fraternity for life, implying a constant and faithful friendship to each other. This practice enters largely into the plot of several of the medieval stories, as in that of *Amis and Amiloun*. The desire for this true friendship began when pages or young esquires, living together, was not unnaturally fostered by the general prevalence of hateful feuds.

As described in the adjacent sidebar, the youthful esquires were typically classed in six specific categories of employment in the household. As noted, the most honorable were the first and the sixth — i.e., those who were appointed to wait on the persons of their lord and lady, and those who were appointed to "the Honors," as they were called.

The first were admitted to great familiarity by these distinguished persons. They took part in their courts and assemblies. They were enabled to mold their conversation and conduct by those they mixed with. They accompanied them when they made visits to their neighbors. They often took part (instead of those detailed for that duty) in the Honors. They were enabled by this constant personal service, in the more refined presence of their master and mistress, to become skilled in elegant manners and modes of speech, to cultivate, by their bright example, modesty, and a facility for witty conversation.

Second, those who were esquires of the Honors were so named as taking part in and marshalling the ceremonies of the lord's court. The word "honors" here signifies the ceremonial of such, and the articles pertaining to these stately functions. Thus, the esquire of honor carried his lord's sword of honor; he stood by the lord's chair or throne of state; he carried his master's helmet of honor; he led his state horse with all its glittering caparisons; he carried (if not worn) his lord's mantle of state; and had, besides, all the duties thrown on him of any great reception at which the lord's neighbors and vassals were entertained. Perhaps the duty they most thought of was that of carrying their knight's banner and of raising his battle cry, as was depicted in the life of the celebrated Du Gueslin.

In addition to these duties, these esquires were often dispatched in the place of heralds, and indeed often took the office of such — to throw down their master's "gauge" of battle before his adversary.

Third, the esquire of the table had many onerous duties, such as we now look on as those fit only for persons of a low degree, but were then considered as marks of honor and to be sought after by youths of noble lineage.

To enforce the submission of high-spirited youths to these menial offices, the "Order of Chivalry," in its dissertation "How to Acquire Knighthood," lays down: "It is fitting that the son of a knight, while he is an esquire, should know how to take care of a horse, and it is fitting that he serve (at table) first, and be subject before he himself is a lord (or knight) for otherwise he will never know the nobleness of his knighthood when he comes himself to be a knight. For this reason should every knight put his son into the service of another knight so that he may learn to carve at table and to serve thereat, and to arm and robe a knight in his youth. Thus, like a man who would learn to be a tailor or a carpen-

ter it is fitting that such a one should have a master who is a tailor or a carpenter; so too it is fitting that every nobleman who loves the order of his knighthood should have had first a master who was a knight."

To serve, therefore, whatever his family's rank, at his lord's table, was one of the usual duties of the young esquire. Sometimes — if his instruction was conducted at home — this service was rendered to the knight who was his father. The duties of these young esquires were not confined to domestic tasks. In a warlike household the preeminent duty of such was to attend to his lord's convenience when preparing for joust or battle, and to the arming of the latter before a fight. Doubtless the armorer was needed, when chain armor was discarded for plate, to rivet the many pieces which made a knight a veritable man of steel, but he was always overlooked by the faithful squire.

On a journey, the esquire also carried — until the knight needed such to meet his adversary — the arms of his master. Some young esquires therefore bore after him his steel gauntlets and the arm pieces of his coat of mail. Others bore his lance, and his sword and his pennon, or — if entitled as a banneret — his square banner. They also, unless it was slung on the saddlebow of his destrier or warhorse, bore his helmet, ready to give it at the least approach of danger. With the exception of bearing the pennon or banner, the most coveted distinction of these youthful squires was adjudged to be he who carried the lord's shield. Not less a service was that assigned to the esquire who led the great warhorse, covered with plates of mail for any knightly adventure which demanded strength rather than speed.

Not only did the youthful esquires superintend the arming and carrying of the armor when it was not required of their lord but they of course accompanied him to the frequent tournaments of the time. Hardouin de la Jaille, in his book *Du Champ de Bataille*, writes, "One of his esquires should walk his horse in his part of the lists, about halfway,

CLASSES OF ESQUIRES

The youthful esquires were typically divided into six different classes, or types of employment, in their lord's household.

1. The Squire of the Body
   (That is to say, he who rendered personal service on the knight's person and that of his lady).
2. The Squire of the Chamber
   (the Chamberlain).
3. The Squire of the Table or Carver.
4. The Squire of the Wines.
5. The Squire of the Pantry.
6. The Squire of Honor or "the Honorus."

Of these, probably the most honorable were the first and the sixth, i.e., those who were appointed to wait on the persons of their lord and lady, and those who were appointed to "the Honors."

and the other esquire a little more in front, taking care that the horses do not annoy each other, nor fight, which they might do; nor need they restrain them further than when it comes to mounting (or when they proceed to mount) in order each one to aid his master and to go beyond the pavilions.

"The young men followed. Lances and bassinets they carried for the older knights, and learned the way to ride, and they saw the three modes of arms.

"Then they became archers. At table and everywhere they served, and the baggage they packed, behind them right willingly. Thus, they used to do and in the kitchen did offer themselves. The esquires at this time, then did they become men-at-arms and proved their worth eight or 10 years altogether.

"And they used to go on long journeys. Then they became knights [i.e., fitted for knighthood], humble, strong, prompt and agile in honoring strangers.

"By honors they maintained themselves, At jousts then they tilted, for this were a right they held dear, and they honored the ladies, who for their well-doing, loved them."

They, moreover, were bold and proud against their enemies and courteous to their friends. Yet in these outings and more domestic duties in which the young esquires took their share, whether in tournament or enterprise, theirs was always a secondary place. Their education was not over, and until it was, immediately after attending their lord afield, they returned to his castle or manor to engage again in their military training. They practiced putting on the chain mail and, later in the century, plate armor to accustom their limbs to bearing its weight and confinement.

They put on the heavy gauntlets of a knight and practiced holding a battle-ax and lance. They learned to use a shield deftly in mimic warfare with their companions. There they used to ride on the destrier fully armed and at full tilt, as against an adversary in a tournament. Often they were purposely without a fire in winter in the hall to condition themselves for future forays and encounters in the open country.

They practiced leaping and scaling walls, to fit them to make good war on beleaguered and fortified towns in the future. All these martial trials and exercises, despite their youth and sometimes almost a girlish figure and face, were deemed essential to the training of a future good knight, and were eagerly pursued day after day by these lads.

Despite their youth, many arduous tasks even outside in the world were often confided to the esquires — such tasks continually appear for the young page in the old ballads and in the pages of Froissart. Despite their youth, too, their lords seemed to have had great confidence in them. They used to confide the prisoners they took in a tournament to their keeping to hold for ransom.

Thus, in *The Ballad of Brut,* it is said of them, "The prisoners they caused to be arrested, And instead of turning back [i.e., to put them in ward] To the squires they delivered them And to guard them they bade them."

Alternative Paths to Knighthood

The grade or status of esquire, which was held necessary to obtain knighthood, was dispensed with frequently when the postulant for the latter was of royal or princely birth. Thus, the celebrated Dunois, Bastard of Orléans, was created a knight banneret, though he had never been an esquire. Geoffrey of Anjou in 1127 obtained knighthood at the hands of his father, King Henry, without passing through the grade of squire. Either for their high birth, considered to be unfitting for the menial condition of an esquire, or for their special valor on the field of battle, such as these were excused the long years a squire received of training ere he obtained knighthood.

Princes and kings often waived this ordinary rule — of being an esquire before receiving knighthood — in the case of noble children, whom at a very early age they conferred knighthood on. Thus, Charles of Valois, brother of Philip le Bel, passing through Bologna in 1301, conferred knighthood on Philip and Albert Degli Asinelli, one boy of 12, the other of 14, who had never attained the rank of esquire. So, too, he conferred it on Francis Bentivogli, who was only 13.

In Gherardacci's *History of Bologna*, we find Jean de Pepoli, son of the governor of the city, conferring knighthood on the two boys of a certain Macagrano, lately deceased, on account of their dead father's great services to the state. He knighted them on the day of their father's burial, at his tomb, and neither of these lads, of course, had previously passed through squiredom.

However, with such exceptions, which were not rare, there are also cases of older squires who refused to receive knighthood. Some waited their whole lives, enduring the necessity of passing through the rank of esquire, yearning for knighthood, yet never winning their spurs.

Above: The Holy Roman Emperor Frederick Barbarossa (1123–1190) conferring Knighthood upon a pair of noble young esquires.

It was a wise provision, for as we have seen, they were brought up in a military household from the day they entered it as pages, and were taught in all martial science by their instructors. Their bodies, by constant exercise hardened for a knight's life in battle and in tournament, they, upon attaining knighthood, were perfectly fitted to carry out all the duties that high dignity demanded of them. From the above description of the early training of a child through the grades of pagedom and squiredom, the reader will easily perceive that training was carefully undertaken for one purpose: to enable the youth, when he had attained the proper age, to receive the semi-sacred rite of knighthood.

It was a romantic and glorious career opened up to him, the highest ideal that warlike age possessed for a perfect Christian and a perfect gentleman.

Knighthood was a state earnestly desired by the youthful esquires. It was at their attaining the age of 21 and after serving successively as a page and an esquire, that knighthood was bestowed. At that ripe age, the youthful postulant for that coveted honor was considered, by virtue of the military education and the military exercises he had passed through, to be suitable to enter the ranks of chivalry. As has been noted above, there were exceptions, frequently and principally among royal persons, to this rule. Thus, Fulk of Anjou was knighted by his uncle Geoffrey when he was 17.

In the ballads and stories, there are frequent instances of lads being knighted at the age of 15, but for the generality, 21 was the obligatory age. It was upon attaining this age that the heir — if his father was dead — was allowed to enter on the paternal or ancestral fief. This entailed service in the overlord's wars, and it demanded from the holder of the fief strength and aptitude to fulfill those obligations successfully.

CONFESSION

Those who were about to become knights, had to first confess all the acts of their past lives — or if time was not given for that, then a short general summary of them. Indeed, it was always customary in those ages of faith for a knight to confess before he took part in a judicial combat, or before he took a ship overseas, or on any occasion where he adventured his life.

This confession took place on the field of battle just before engaging, or in some adjacent chapel or church, or even in one of those cells of hermits found scattered throughout France and England. If a man was mortally wounded on the field of battle and a priest could not be found, it was not unusual for him to make his confession to a brother knight. The Church, though she regretted the necessity, did not censure it.

There was also a symbolic rite often performed by knights at this period, the origin of which is veiled in obscurity. It was done with three blades of grass, or herb, or else three leaves plucked from a tree. The explanation most feasible seems to be that the three blades or leaves represented the Blessed Trinity.

The Calendar of Investiture

The usual time for bestowing knighthood was at one of the five great festivals of the Christian year. These were Christmas, Easter, Ascension, Pentecost, and the Feast of St. John the Baptist. Christmas, occurring in the winter, did not commend itself so readily as the others.

Chivalry was especially for the young and spirited, emblematic of the spring of the year, and therefore Easter or Pentecost was considered the most suitable. It was at Pentecost that Fulk Rechin was armed as a knight by his uncle, Charles Martel. On that feast, Henry, the son of William the Conqueror, was knighted. So also on that day his father knighted Geoffrey Plantagenet. On the Festival of the Ascension, Renaud de Montauban, in his chronicle, says, "Many young men were knighted." In *The Ballad of the Knight of the Swan*, he is represented to have created five or six knights on the Feast of St. John the Baptist.

Besides the church festivals there were many other occasions on which the accolade was conferred, such as on the marriage or baptism of a prince, or upon the latter himself receiving it. Thus, when Geoffrey, son of the Count of Anjou, was knighted by Henry, the English king, 25 noble youths were also knighted.

The field of battle was the most glorious place to win the golden spurs, and it often saw, after an engagement, these conferred on some gallant squire. Places held in great sanctity, too, were considered peculiarly adapted to conferring this high honor of knighting. The pilgrimage to the Holy City and the Tomb of the Holy Sepulcher were held in high estimation for this purpose. When the English Earl of Essex was there with Lord Robert de Severino, he

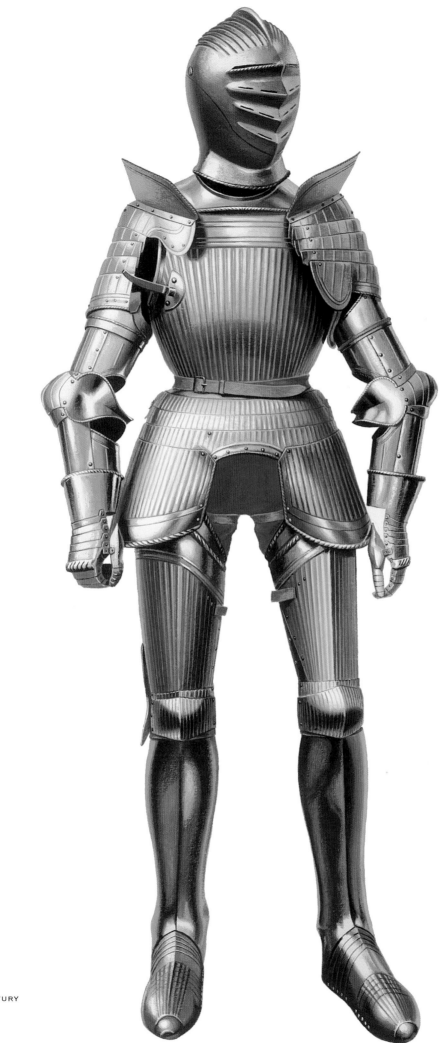

Right: Sixteenth-century
German Armor.

created several knights. In 1398, Count Rudolf de Montfort created there Albert IV, "The Patient," Duke of Austria.

Nicolas III d'Este, Lord of Modena, would not put his spurs on when at Golgotha, or on those he created knights. He also created several, therefore, on the Holy Sepulcher. Friedrich of Brandenburg, in 1453, created 24 of his followers as knights on the Sepulcher. There the Duke Ernest of Austria was created knight in 1414 with 26 of his companions.

Sometimes the place chosen was after a battle, when a knight was taken prisoner. As it was the rule, a knight could yield only to another knight, so the captive would knight his captor before he surrendered to him.

"Are you a knight and a gentleman?" asked the English Earl of Suffolk when long ago he yielded to his captor, the Frenchman Regnault. "I am a gentleman," said Regnault, "but not yet a knight." Whereupon Suffolk bade him kneel, dubbed him, received from him the accustomed oaths, and then — and then only — gave up his own sword to the new chevalier.

Conferring Knighthood

Who was deemed fit to confer knighthood? It was, and has always been held, that every knight, whatever his social circumstances, has in himself the inherent power of creating others to his order.

Many instances are to be found in the old chronicles of such knights using this power, yet it is understandable that, for the youthful aspirant to knighthood, when all the future of his life seemed unknown and strange, one of the most likely persons he would wish to confer this grace upon him was often his own knightly father. So in the medieval ballads nothing is more common than this conference by the father. In that of Hervis de Metz, he is armed and knighted by his father, Duke Pierre.

In another ballad, the young hero is knighted by his father before starting for the court of King Louis. His mother is depicted as standing weeping at his going, and exclaiming, "My son, forget not while away thy father who is ill and left here alone." Thereupon the sick man, raising himself up, gives his son the accolade.

Sometimes instead of the father, the uncle creates the nephew a knight. Thus, in the ballad *Covenans Vivien*, William of Orange is portrayed giving knighthood to his nephew *"Vivien Guillaumes et Vivien adoube."*

Another conferrer of knighthood, and generally preferred by the parents to their own relative, to give the accolade to their son, was some rich and powerful lord in the vicinity. Often such are now chosen, with a like view, as sponsors in baptism — with a view of their powerful assistance afterward, in peace as well as in war, to the youthful chevaliers they had created. Thus, in *The Ballad of Girart de Rousillon*, it is clearly stated that such was their obligation.

"The young warriors said the war is over, there will be no more skirmishes, no more wounded knights, no more broken shields! That none be discouraged at that," said Lord Fulk, "I will willingly give them more."

Fulk told Girart to go to King Charles Martel: "Now," said the latter, "see to it that each of you Counts and rich Barons give the poor young knights enough to assure their subsistence. Let some more of them be enrolled for the defense of the land as has become the fashion, and if there be any rich avaricious man, a felon at heart, who thinks their maintenance and gifts cost him too much, he shall be deprived of his fief and it shall be given to a more valiant, for hoarded treasure is not worth a coal."

Perhaps the most popular person to confer knighthood was a prince or king. Receiving the accolade from such in the midst of a brilliant court, the newly created chevalier became the cynosure of all fair eyes — or mounted on his horse, or engaged in the martial game of quintain, he became the admiration of the populace standing round the castle green.

It was open to him as then knighted to take a vow to perform some chivalrous service for the fair one he then picked out, or, if he was to be a troubadour knight, to sing her praises at many a castle and manor throughout the land.

Other conferrers of knighthood in rare cases seem to have been certain ladies themselves. For instance, Cecile, daughter of Philip I of France, and widow of Tancred, Prince of Antioch, conferred knighthood not only on Gervais, son of the Count of Dol, but also on many more esquires. It is also said that Blanche, mother of St. Louis, a little before her death in 1343, conferred knighthood on the Seigneur de Saint-Yen. In 1343, Joan, Queen of Naples, on behalf of Andrew, her husband, conferred knighthood on James Leparito.

In *The History of Du Guesclin*, Jeanne de Laval, widow of the celebrated constable of that name, girded her husband's sword on Andre de Laval, a mere boy, and so made him a knight.

The Vigil and Bath

The preparations for conferring chivalry upon the esquire were of the strictest and most solemn nature. Indeed, they followed their counterpart in the rites of baptism and marriage. We have noted above how strict the rule was that confession of sins should always and frequently be made by knights. It is no wonder, therefore, that before admittance to that order, the young neophyte had to fast the day before his initiation, and make a general confession embracing the whole of his past life (see sidebar on page 42).

A prayer vigil began during the night preceding his knighting. Often the vigil was shared in by the young aspirant's godfather in chivalry (patron) or some friendly priest who, through the long night — in the shadows of some great cathedral or medieval church — helped the aspirant to keep his drowsy eyes awake. It corresponded to the neophyte's vigil before the Feast of Pentecost, when he was to receive the sacrament of baptism.

A vivid description is given of the time, in the early twelfth century, when young Geoffrey Plantagenet, son of the Count of Anjou, received the accolade at the hands of the English King Henry (1129). Geoffrey was 15 years old, and had always been an expert horseman, remarkably good-looking, and, according to the old chronicles, full of chivalric virtues. King Henry says to the Count, "Send me your son and I will marry him to my daughter (Maud), and as he is not yet a knight, I will knight him with my own hands." Accordingly, Anjou consented, and sent his son with five picked companions to Rouen — namely Hardouin of St. Mar, Jacquelin of Maille, Robert de Lemblancai, John of Charvans, and Robert of Blois.

The King of England, who was not used to rising from his seat at anyone's approach, rose at the entry of young Geoffrey and threw his arms around him, and showed the greatest affection. However, he did not let his feelings overcome his prudence, for he immediately put searching questions to the young count as to his aptitude in learning and in arms. The answers were satisfactory, and the interview was terminated. That night, the Vigil of Pentecost, the lad was conducted to his bedroom, where he and his 25 young companions were provided with the symbolic bath.

ABOVE: A MEDIEVAL CELTIC DESIGN.

Antoine de la Sale, a medieval writer, describes the ways in which an esquire becomes a knight: "The squire, when he had traveled much and has been on several deeds of arms by which he had attained to honor, and if he has sufficient of what is necessary to maintain the estate of knighthood (for otherwise there is no honor for him and it is better worthwhile to be a good squire than an impoverished knight). Since that it is most honorable to be made so before a battle, an assault or encounter, where the banners of princes are, then he might request some lord or noble knight in the name of God, of our Lady and Monseigneur St. George. The good knight, handed him his naked sword, and then kissed the cross. Other good knights are dubbed at the Holy Sepulcher of our Lord for his love and honor of others at St. Katherine, or where they perform their devotions. Others are made (knights) who are bathed in tubs, and then re-clothed in new (garments) and that night they go to watch in the Church where they must be at their devotions until after High Mass is sung. Then the prince or some other knighted lord girds him with the golden sword and also in several other easier ways."

The latter part of this passage is important as mentioning both the bath and the vigil, and evidently refers to the more elaborate ritual observed when being knighted in peacetime and not on the field of battle — which the commencement does, where all ceremonious giving of the accolade was necessarily omitted.

The bath mentioned was no doubt a wooden one. The old Roman baths of marble had long since perished and been forgotten. Metal was never employed, so if ever a bath was used, it was a round wooden tub.

When an esquire came to court to seek the accolade in time of peace, two esquires, sage and well nourished in courtesy and expert in deeds of knighthood, were assigned to him as teachers. If he arrived in the morning he was to serve the king with water at dinner or else place a dish on the table — this was his farewell to his past services as a squire. His governor then led him to his chamber, where he remained until the evening, when they sent a barber to him and his beard was shaved and his head rounded. All illuminations of this period show the young squires beardless. It was probably to show their semi-ecclesiastical position as future Soldiers of the Cross.

In order to prepare worthily for the feast, the body was purified by baths and the hair and the beard were cut as a token of the care with which the Christian ought to preserve the purity of his soul and to remove all vices.

Forms of Investiture

The vigil of arms, the strict fasts, the three nights spent in prayer in a lonely chapel, the white garments of the neophyte, and the consecration of his sword in front of the altar were sufficient to prove to the novice the gravity of the engagement he was contracting under the auspices of religion. At last, a day was fixed for the great ceremony, and the neophyte — after hearing Mass on bended knees, and with his sword, which he had not yet acquired the right to gird to his side, suspended from his neck received from the hands of some noble or some noble lady his spurs, his helmet, his cuirass, his gauntlets, and his sword.

Turning to the ceremonies that followed the vigil and the bath, there is considerable difference between the more primitive conference of knighthood and that which was customary when chivalry had attained its zenith. In the earlier, it was greatly shortened and almost exclusively nonsacramental. In the latter, it was the reverse. In the former it was lay, in the latter ecclesiastical.

There seems also to have been something mysterious implied in the manner by which the honor of chivalry was transmitted from one knight to another. It is no wonder that a resemblance has often been traced between the admission of knights and churchmen to their respective functions, and a close resemblance really did exist in the different ceremonies we are considering on the two occasions. But perhaps the most

ABOVE: A MEDIEVAL ITALIAN ALTARPIECE BY LORENZETTI.

singular circumstance of the whole is this solemn necessity, which in both cases was insisted on, as to the validity of the original fountain, and the genuine transmission of the honor, or the sanctity, to be conferred.

The earlier and simpler form of conferring is to be found in many of the old chronicles and ballads. Thus, Lambert, chronicler of Guisnes and Seigneune of Ardes, describes the knighting of young Arnoul, son of Count Baldwin II, in 1181: "The Count called together his sons, his legitimate and natural ones, besides his friends, to attend his Court. Then in their presence he dubbed his son, Arnoul, knight, by giving him a light blow with his fist in the nape of his neck, the principal sign of knighthood. This was all."

In the same simple fashion another chronicle, *Magnum Belgii Chronicon* (1247), recounts how the King of Bohemia knighted William of Holland. He conferred it by simply giving the blow with his sword on the young count's neck. When Geoffrey Plantagenet, son of the Count of Anjou, was knighted at the hands of King Henry in 1129, he was 15 years of age, so the ceremony of conferring it was the simplest, though he certainly was bathed with his companions the night before receiving the accolade. Clothed in a rich garment, he marched next morning into the presence of the king, who thereupon knighted him.

Generally, several squires were knighted on the same day, and the exhortation was shared by all. One reason for this might be that, after the ceremony, they might, on their fiery steeds, caracole along the course together before the assembled multitude, *"en cadence,"* and show off their horsemanship among the crowd of burghers and others attached to the court.

After receiving Communion, the young esquire presented his sword to the officiating priest, who laid it on the altar, blessed it, and returned it. The custom of being armed by a fair lady (assisted, of course, by the squires or armorers riveting the various pieces of the armor together) was a common proceeding. Sometimes a king or queen provided the sword to be belted on. In *The Ballad of Lancelot*, Arthur's Queen Guinevere gives him a sword and he becomes in future the knight of the fair queen.

During his armoring, the young squire is supposed to be receiving the sword and the belting with the utmost humility and piety, to lift, during the belting, his eyes to God and his hands to heaven, and to realize the belted sword now round him as the silent memorial, ever after, of chastity, justice, and charity.

The Christian symbolism which accompanied the first steps of the novice followed and accompanied him in some way or other during the whole of his knightly career. The vigil of arms, the strict fasts, the nights spent in prayer in some lonely chapel, the white garments of the postulant for knighthood, and the consecration of his sword were engraved on his memory ever after, a constraining force, against a constraining world.

Ecclesiastical Knighting

Another conferrer of knighthood, as its initiatory ceremonies developed as the years went by, was a representative of the Church. The young squire fell into the habit of placing his arms on the altar of some church to imbue them with a sanctity — the priest was asked to bless his sword (though not gird it on him).

As we have seen, the great festivals of the Church were generally chosen as the times to confer knighthood. Almost imperceptibly, the mitered bishop often began to take the place of the neophyte's father or overlord, and it was he who bid him, "Rise, knight," and it was he who gave him the accolade, not indeed with the vigorous blow of the rough knight, but with a gentle touch of his hand.

However, in a synod held at Westminster in 1102, abbots in England were forbidden to make knights, probably from the dangerous increase it gave to ecclesiastical power. Again, from the habit often in this warlike age of bishops and monks themselves arming and joining in the feudal battles, either to defend their patrimonies or to side with the cause of one of the princes whose lands surrounded their own, the hard line was broken down which had existed between an ecclesiastic and a layman — and if the former was a powerful and warlike prelate, knighthood at his hands was considered no disgrace but an honor.

This custom was helped by the Crusades — these *were* holy wars. What was more suitable than that the men wearing the cross should often receive from holy hands their accolade? Thus, Martin V conferred knighthood on Nicholas, Ambassador of Venice. In 1289, the Patriarch of Aquileia conferred knighthood on Albert of Goritz, and Nicolas of Cividale.

The historian of Aquileia, when writing of Friuli, gives an account of one of these ecclesiastical knightings: "The patriarch, after celebrating mass, mounted a step in sight of all the people, and, after a discourse on the duties of a true knight, solemnly blest the young squire who sought it, and called upon God to protect him because he would never engage in any but just wars.

"Then he threw over his neck a chain or collar of gold [the knight's usual collar] and girded him with the sword. The young knight, leaping thereupon to his feet and drawing his consecrated sword out of its sheath, swore to defend the Church and never do anything unfitting to a Christian knight. He swore also to protect the widowed and the fatherless and the servants of Jesus Christ against the infidels."

Such ecclesiastical knighting was conferred both by the patriarchs of Jerusalem and by Constantinople. It was the custom, particularly in the late eleventh century at the time of the First Crusade, for those seeking knighthood and who had made the pilgrimage overseas to the Holy Land, to seek the accolade at the hands of the chief ecclesiastical dignitary in the Holy City or some knight of great prowess who happened to be there.

Again, from the immense lands of which the Church in Western Christendom gradually took possession, it became the custom for the abbeys to retain in their service men-at-arms and squires and knights who should lead to the field the men when called upon for military service. Hence, often a brave squire was raised, in gratitude, by the lord abbot for his good services to the rank of knighthood. A famous example of ecclesiastical knighting is that of Amauri, son of Simon de Montfort, who was at Castelnaudary at the time of the Feast of St. John with the two bishops of Orléans and Auxerre. He asked the former to confer knighthood upon his son by putting the baldric on him.

The bishop for a long time refused, says Peter de Vaux-de-Cernay. He knew it was contrary to the usual custom, and that ordinarily only a knight could create a knight. However, at the insistence of the count, he ultimately consented. It was in summertime. Simon de Montfort pitched large tents on the plain outside the city wall, which was much too small to contain the spectators. On the day that had been fixed, the Bishop of Orléans celebrated Mass in a tent.

The young Amauri, his father on one hand, his mother on the other, approached the altar. His parents offered him to the Lord, and asked the bishop to consecrate him knight in the service of Christ. Immediately, the two prelates knelt before the altar, belted the sword on him, and sang the Veni Creator with profound devotion. The chronicler adds these significant words: "What a new and unusual way of conferring knighthood."

However, this mode of conferring knighthood is not as extraordinary as Peter of Vaux-de-Cernay thought, for in the Roman Church there was already a formula of prayer — drawn up at the beginning of the eleventh century — to be used by bishops conferring knighthood. So much had the spirit of chivalry invaded even the peaceful fold of the Church, that what to an earlier age would have seemed alien to its spirit — an ecclesiastic creating a knight — became an event which was passed without censure. Chivalric terms, and chivalric customs, were so in vogue, that they were later used in describing even sacred things.

The English *Piers Plowman*, describing the Crucifixion and speaking of the soldier who pierced our Lord's side, calls him "a knight," and says, "He came forth with his spear in hand and jousted with Jesus."

Afterward, for doing so base an act on a dead body he is pronounced "a disgrace to knighthood," and our "champion

L'ORDENE DE CHEVALERIE

An intriguing poem entitled *L'Ordene de Chevalerie* was written by Hugues de Tabarie (or de Tiberiade), in which he undertook the task of explaining all the forms of investiture. In order to make his explanations more intelligible, Hugues de Tabarie supposes himself before an aspirant entirely ignorant of all the usages of chivalry. He pretends that he has been forced to confer the order of knighthood upon his prisoner, the Sultan Saladin.

The first thing Hugues does is to order Saladin to comb his hair and beard, and to carefully wash his face. His hair, his beard, and his face are then carefully arranged, as is the duty of a new knight. Then he made him enter a bath, and Saladin began to ask what all this signified.

"Sire," answers Hugues, "like the babe that leaves the font cleansed from original sin, it is thus that you must emerge without any stain from this bath; for knighthood must be clothed with honesty, with courtesy, and with goodness, and make itself beloved by all."

"By the great God," says Saladin, "this is a wonderful beginning!"

"Now," answers Hugues, "leave the bath and recline on this great bed as an emblem of the one you will obtain in paradise, the bed of rest that God grants to his followers, the brave knights."

Shortly after, while dressing Saladin from head to foot, Hugues says: "The snow-white linen shirt with which I am clothing you, and which touches your skin, is to teach you to keep your flesh from every stain if you wish to reach heaven. This crimson robe indicates 'That you must pour out your blood To serve and honor God. And to defend the Holy

Church; For all this must a knight do If he wishes entirely to please God; Such is the meaning of the crimson.

"These trunk-hose of brown silk, by their somber hue, are meant to remind you of death, and the earth where you will rest, Thence you came and whither you will return. This is what you must keep before your eyes. Thus, you will not fall into pride, For pride should never govern A knight nor reign within him. Humility should always be his trim.

"This white girdle which I place around your loins is to teach you to keep your body pure and to avoid luxury. These two golden spurs are to urge on your horse. Imitate its ardor and its docility, and as it obeys you, so be you obedient to the Lord. Now I fasten your sword to your side; strike your enemies with its double edge, prevent the poor from being crushed by the rich, the weak from being oppressed by the strong. I put upon your head a pure white coif to indicate that your soul similarly should be stainless."

Every pursuivant was perfectly acquainted with the meaning of the ordination of knighthood.

The ceremony was then completed by the investing knight. Before presenting Saladin with the sword, the investing knight struck him across the shoulder with its flat side, and then gave him the accolade as a sign of brotherly adoption. His shield, his lance, and his charger were then brought to the new-made knight, and he was thereafter at liberty to commence the career of glory, of devotion, and of combat, to which for so many years he had aspired.

The Christian symbolism, which had accompanied the first steps of the novice, followed and surrounded him in some way or other during the whole of his knightly career.

chevalier chief knight" is ordered to yield himself "recreant." So, too, in the *Morte d'Arthur*, Joseph of Arimathea is called "the gentle knight." St. James of Compostella is named, in one chronicle, "the Baron St. James."

The Vows of Knighthood

The vows or promises which the young knight, previous to his admission, made were varied and to be kept as the occasion arose:

1. The first one, according to some medieval writers, bound him, whenever he went on a quest or a strange adventure, never to lighten himself of his arms, except to sleep at night.

2. By the next, he promised, whenever in pursuit of adventure, not to avoid perilous "passes," nor to turn out of his way for fear of meeting powerful enemies, or from any dread of monsters, savage beasts or spirits, or anything which could only harm, or might be resisted by, the body of a man.

3. The knight was committed to defending a lady. He was rather to die than desert her, or suffer her to be offended.

4. He should be punctual to the day and hour in which he had been engaged to contend in arms with a brother knight.

5. Upon returning to court after having been about in quest of adventure, he should give an exact account of all he had done, even if his actions should have been to his disgrace, his knighthood being the forfeit if he should disobey this ordinance.

6. Upon being taken prisoner at a tournament, he should, besides rendering up his arms and horses to the victor, not again contend without the special leave of the latter.

7. Finally, he should not, in company, fight against a solitary enemy, nor carry two swords, if he was unwilling to contend with two opponents. Arms, especially the destrier or warhorse, were rendered up to the victor as his right.

Failing to Achieve Knighthood

Several things may have delayed or prevented certain of these squires from seeking knighthood. These might have included the consciousness that they were unfit, owing to a licentious life or an unreadiness in command, or to their own or their family's poverty, to enter this exalted state.

ABOVE: TEUTONIC KNIGHTS OF THE TWELFTH CENTURY.

The yearly largesse alone a knight was expected to give was a considerable outlay. The brilliant entourage he was also expected to bring with him on entering, or holding a tournament, was another. So was the large entourage he was called upon in his hall or castle every day to provide an open table for. All these demanded wealth. Even in the case of the poorer knights, they had horses and a squire to keep, and in certain places a tax was levied on their knighthood. Thus, in the *Costume de Hainaut* it was laid down: *"Un chevalier, non pair"* is to pay *"sept livres dix sols."* The knight, however, got some return in another county, for in Brabant, according to the *Costume de Brabant*, if a peasant struck a knight he lost his hand, though if his squire was struck, the peasant lost not his hand but his money, being heavily fined.

In *Romance of King Meliadus*, one of the Arthurian companions of the Round Table is found to be an elderly squire very different from the slim, graceful, frizzled-haired lad one is accustomed to associate with that degree. He is a clumsy enough looking man, with a jocular face, and on his head is a cap containing one long feather. The artist portrayed a squire often seen at that period. The illuminators drew men and women they saw around them.

In this respect these old and delicate illuminations are very valuable, as are the old stained glass left in Gothic cathedrals in France and England, providing us with what we should otherwise have failed to learn — the dress, armor, and figures of the Middle Ages.

Chaucer, who noted, too, the life going on around him and then wove it into verse, had such a squire — rough and faithful but getting on in years when he wrote: "A worthy man That from the time he first began To ridden out, he loves chivalry, truth and honor, freedom and courtesy in his lord's war, And thereto had he ridden no man fare As well in Christendom as in Heathenesse and ever honored for his worthiness."

That these older squires who had never risen to knighthood served for hire, is demonstrated by Leber, in his *Collection Relative to the History of France*, when asking a knotty question in an intriguing passage. "A knight has two squires hired for the tournaments and for a year. The said knight comes to a town where he finds it necessary to enter the lists hastily, and he cannot find his squires, so hires two others on the eve of the tournament, but when the morrow comes these two squires hired for a year turn up before the hour of arming, and present themselves to their master, to serve him. But the master says, 'Not so, as far as today,' for this day he had hired these two others now. Thereupon these two squires, hired for a year, go out and seek their livelihood with other masters for that year, and they say they are justified in doing so. But their first master says, 'Not so, they are still engaged to him.' How would this be decided by the Law of Arms for Tournaments?"

This passage is valuable, as it shows that squires older than 21 — or they still would be in tutelage and not, as these were, able to do what they chose — existed and also that not only for pure honor but for subsistence, a good sword was then bartered. If it be asked how the younger squires accompanied their lords to battle or tournament, we mean those still in training for the knightly degree. All contemporary writers declare that they did so unarmed — with the exception probably of the sword they received on being admitted to the rank of squire, and also probably with the short knife or poniard they carried at their side, which is constantly seen in pictures of them from this era.

ABOVE: A MEDIEVAL CELTIC INSIGNIA.

The esquires at that time were therefore merely spectators, and stood ready to assist their lords, if dismounted, by leading in a fresh horse, or carrying them off the lists, if incapacitated or wounded.

The evening before the tournament, it was a custom to allow the young esquires to compete in the lists among themselves. In *The Ballad of Perceforest*, these young lads under the name of *"la jeune Chevalerie"* are stated at the hour of Vespers to so muster *"pour celebrer les vespers de tournoi de la haulte journee au lendemain."* These contests were named "essays," or "escrimie" (fencing matches).

The weapons employed by these young esquires were light and easily handled, and the lances often blunted in order to avoid wounding.

Again, it seems that often in the second day of a tournament, which generally lasted three days, esquires were allowed to appear on foot and engage among themselves in light contests.

The elevation of the squires therefore contributed greatly to the decay of medieval society, so much so that our later kings had to insist on knighthood being taken up in rank.

Again, the practice of the heralds, when they obtained royal sanction for their college, was to establish on quasi-legal footing the squire's right, if of gentle descent, to coat armor.

In older days, it was sufficient honor to the squire that he carried his lord's or knight's own shield when he required it, but in these later days he aspired and asked for his own. The heralds granting this — while they raised the state of an esquire — debased the state of a knight.

Those squires who had not been able, or were unwilling, to gain knighthood, seem to have been permitted to carry certain arms of war of their own, other than the sword, which was the only arm the young squire looked forward to and, training for knighthood, was permitted to wear.

The general inability of a squire to bear a device of his own in medieval days precluded, as we have said, many from transmitting to their children records of their brave deeds. It is probable that their desire to do so in the only way they could, by acquiring the right as a medieval warrior to blazon the tale on their shields, was another reason the young squire so ardently looked forward to knighthood.

The First Act by the New Knight

The first thing a newly knighted young warrior is represented to have done — in the many ballads and chansons — was to mount his destrier and, by himself, or with other youths who may that day have been knighted, show himself in all his newly acquired bravery to the fair ones looking on from the castle door, and to the villagers and burghers congregated on the castle green.

There two martial games awaited his dexterity. One was the quintain, the other the behourd. The quintain was a manikin covered with a hauberk and a shield, and fastened to the top of a post.

The play consisted in the young knight's dashing on the post, his horse at a gallop, and his lance couched, and piercing the hauberk and buckler in one attempt. Sometimes, to increase the difficulty of the play, several armed manikins were arranged in a row, and the point was to run through and overthrow them all. This was the test that was ordinarily imposed upon newly created knights, which took place before the witnesses of dubbing — the ladies and the knight's friends.

As to the behourd, it was simply a form of training for tournaments and was a sort of fencing or tilting on horseback. The knights arranged themselves two by two, and one of them turned on his partner, trying to pierce his shield with a lance. This was sometimes dangerous play, for one grew excited in it, and in the heat of the strife forgot that it was an amusement.

PUNISHMENT AND DEGRADATION

Christian symbolism took part in the knight's punishment and degradation if he broke his plighted faith or forfeited his honor. Exposed on a scaffold in nothing but his shirt, he was stripped of his armor, which was broken to pieces before his eyes and thrown at his feet, while his spurs were thrown upon a dunghill. His shield was fastened to the croup of a cart horse and dragged through the dust, and his charger's tail was cut off. A herald-at-arms asked thrice, "Who is there?"

Three times an answer was given, naming the knight about to be degraded, and three times the herald rejoined, "No, it is not so. I see no knight here, I see only a coward who has been false to his plighted faith."

Carried thence to the church on a litter like a dead body, the culprit was forced to listen while the burial service was read over him, for he had lost his honor, and was now only looked upon as a corpse. Although the Church was the protectress of chivalry, and even invested it with an almost sacred dignity, she always refused to extend her protection to tournaments, tilts, and assaults of arms, brilliant, but often dangerous, manifestations of the chivalric spirit, and particularly to judicial duels, which were of German origin, and which dated from a period long prior to the institution of Christian chivalry.

When the Church found itself obliged to show indulgence to these medieval traditions, which custom had interwoven with the habits of the Middle Ages, she did so in as reserved a manner as possible. The Church was always indignantly protesting against the barbarous custom which compelled or allowed women, children, churches, and convents to choose from among the knights a special champion who should always be ready to sustain against all the patron's cause.

In *The Ballad of Girart de Roussillon* there is a description of the game of quintain in the recital of the marriage of Fulk: "On that day he dubbed a hundred knights, giving horses and arms to each. Then in a meadow which bordered on Arsen he arranged for them a quintain equipped with a new shield and a strong and glittering hauberk. The young men ran their courses, and other people came to watch them. Girart saw that they were beginning to quarrel with each other, and he was much troubled. The crowd pushed toward the quintain. The hundred young men had made their trial. Some had succeeded others had failed, but no one had more than indented the mail of the hauberk.

"The Count called for his boar-spear. Droon brought it to him. It was the spear which Arthur of Cornwall had carried when formerly fighting in a battle in Burgundy. The Count spurred his horse into the lists, struck the target, and made a hole of such a size that a quail could have flown through it. Then he broke and cut the shield under the ventail. There was no knight who equalled him or could ever have sustained a struggle against him. The Count struck out with such force that with a blow he split one of the straps and tore off the other, all the while holding his weapon so firmly in hand that he again drew it out. And his men said, 'What strength!' When he makes war it is not to take sheep or cattle that he is intent against his enemies, but he had drawn much blood from their bodies."

When these games had ended, the whole knightly company sat down to a rich banquet. It was here that all the superb costumes of the knights and the exquisite dresses of the ladies were best displayed.

The Code of the Knight

The code of the medieval knight was founded on respect for his engagements, which led him to loathe a lie. It mattered not whether his oath was given on the book of the Evangels or relics of the saints, or sworn to with his bare, uplifted hand.

The high moral character — which is characterized by an absence of deceit and lying — is well expressed by a ballad of Eustache Deschamps: "You who would (take upon you) the order of knighthood, It is fitting you should lead a new life; Devoutly watching in prayer, Fleeing from sin, pride and villainy. The Church you must defend And succor the widow and orphan; Be bold and guard the people; Loyal and valiant (knights) taking naught from others, Thus, should a knight rule himself. He should have a humble heart, should work always, and follow deeds of chivalry; Loyal in war, and a great traveler He should frequent Tournaments and joust for his lady love. He must keep honor with all So that he cannot be held to blame Nor cowardice be found in his doings. And above all he should uphold the weak. Thus, should a knight rule himself. He should love his rightful lord And above all guard his domain, Have generosity, be a faithful judge, so Seek the company of valiant knights, Harkening to their words and learning from them."

Another virtue inculcated in the same code was active charity. Sometimes these rough and mail-clad knights in the license of a camp forgot this virtue, but many were found to be truly animated with its spirit. Godfrey de Bouillon, in the First Crusade, by his obedience to this virtue, was called "a brother of the poor." Hugo of Bordeaux, another knight, was so noted for his charitable deeds that he has been compared to St. Laurence come to life.

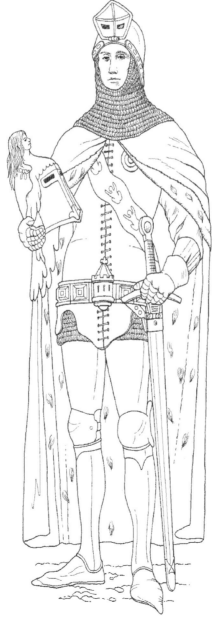

ABOVE: A KNIGHT IN FULL ARMOR.

When in danger, by sea or land, it was frequently the custom of the time for a knight to vow for his deliverance a "Hospital for the Poor," as Godfrey of Bouillon, in danger, called on the King of Heaven and he vowed to found such for the poor. Though some forgot this virtue, many remembered in those rough ages to practice charity.

There was a certain king of the Moslem Arabs (Saracens) who had been taken prisoner by Charlemagne. The latter offered the Moslem Arab his freedom if he embraced Christianity and was baptized, or, on the other hand, death, if he refused. The Moslem Arab chose death, asking, "Who are those fat and luxurious men sitting at your table, clothed in furs and fine raiment?"

"They are," replied Charlemagne, "my bishops and abbots."

"Who again," he asked, "are those thin and wasted men in poor garments of black and gray, who also are fed at your table?"

"They were the mendicant friars."

"Who, then, are those I see sitting on the ground and who get but the crumbs from your table?"

"Those," said the Christian king, "are the poor."

"Ah," cried the Moslem Arab, "is that the way you honor Him who is the author of your religion? If that is the way you follow your Christ, then I would refuse to be a Christian — I prefer death."

The obligation of charity, and acts of defense on behalf of the widow and orphans and the weak, was one of those laws down in the celebrated code or office of chivalry.

Another virtue — at least, in the Middle Ages it was considered to be such — was courtesy. Again and again, in the writings of the period, the young knight is bidden to be "courteous." However, in the days before chivalry came to its full flower, simple alms to the poor, or gifts to "Mother Church," were the only forms of "largesse" that were practiced.

The Virtue of Gallantry

An essential virtue or, rather qualification, necessary for knighthood was gallantry. Held originally in a poetic, but perfectly chaste, manner, its cult became rapidly "corrupted" from interaction with Provence and other southern portions of France, which largely felt the licentious influence of their Moorish neighbors.

It was a good and restraining influence for the young squire, and afterward for the young knight, to have a lady whom he had taken, as the object of his platonic affection, to serve, honor, and obey. To be without such, not to have "gallantry," as it was called, a young lad would have been considered wanting, and not really fit for the accolade. Thus, in the romance of "Little Saintry," his protectress taught him how needful, even while still a page, it was to have some fair one as the object of his service, and she herself the protectress of his interests.

The symbolic ritual of conferring knighthood, when in its zenith, so nearly figured the more sacred ritual of the Church when administering her sacraments of Baptism, Marriage and Holy Orders, that it is not surprising that a platonic devotion between men and women grew, and this caused the knight to dedicate knightly swords and knightly adventures to her service. At about this time, the greater Cult of the Virgin was spreading through Christendom, so that a woman's place in medieval society came to be considered much more.

Also at this time, the Virgin herself, from being the dogmatic Mother of God, was brought forth from her celestial niche in dogma and made more human, and so more popular by being appealed to with greater freedom of language, while she also became a center, like her earthly sisters, of poetic fancies and knightly vows.

Knights' ladies could not — except as spectators — take their places in tournaments, but so had the platonic gallantry of the age grouped itself around their sex, that the Virgin herself was interwoven into the fierce encounters of chivalry. It is on

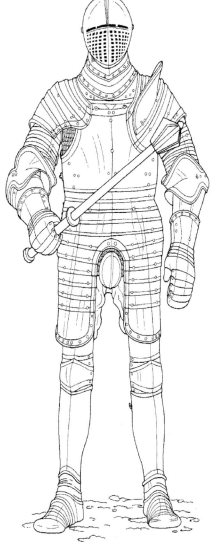

ABOVE: A KNIGHT WITH A MACE.

record that, in a tournament held close to the walls of an abbey (dedicated, probably, to her), the Virgin took the place of the chief knight — Walter de Birklede — and fought in the bloody melee.

Gallantry, therefore devotion to the fair sex, was a necessity in him who would be a knight. It embraced the highest ideal of womanhood (the Virgin Mother) as well as the Chatelaines and their daughters.

During this period, the grand distinction of the chivalrous character, in regard to the other sex, was gallantry, not love. Gallantry meant to refine manners, to throw over the face of society a rich and golden veil, and help the fancy to many sparkling and seductive images, but it produced few of those mighty and permanent impressions, either on individuals or communities which love, in its strength had accomplished. Endowed with courtesy, gallantry, and largesse, the young aspirant for knighthood stood ready for that high profession. He had passed through the ranks of page or squire, he had been thoroughly trained to arms, and he had received what was considered, at that time, sufficient profane education to write a letter, sign his name, and tolerably read a book in the Roman or Norman language. He also, under the chaplain who resided with him in the castle or manor of the lord who supervised his training, had been instructed in religious knowledge. He therefore was fully ready for the accolade of chivalry, and to pass through the prescribed formulas attached to his admittance thereto.

Pursuit of Good

Loyalty, courtesy, liberality, and justice were the virtues essential in the estimation of mankind to the character of a knight in the days of chivalry. A more splendid virtue than all others demanded of the young aspirant for knighthood, both before and after initiation, was the pursuit of good, the detestation of evil, not solely when found in his own soul but also in that of the world.

The liturgy of the Church reiterated the same exhortation when youths were

ABOVE: AN ITALIAN KNIGHT FROM THE END OF THE FIFTEENTH CENTURY.

admitted to knighthood. At Rome, on the creation of a knight, it was solemnly said, reading the *Pontificate Romanum:* "Call to mind, O knight, that thou art to be the defender of the Order and the punisher of Injustice. On this condition — the living copy of Christ — thou may reign eternally above with your Divine Model."

Well was it with a consecrated sword — a soul absolved — the young knight should be clothed in his spiritual, as well as his natural, armor. Perhaps we cannot do better than to finish these moral requisites in a young man seeking knighthood, to sum them up in the description taken from the *Morte d'Arthur,* where the excellence of the true knight is well portrayed. Sir Ector, in his eulogy over the body of Sir Lancelot du Lac, thus bewails him: "Ah, Sir Lancelot, thou wert head of all Christian knights, now there thou lied. Thou wert never matched of more earthly knights' hands, and thou wert the curtiest knight that ever bore a shield. And thou wert the truest friend to thy lover that ever bestrode horse. And thou wert the truest lover of a sinful man that ever loved woman. And thou wert the kindest man that ever struck sword. And thou wert the goodliest person that ever came among a press of knights. And thou wert the meekest man and the gentlest man that ever eat in hall among ladies. And thou wert the sternest foe to thy mortal enemy that ever set spear in rest."

The Knight's Finery

At the end of the fourteenth century, the chevaliers were accustomed to receive long mantles of scarlet upon their admittance to chivalry, reviving the color of the ancient military cloaks of the Romans. These the French kings were accustomed, at the two seasons of winter and summer, to renew for their knights. It was also usual for the king, at the time he gave the young newly created knight a scarlet mantle, a horse, or if not that, then a bit for the same, ornamented with gold, which represented the pledge used in investitures, as a sign of an alienated fief.

A Knight's Garments

The early military knights had one garment to cover them, and one horse to carry them. However, when medieval society was at its zenith, the garments worn by the knight and his friends were of the richest fabric. For instance, in the period between 1350 and 1364 for King John II of France, 670 marten skins were used in one cloak. One of his sons had 10,000 martens brought to line five such cloaks and five court ladies' doublets. To line a cloak for one of his grandsons, 2,700 squirrel skins were procured.

Precious gems were also lavishly used. Pearls were quaintly employed to embroider texts and songs and mottoes on clothes. The robe of state of Jean sans Peur of Burgundy was set with pearls and gems, valued at 200,000 ducats. His consort's ladies-in-waiting received 400,000 Brabant thalers a year from the ducal exchequer for ornaments.

At the banquet of his initiation in chivalry, the knight would, for the first time, put on the gold collar pertaining to that order. Here again, these collars of gold revived the practice of the Equestrian order of ancient Roman days. These knight's collars were probably, in the early ages of medieval society, plain gold circles. They obtained them, not from the favor of a sovereign lord but as a personal right appertaining to their status as chevaliers. This was a right descended from a long ancestry of warriors, for twisted collars of metal and torques are found in the burying places of all the older dwellers in northern Europe.

The ancient British chiefs wore them, and golden torques were around the necks of the leaders of the first Saxon — and afterward Danish — invaders of Britain. In turn, they continued to be worn by the Saxon warriors down to the time of their last king — Edward the Confessor — who was buried with a chain-collar of gold two feet long, carrying a jeweled cross.

Wearing Their Lady's Colors

Knights about to enter a tournament were given scarves, or "honors," related to their devotion to a lady to place on their helms or harness. Many of the legends inscribed on these scarves or elsewhere were decipherable only to the loved and the loving — all were to show the "devoir" the bearer was to render to the object of his affection. Menestrier, writing on the origin of armorial bearings, noted that the amorous medieval warrior often adopted "the colors" of his lady-love. Instead of their own blazon on their shield, they would substitute some device, the meaning of which, though puzzling to those who saw a knight wearing it, was known to the lady. Hence arose so often in the ballads such fanciful names as "the Knight of the Swan, of the Dragon, of the Eagle, of the Lion."

For the same amorous reason they assumed, as before said, the lady's livery or colors. Hence we read of the White Knight, the Chevalier Noir, the Green Count, or the Red Count, and no woman in that gallant age felt so honored as when her device and colors were triumphantly borne by her knight, in tournament and on the field of battle, not alone in his own country but far afield in Europe.

Sometimes, however, a fair one did not reward the knight. This is found in an instance given by the author of *Aresta Amorum*. He tells of a certain lady whose chevalier had mounted her colors and liveries and came before her armed and mounted for her benediction, ere he entered the lists, and made an excuse for not doing so, on the ground that she was too unwell to appear.

The "Parliament of Love," before which the case was brought, condemned her conduct and ordered her, the next time this knight rode to the tournament, to robe and arm him herself, and take his horse by the bridle. After he had mounted, she must lead him down the lists and, giving him his lance, say to him, "God be with you, my friend, fear nothing, because I pray for you."

This wearing of a lady's favors was far from infringing on the honor due to knighthood. Conversely, it was one of its glories, even if shown in an extravagant degree. Thus, at a certain tournament, a medieval warrior appeared with strange "honors" — with chains attached to his hands and feet to show that he was chained by his word of honor to his lady. Another came into the lists, chained, one end of the chain held by his lady-love.

At a tournament held in 1388 by the King of Sicily, the knights marched to the barrier and with them the ladies, who then decorated them with colored ribbons and scarves of their own devices and liveries of silk.

Sometimes to reward her chevalier the lady gave him a costly jewel. These, like the collars given for knightly brotherhood, were very much used in different articles of jewelry between lovers and friends, lords and ladies, princes and those they wished. This was done for the same purpose the ladies gave collars — to bind the knights to their interests and service.

The Privileges of Knighthood

The certain privileges which a squire, attaining knighthood, obtained were not simply of honor; knighthood carried with it many prerogatives, privileges, and franchises, which, often later in the Middle Ages, were particularly named in the letters of the sovereign who made the squire a knight.

These included:

1. JURISDICTION. The knight was empowered to assemble his retainers for services in any war he might be about to engage in. And also, on such vassals of his, to dispense justice both of the high and the low kind (*moyenne et basse*), or, as the old Saxons expressed it, "outfang and infang."

2. PRECEDENCE. In France, the different estates of the province or realm assembled, knights took precedence of all those not such — so in the Parliament of the year 1322 in the forest of Vincennes, those who were knights were first announced. So in the Parliament of Paris all those councilors who were knights had precedence of those who were not.

3. TITLE. In France, a knight had bestowed upon him the prefix of "Monsieur" or "Monseigneur." In Gascony, the title was "Mossen," in Spain, "Dom" or "Don," in Italy, "Messer," and in England, it was "Sir." The wives of such, in France, obtained the prefix "Madame," but anciently that of "dam," which had been the older prefix of knights themselves, so we find in the old French chronicles "dam chevalier." In England, the wife of a knight evidently obtained her prefix from this, as she was called "Dame."

4. ARMOR. Another privilege attaching to knighthood was to go into battle fully armed, not alone themselves, but for their horses also to be thus equipped. Indeed, it was one of the privileges of a new-made knight to be granted money for a knightly mantle and a horse.

5. A PLACE AT THE TABLE. From earliest times (even among the Lombards in A.D. 571), the sons of princes and the highest nobles were not permitted to sit at the table of their parents, unless of chivalric rank. But from that time onward and during the noblest time of knighthood, a belted knight was permitted not alone to sit at his lord's, but even at a king's table, when invited to do so. Without having received the accolade, however high his birth, he could not do so.

6. PRESENTING ARMS. Knights, particularly in Germany, were allowed, at Mass, to unsheathe their swords, and hold them aloft during the Gospel to demonstrate that they were ready above all men, by their knightly oath, to defend the Christian faith with their lives.

Above: Ladies mourn and minstrels play as twelfth-century knights go off to battle.

The Death of a Knight

HE PARTICULARS CONCERNING THE DEATHS and funeral obsequies of the ordinary knight are found few and far between in the chronicles of the Middle Ages, simply because there was nothing extraordinary in their deaths nor was the debt they paid to nature other than that of all mankind. The tumultuous days they lived in, the constant feuds, the inefficiency of medical science, even the many mortuary Masses they attended for their departed brother knights, made death a very familiar thing to them. As has been mentioned, they very frequently welcomed it as bringing them that gift the age they lived in could not give — rest.

For this reason, the few instances given here of deathbeds are those of highly placed medieval warriors and those of royal birth, but these instances are useful in so far as they show us what, no doubt, was the usual trend of mind among brother knights of a lower rank in the presence of death, for "death," as it has been well said "makes all men equal."

One feature in these instances is common to all — that whatever errors the knights had committed in their past, at the prospect of death they became sincerely penitent. Nor is this to be wondered at, for unlike many people of the present age, they thoroughly believed in

Above: Death visits a medieval warlord.

another life beyond the grave, and in a judge who would then take account for all their earthly life. A happy issue to death was often expected by a medieval warrior on account of having taken the Cross to the Holy Land.

Warlords on Their Deathbeds

At the death of King Louis le Gros in 1137, he distributed all his gold and silver, giving even his clothes and the rich hangings of his bed away. He received the last sacraments. He caused a tapestry to be spread on the ground and ashes, in the form of a cross, to be strewn over it. Upon this bed of penitence he expired in the act of making the sign of the Cross.

In like manner, in 1272 Henry III of England, after confessing his sins at first privately, and afterward in public before all the bishops and monks around, caused himself to be placed on a bed of ashes, on which he finally died.

One of the finest examples of a dying knight is of a much later age. To Villars, the French marshal wounded at the Battle of Malplaquet, it was proposed that he be given the viaticum privately. "No, no," said he,

Above: Knight, Death, and the Devil, originally engraved by Albrecht Dürer in 1513 and copied by the Wiericx Brothers in 1564.

"since this army has not been able to see Villars die like a hero, it shall see him die like a Christian."

Charles V of France, on the day he was dying in 1380, desired to see the relic of the Crown of Thorns and his own coronation crown. When both were brought, he placed the Crown of Thorns before him, crying, "Oh precious crown, diadem of our salvation, how sweet, how precious is the mystery comprised in thee."

Then, turning to the crown of France, he said, "Oh crown of France, precious art thou considering the mystery of justice contained in thee, but vile and viler than all things if one regards the labor and anguish, torment of heart and conscience, yea peril to the soul thou bringest those who bear thee."

Ulrich Baier, a knight of the Teutonic order, died in battle in 1281, fighting against the infidels in Prussia. His wish was that he might die as his Savior did, with wounds in his hands and feet and side — and so it was. He received from the enemy exactly those wounds. It was at the attack of Brescia by Gaston de Foix that he was dangerously wounded. Finding himself so, he exclaimed, "Jesus, my God, I am a dead, dead man."

He then kissed the cross of his sword, repeated some prayers aloud, and, no priest being present, made his confession to his house steward. He then caused himself to be laid at the foot of a tree with a stone under his head and his face toward the enemy, showing, in that last hour of his life, that he would not turn his back on them. When the Duke of Bourbon stood weeping over him, he cried, "Weep not for me, I die in the service of my country — you triumph in the ruin of your own and have far more cause to lament your victory, than I my defeat by death."

Sometimes before death, knights of an order of chivalry voluntarily degraded themselves of such, so impressed were they with the humility necessary to approach the next world. Thus, the Emperor Charles V renounced, before retiring into the convent of St. Just, his membership of the Golden Fleece. He gave it to his son and successor.

In 1312, Ferdinand, King of Spain, was summoned by two brothers, Peter and John, of the knightly order of Caravalla (who were by him unjustly condemned to death) to appear in 30 days before the Eternal Judge. Upon the thirtieth day, the king was found dead in his bed.

Penance by Proxy

In the Middle Ages, the performance of religious duties and penances by proxy was no doubt largely resorted to by many who, cut off by death, had not themselves been able to perform their vows and religious obligations. It would be interesting to know whether the monks, to whom so many gifts and alms by the dying, both in money and real estate were made, accepted them without disturbing themselves about their source. The monks accepted such without inquiring to what extent the donor had rightfully or wrongfully acquired the gifts he made or sent by his executors.

The truth is, this scruple did not worry the monks very much, for the very simple reason that, at bottom, the great mass of the faithful were convinced that giving to a saint or to God was a pious deed which, in itself, justified everything. It mattered little whether the source of the gift was pure or impure; from the moment that the Church was enriched even with possessions wrongfully acquired, the sin was expiated and the wrong repaired. A letter which a certain Simon of Namur addressed to Henry, Bishop of Villiers, in the first years of the thirteenth century on that delicate subject, was answered after many reservations. It stipulated that if the donor's possessions be of a mixed nature, part of it was gained honestly, part dishonestly, the monks may always accept it, as they can go on the hypothesis each thing, money or lands, was acquired honestly, it being impossible for them to show to the contrary. It was the monks who usually performed the service of internment for the dead, and the medieval warrior always, if he could, desired to be bestowed in an abbey, and was happy — as has been noted — if he could, before death, assume the monastic habit, since it was always good for the dying knight to stand well with the Church.

Not only did the religious houses receive gifts of money

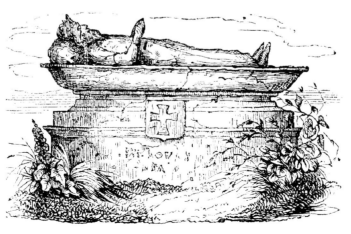

ABOVE: THE CRYPT OF A FALLEN MEDIEVAL WARRIOR.

from the dying warriors and landed proprietors — or "post mortem" benefactions by their wills and at the hands of those they had designated — but they received properties, including lands, woods, meadows, vineyards, wheat, barley, oats, flocks, even iron and coal, and also rights to pastures, to mills, and judicial rights.

From 1164 to 1201, the French Abbey of Clairveaux alone received 964 donations. At Vauluissant, one of the medieval abbeys of the order of Citeaux founded in 1127, in the cartularies between 1180 and 1213, there are 60 which mention such gifts to the monks.

ABOVE: DEATH VISITS THE BISHOP AND THE KNIGHT.

And the motives were nearly always the same. Here a woman enriched Vauluissant "for the salvation of her soul, for that of her husband, her children and of her ancestors." Some made donations "for the expiation of their sins," and others because they were leaving for one of the Crusades.

In 1216, a noble knight "on the point of setting out against the Albigenses made his will and the priest made him give the abbey six pieces of land."

A point is that a great many of these donations — as those left in wills — were to come into operation only when the medieval warrior who was the testator died. They were valid only "post mortem."

As the vows, unfulfilled in lifetime, to go on a pilgrimage or to take the Cross were afterward performed by deputy, the efficacy to the soul passed away, and was supposed to be benefited and freed. However, the medieval warriors and their ladies did not leave money alone. Those who wished that their souls should not suffer too long in the other world left endowments for the distribution of food.

Funeral Preparations

Sometimes the dying noble and knight made provisions for vows unfulfilled in his life, to be fulfilled for him by others after his decease, but he left directions how he should be buried and the anniversaries of his death celebrated. Edward the Black Prince — in his will still extant in the register of Archbishop Sudbury at Lambeth — directed that at every anniversary of his death, his coffin should be opened and his corpse wrapped in a new cerecloth. This precept was obeyed until the deposition of Richard II in 1399.

Henry VII agreed with the abbot and convent of Westminster that there should be four tapers burning continually at his tomb, two at the side and two at the ends, each 11 feet long and 12 pounds in weight. There were to be 30 tapers in the hearse, and four torches to be held about it at his weekly obit, plus 100 tapers 9 feet long, and 24 torches of twice the weight, to be lighted at his anniversary.

Funerals were often much longer delayed in the Middle Ages than now, especially in the case of the highest knights and nobles. The Black Prince, who died on June 8, 1376, was not buried until after Michaelmas. His consort Joan, who died August 7, 1385, was still unburied on the December 7 following.

One important item at a funeral was the torch bearers clad in white, equal to the number of the years of the deceased person. The record that 24 torch bearers held the pall of Blanche, Duchess of Lancaster, sets at rest the otherwise disputed date of her birth. This princess had one of the costliest tombs on record in England, no less than 486 pounds having been paid for it to Henry Yeuley, Mason of London.

For her mother-in-law, Queen Phillipa, "the iron tomb over the grave of the Venerable Father Michael, late Bishop of London, outside the western door of the Cathedral Church of St. Paul," was bought at a cost of 40 pounds and adapted for its new tenant.

The custom of lighting candles to burn a long while around a dead body, and watching at its side all night, was originally owing to the belief that a corpse was specially liable to the assaults of demons. The practice of tolling a bell at death must have had a similar origin, for it was a common medieval belief that the sound of a blessed bell had a similar efficacy to drive off the demons who, when a man dies, gather near to waylay his fleeting soul.

Above: A deceased warrior.

It was also a belief that demons raised storms and tempests in the material world. St. Thomas Aquinas gives his sanction to this belief. Blessed bells were therefore used to allay tempests. Albert le Grand, in his *De Potentia Demonum*, says of such bells, "Every time that they sound they chase far away the malignant spirits of temptation, the calamities of storms, and the spirits causing tempests."

The custom of tolling was slightly varied in England and France. In England, the consecrated death bell was tolled after the death, according to the custom of the time of Bede. In France, it tolled at the time the soul was departing. It was rung, according to the great liturgist Durandus, thrice to denote the absolution which had been given to the penitent for the three modes of sin — by thought, word, and deed — while for a clerk it was tolled as many times as denoted the number of his orders. For a like reason — to keep evil spirits from the dead — the consecrated wafer was often buried with the dead, and St. Basil is said to have specially consecrated a Host to be placed in his coffin. It was probably also the fear of such demoniacal assaults that inspired, for one reason, the custom of burying the dead under the floors of churches and as near as possible to the altar. Another reason is probable from the usage handed down from the primitive Church of burying their dead in the catacombs, where their place of worship was carved out, with those who had departed lying all round in their niches.

Coffins and Burial Rituals

The coffins that the medieval warriors were placed in were made chiefly of lead and shaped like the mummy cases of ancient Egypt. Iron coffins are extremely rare. In the earliest years of the Middle Ages, stone coffins in England were fre-

quently used, but only by the nobility and the wealthy. When the dead were about to be buried, it was customary to place their feet and faces toward the quarter where it was hoped their future would to be spent.

From the earliest times, the Christians placed the dead toward the rising sun (the East) because, according to the old tradition, that is the attitude of prayer and because at the last trump, the holy dead will hurry eastward.

The body was washed in spiced wine and water, and a cross placed in the hands or on the breast. The coffin was left open until the day of burial, often with an elaborate silken pall, brought back, if the knight had been crusading, by him for this very purpose, from the Holy Land. In the room where these last offices were rendered to the dead, many tapers and a great deal of incense were burned. It is difficult to reckon the number of candles or torches that were burned for a simple knight, however gallant had been his life. They amounted probably to about a quarter of those bestowed on a royal person. Four hundred torches of wax, each weighing six pounds, were burned before the coffin of the Queen of Charles V of France.

The body of the dead knight was conveyed in a carriage drawn by seven horses as far as the churchyard, and thence carried on the shoulders of knights into the nave of the cathedral, where the abbot performed the funeral service, at which alms were offered.

If the knight had fallen on the field of battle, many of these elaborate ceremonies were left wanting, unless his squires brought his body home for burial. A nephew of the Earl of Essex, who had fallen in 1301 at the siege of Rouen, was brought back overseas to his native land for interment, but very often, when the knight fell, he was either buried on the spot or conveyed to the nearest church for that purpose after the town had been taken by his army. From the ballads and stories it seems a very usual practice when a knight thus fell on the battlefield for his companions, when he succumbed, to make a short prayer over him — thus in the early Chanson de Geste of *La Mort de Roland*. The hero finds Turpin, the celebrated archbishop of the Carolingian Cycle, fallen, and so he cries, "Alas, gentle soul! Knight of noble lineage, I commend you to the glorious heavenly father. Never shall I serve a man with greater willingness with the exception of the apostles. No one has been a greater prophet to maintain the law and to attract men. May your soul endure no evil or suffering, May the gate of heaven be opened to you."

The good knight buried, and the task of describing his obsequies finished, a word about the memorials. They would display armor over his tomb, or valuables, chiefly brasses, laid over his remains still found on many a now-forgotten churchyard or aisle, but which, examined by a discerning eye, are most valuable both for family and for history.

The remains in England of any armor found suspended over a medieval warrior's tomb are few and far between. The best known is that of the Black Prince in Canterbury Cathedral, but one part of the armor — the helmet — is found frequently in that position. As helmets were always a knight's peculiar cognizance, it seemed fitting therefore, over his last long sleep, that they were so often suspended. Even while living, it became a custom peculiar to this country to use them as a token of hospitality outside the dwellings of the "gentle born," to denote to the wandering brother knight or his lady therein they would meet with both fraternity and lodging.

Though but a small proportion of the vast number of suits, helmets, and weapons that have come down to us can be assigned to definite wearers, most of these owe their origin to this medieval custom of hanging those of the knightly persons over their tombs. This custom is linked with the still older dedication of arms and armor at the obsequies of the dead, by either placing them in the grave or in the temples of the gods.

This reality of the connection between pagan and Christian customs is apparent by such incidents as that of William of Toulouse, early in the thirteenth century, who dedicated his helmet, shield, and sword to St. Julian, hang-

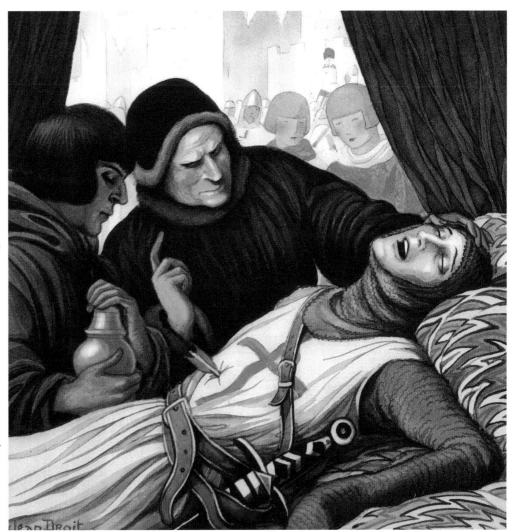

Above: The death of a medieval warrior.

ing them over his shrine; or that of the King of France, who, after the Battle of Cassel in 1327, presented his victorious arms to the neighboring church. Unfortunately, the early medieval veneration for the person of the dead, which led to the consecration of the armor and weapons he had actually used, hardly survived the thirteenth century.

Though the helmet and sword were frequently displayed over a knightly tomb, only a medieval warrior who died on the battlefield was allowed, in the days when medieval culture was at its prime, to have his banner (if he was a banneret) or pennon (if he was a simple knight) displayed over his last resting place.

From the earliest years of the Middle Ages, it was a frequent custom to place small hearts in the hands of the knights and ladies commemorated on brasses — just as the chalice was placed in those of priests — either to indicate that the deceased had been enabled to fulfill some vow, or simply to suggest that their heart was given to God, a new heart was desired, or as a symbol of a complete trust in the Sacred Heart of Jesus.

Medieval Arms and Armor

N THE TWELFTH AND THIRTEENTH CENTURIES, and well into the fifteenth, the principal weapons of the medieval warrior were the sword and the spear, or lance. Secondary weapons included the dagger, the ax, and the mace. The lance's head is sometimes of the lozenge shape, and very seldom barbed. In the eleventh century, nearly all the Norman spears were adorned with pennons having two to five points. The Saxon ax was eventually superceded by the mace, although at a later date the ax again came into favor with the medieval warriors.

Chain armor had its origin in remote antiquity. It came from the East and penetrated to the north and west of Europe. As far as England is concerned, the epoch of chain mail, pure and simple, may be said to have closed with the reign of Edward I in 1307.

From the time of the Norman Conquest until the introduction of plate armor there was little alteration in a medieval warrior's equipment. When the Normans arrived in England in 1066, the subject of armor and arms in that island nation became more definite to trace and to describe. This is owing chiefly to the famous Bayeux Tapestry, and also to the multiplication of manuscripts, carvings, ivories, and brasses preserved in France and England. Both countries, though often at war, had a common tradition in the manner of their armor.

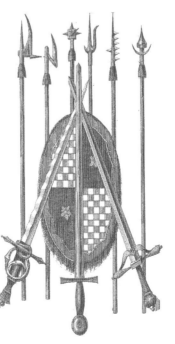

ABOVE: MEDIEVAL WEAPONS.

The Sword

To the Vikings, the sword had been their most precious weapon. Fighting as they did along the coasts of the countries they made descents upon, their weapons alone saved their lives, and such were cared for with the utmost diligence. To them, the sword had surrounding it a mystic glamour which was handed on to the medieval knights, their successors, and which lingers yet in regal functions. At the time of Bayard, the epitome of French chivalry, this mystic glamour still hovered around the sword. This was what he considered to be the greatest reward of all.

Tradition elevated the forger of Odin's sword into a demigod. Athelstan, Ethelwulf, and Alfred, in Saxon England, bequeathed — as their dearest treasure — their swords to their next of kin. Thence, it passed in the Arthurian circle to Arthur's mystic sword Excalibur, which is said to have been presented by Richard I to Tancred of Sicily.

All the better armor in the twelfth and thirteenth centuries was brought from Germany. There, the constant feuds of the Hanseatic and other towns with the neighboring nobles made the manufacture of arms a personal necessity, and the best armed gained the day. This armor was continually brought into France and England, and, among the chivalrous of both kingdoms, was eagerly pur-

Above: A fifteenth-century German knight, armed and armored in the manner of the period.

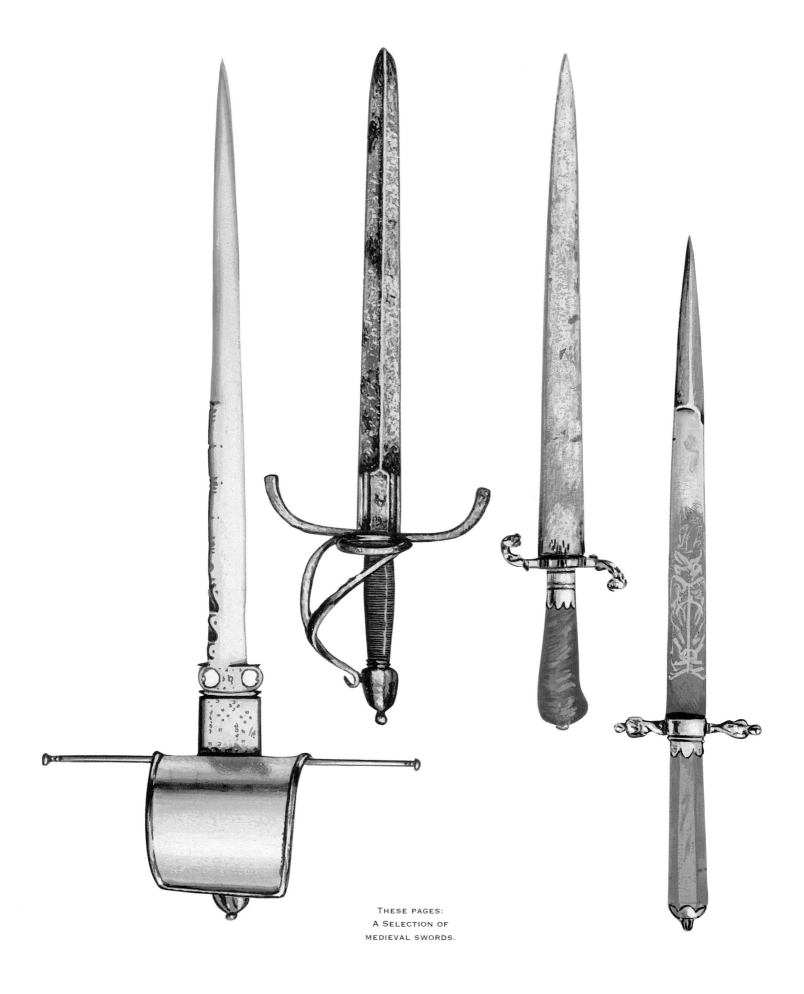

THESE PAGES:
A SELECTION OF
MEDIEVAL SWORDS.

chased. Cologne was a great center for this warlike commodity, and is spoken of in many an early ballad. The Battle of Otterbourne was fought with swords of "fyne collayne." King Arthur's mystic sword was said to have been made there: "For all of Coleyne was the blade, and all the hilte of precious stone." As to France, the sword that St. Louis, in the thirteenth century, bore in the Crusade which he undertook, was of German workmanship.

Later, Italian — particularly Milanese — arms and armor were the fashion, but this only when plate had taken the place of the older chain-mail armor.

The sword of the medieval warrior varied little in form from the twelfth to the end of the fifteenth century. The swords in use at this period can be divided into three classes:

1. Those having the character of a broadsword, with parallel sharp edges and an acute point and the tang (the prolongation of the blade which fits into the handle is the tang) only for a grip.

2. A similar variety having a cross-guard arm.

3. A sword with the blade slightly curved.

The sheaths were usually of leather stiffened with a wooden framing. The sword had short "quillons" drooping toward the blade. The grip was slightly swelling, and the circular pommel, if not a cross-hilted sword, was enriched with a design. The method of suspending the sword is peculiar to the period, gripping the scabbard in two places, between which a small strap runs as a "guide." The weapon thus hangs diagonally across the left front of the medieval warrior.

The two-handled sword seems seldom to have been used. It rarely occurs on the monumental brasses of the period. It required great strength of arm to handle it, but that redoubtable knight, Richard I, is said to have been proficient in its use.

The swords were generally cross-hilted. Hence, often in battle a knight sorely wounded would (as the celebrated Bayard is said to have done) place before his dying eyes his sword, upright-bearing his last thoughts heavenward.

Helmets and Body Armor

During the Middle Ages, the helmet, another necessity in the medieval warrior's equipment, was conical with a "nasal" (nose protection). This is seen clearly in the Bayeux Tapestry. The nasal continued in use until about 1140. This conical shape was gradually superseded by a cylinder shape, made of iron with a vertical slit for the eyes, one on each side

Above: Fifteenth-century Italian armor.

Above: Full chain-mail armor.

of the helm, called "occularii." Holes for breathing were rare in specimens left us. The medieval warrior had to breathe through the small holes provided for his nose and eyes. An example of this sort of helmet is to be found on the monumental effigy in Kirkstead Chapel, Lincolnshire.

The helmet itself was generally flat-topped and had very much the appearance of a chimney pot. A slightly more graceful one was brought in at the end of the fourteenth century, called the "armet" (from "elmette" or "armette"). This differed from those previously used in that, while the older forms had been put on by lowering them over the head, and the weight had in all cases been borne by the head, the armets opened out their lowest part on hinges, and could be closed around the head and neck, while the weight was transferred to the gorget (collar) and thence to the shoulders. It is very likely that the present heraldic way of portraying helmets is derived from this "armet," as both are singularly alike. There is a fine specimen of an armet in London's Wallace Collection.

The conical helmet, which the armet afterward often took the place of, was of great weight and so either hung at the saddlebow or was carried by the squire when not in use. Inside — as were all the other forms — it was thickly padded and went over the mailed *chapelle de fer.*

At first, no crest appeared on these helmets. The earliest form of the latter was a painted emblem on the side of the helmet, such as is found on that of Philip d'Alsace, Count of Flanders, in 1181. So, too, on the cap of Geoffrey, Count of Anjou, in 1150.

The earliest authentic example — predecessor of all others — is that of Richard Coeur de Lion, who shows on his great seal a fan-shaped ornament surmounting the helmet.

The introduction of a crest on the helmet seems originally to have been for defense — from their indented and serrat-

Above: Partial chain-mail armor.

ed edges — which served to deaden the blow of a sword or mace. The immense crests also used were for an entirely different purpose, that of ostentation and ornament in tournaments, and were generally made of painted *cuir bouilli. Ailettes* also must be mentioned. These came into vogue toward the end of the thirteenth century and have often puzzled the uninitiated. They were small shields or defenses fastened at right angles across the shoulders, designed to lessen the effect of a sweeping cut from a sword or an ax.

An early notice of ailettes occurs in the "Roll of Purchases" for the great tournament held at Windsor in 1278, where they were stated to have been made of leather covered with a sort of cloth. Silk laces were employed sometimes to fasten them. It is remarkable that the brass of Sir Roger de Trumpington, who was one of the 35 knights taking part in this tournament, should show one of the earliest examples extant of these ailettes.

The use of ailettes is rather perplexing. That they were merely ornamental is improbable. The only supposition is that they were little shields for the neck and shoulders, but more especially for the latter. Occasionally for tournaments and pageants, ailettes appear to have been made very elaborately. Thus, in the Inventory of Piers Gaveston in 1313, mention is made of a pair garnished and fretted with pearls.

The gambeson was another article in the medieval warrior's equipment. It generally was worn under the mail, but it also, on one or two brasses, has been found over the chain mail. It was made chiefly of leather prepared by previous boiling and so extremely tough, and had various snips and discs of iron sewn on its surface. It, like the coat of mail or hauberk, had a thick stuffing underneath, to prevent it, or the mail, from chafing the warrior's skin. The tunic was worn under both the gambeson and hauberk. Sometimes the tunic was worn much longer than at other times, so in some sepulchral brasses it is quite clearly seen beneath the ringed hauberk.

The hauberk itself was the chief method of bodily defense. Its coif, which generally went over the head and under the *chapelle de fer* (the other head defense) was usually a part of it, though instances occurred when it was placed detachable round the neck, where afterward the gorget was placed.

This coif had only a small opening for the face. This almost complete covering of the latter sometimes led to medieval warriors in battle mistaking their enemies for friends. Thus, the Englishman Ralph de Courci, in the French wars, mistook the French for his own side and was taken prisoner. At the Battle of Noyon, Peter de Maule and others escaped recognition of the pursuing enemy and mingled in their ranks. William the Conqueror himself is said to have been reported dead by his soldiers, though he was riding in their midst, until he threw back his coif and showed his face.

The hauberk was generally made to open in front in order to afford convenience in riding. Upon the outside of it was, on the chest part, a square or oblong piece to doubly protect the former.

During this era, the hauberk was made of chain mail, and chain mail was a manufacture, of very great antiquity. Antiquarians have traced it on relics of the Assyrian and ancient Persian dynasties. It was certainly known, in a lesser degree, to the Romans, who used rings and discs sewn on a strong stratum of tough textile to arm their soldiery. There is little doubt, however, that chain armor originated in the East, where its comparative coolness and lightness would, as an armor, be peculiarly fitted for a hot country. It came through depredations, far afield, around Europe,

Above: A knight in chain-mail armor.

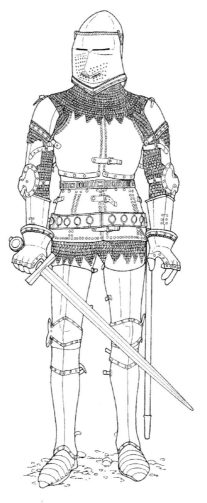

Above: A knight in plate armor.

into the hands and use of the Norsemen, and thence spread rapidly among the Western countries of France and England.

The manufacture of chain-mail armor took a great amount of labor and trouble, for it was hard to forge. Sometimes (from how they appear in the brasses of the time), the mail had rings overlapping each other in the same row; sometimes they look as if each row of rings had been sewn on, and doubtless they often were, upon stout linen or cuir bouilli (*cuir-boilée*). Sometimes the rings are interlinked, as in a nineteenth-century steel purse, so that the coat is entirely of steel rings. The bottom of the hauberk was often scalloped or gilded.

Another item, chausses of chain mail, requisite to preserve the legs of the mailed knight. These came into general use, about the commencement of the twelfth century.

In some they were short, protecting only the knees and shins of the wearer. In others, they were a continuation of the hauberk, and so the latter covered both the legs and the feet. To avoid the difficulty of bending the knee *genouillères* were invented, which generally were of cuir bouilli and often highly ornamented.

The reason for this defense was not alone the protection afforded. The intolerable drag of chain mail upon the knee or elbow when flexed prevented freedom of action in each joint.

However, by ending the ringed mail at the upper part of the genouillere, to which it was affixed, and the continuation of it below, an advantage was achieved which was fully appreciated. A similar device later on was invented to wear at the elbow joints, called *coudieres*. These coudieres were frequently elaborately ornamented.

The hands at this earlier period, were covered with a continuation down the arms

Above: An Austrian helmet and upper-body plate armor of the sixteenth century.

of the linked hauberk and not divided yet into fingers. They were, in fact, ringed mittens.

Perhaps the most interesting — certainly the most showy — of the medieval warrior's equipment was the surcoat, a sleeveless garment reaching nearly to the heels. It was split in front and probably behind for convenience in riding. It was originally introduced to preserve the mail from the rain, which, from its material, was much apt to rust, and indirectly as protection in the early Crusades against the heat of the Middle Eastern sun. But the chief reason for its adoption was that it afforded a means for recognizing the wearer, whose features now were completely hidden by the helmet, thus rendering it impossible, without a distinguishing mark, to recognize friend from foe.

The surcoat indeed took the place of the long, flowing tunic, which had been worn under the hauberk as shown on the two great seals of Richard I, and it was a natural outcome to transfer the latter to the outermost position, leaving the padded and often mail-set gambeson alone the duty of supporting the weight of the hauberk.

The first English monarch who appears in the surcoat is King John, and he is thus located upon his great seal, while his rival, the Dauphin Louis, is similarly represented upon the French seal. So, too, the surcoat appears on the seal of Alexander II of Scotland. Ashdown says it was of white material, sometimes diapered, and nearly always with heraldic charges.

Joinville, in his chronicle, says he spoke to the son of St. Louis of the embroidered coats of arms then in vogue, reminding him that he had never seen such rich ones in his saintly father's time. The young prince (later king) acknowledged that he had such surcoats with arms embroi-

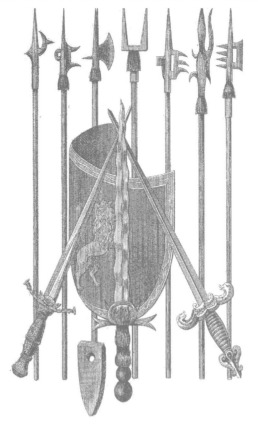

Above: Medieval swords, pikes, and axes.

Above: A warrior in gilt-plate armor.

dered which had cost him 800 pounds. Joinville told him he could have employed the money better if he had given it to God and had his surcoat made of good satin ornamented with his arms, as his father had done.

Another writer (Gardner) says from the time of King John (1199–1216) it was nearly always green, and cites an old adage: "With sharpe weapon and with festive gowns of green to hold their armor clean, and were it from the wette."

The illuminations extant, however, certainly point to the correctness of the first writer — except that the surcoat in them is not always white; sometimes a brilliant blue, sometimes scarlet, in a prince's cloth of gold, but in all charged with heraldic emblems.

The shield of the period was kite-shaped, either flat or a round hollow, so as to encircle the warrior's body to some extent. It was invariably made, at this time, of wood and covered on both sides with leather. The shield was generally about four feet long and two feet across. It was often worn not on the arm, as in action, but slung round the neck, or carried by the youthful squire for its owner. Spurs, of course — for they were essentially the emblem of knighthood — completed the chevalier in armor.

Gilt spurs were fastened on the warrior's heels when knighted. They were hacked off by the cook's ax when degraded. At the famous Battle of Courtrai in 1302, an immense spoil of these fell to the victors and were hung up by them as trophies in the neighboring church.

The gilded spurs were not unknown to the Romans. They were one of the marks of their Equestrian order.

The earlier form of the medieval spur was of a "goad" type fastened on by a single strap. They were probably first used singly and were called "prick spurs." The more modern "rowel" spur appears later, in the thirteenth century, and is seen in the great seal of Henry III. The number of pricks on the ordinary spur of the rowel type was usually eight. Those used at tournaments generally contained sixteen pricks and had very long shanks to reach the horse's flank.

Archers

In the open field, at close grip with the enemy, the medieval warrior was used to the greatest advantage. When medieval society was at its height, the common soldier who fought on foot was scarcely valued or considered. It remained for the battles of Crécy and Poitiers to show how invaluable were his services, and on both occasions the English longbow won the day.

Archers, however, particularly in England from the time of the Norman Conquest, had assumed an importance in all armies under the English banners. The success of the Normans at Hastings was greatly due to the skill and superiority of their archers. The latter are shown on the Bayeux Tapestry, both in hauberks and without, and one is seen on horseback.

The bow then seems to be of the simplest construction and the arrow not the cloth yard shaft of a later age. It became a custom from a very early date for the archer to bear a stake sharpened at both ends. The front ranks drove firmly into the ground, with the second and uppermost points sloping from them, while the rear ranks filled up the intermediate spaces with theirs. When protected thus, in front and on both flanks, it was found that the archers of England could defy the charge of the heaviest cavalry, and the prowess of these archers made them renowned throughout Europe.

At the Siege of Messina by Richard Coeur de Lion, we are told by the chronicler, Richard of Devizes, that the Sicilians were obliged to leave their walls unmanned, "because no one could look abroad but he would have an arrow in his eye before he could shut it."

While Richard himself did not disdain the use of the bow, he used it personally with deadly effect when besieging Nottingham Castle, defended by the adherents of his brother John. During the Norman period the infantry, as a rule, were armed with the bow, though other weapons were placed on the same plane. However, when the long-

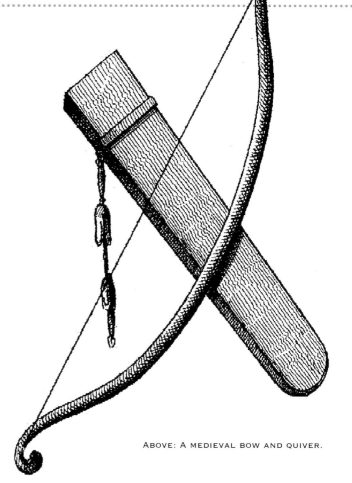

ABOVE: A MEDIEVAL BOW AND QUIVER.

bow proper came into use and the arbalest was invented, the deadly effect of the arrow and the quarrel began to be fully recognized and accepted. The bow, which before had been valued chiefly in sieges and the defense of mountain passes and strongholds, came to be considered of exceptional efficacy in the open field.

The importance of bows was such that yew trees were ordered grown in the churchyards to provide material for them. Every merchant importing merchandise from abroad, where bow staves were exported, was bound to send four bow staves for every ton of merchandise into the kingdom. As to the arrows, an immense number was manufactured, with the vast flocks of geese and swans in medieval England providing the quills. Each archer commonly carried two dozen arrows.

The Saxons at Hastings, as well as the Normans, used the short horseman's bow and drew the arrow to the breast and not the ear. This is well displayed in the Bayeux Tapestry. The longbow is not mentioned, and there is little account of English archery until the wars of Edward I in Wales and Scotland.

The Crusaders, if they used a bow — though against papal injunction — used the crossbow, this because it was smaller, and thus so much more handy on horseback than the six-foot longbow.

The Crossbow

The equipment of the archer began to be considerably augmented. The arbalest, or crossbow, was a very early weapon and was chiefly — at first — used for sport. It was not until the close of the twelfth century that it was recognized as a military weapon and found illustrated as such in manuscripts. Condemned by Pope Innocent II in 1139, it was used by Richard I in his Crusade. In fact, his bodyguard was formed partly of arbalesters.

In the copious records left by Matthew Paris, the crossbowman is constantly mentioned. His particular post was in the forepart of the battle and upon the wings, where the heavy quarrels discharged from his weapon were supposed to check the advance of the enemies' knights. In the thirteenth century, scarcely a battle is recounted where the arbalester is not credited with performing most conspicuous service. In the contest with Louis IX of France, Henry III of England had 700 crossbowmen in his force, while the French had a vastly greater number. In the time of King John, the pay for a crossbowman on foot was three pence a day, while, if mounted, he was paid seven pence half penny or fifteen pence, according to whether he possessed one or two horses.

Superseding the Crossbow

The supersession of the crossbow in England by the longbow was due to natural causes. It was found that as the longbow underwent improvements it out classed the crossbow in more ways than one. A powerful and skillful bowman could discharge half a dozen or more arrows during the time the arbalester was winding up his crossbow for a second shot. Also, the distance covered by the arrow and its penetrative power were found to be greater.

In consequence of the rapidity of the English archers, they invariably beat down the attack of the Continental crossbowmen, where their use was retained much longer than in England.

The great and growing use made of archers in the English battles, prepared the way for infantry gradually to oust the mailed

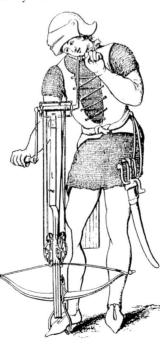

ABOVE: COCKING THE CROSSBOW.

knight on horseback in a fight. An instance of this is found at Crécy.

Edward III was a bad strategist but a good tactician. He ought not to have been found at Crécy on August 28, 1346. However, being there, he did the best that could be done. More than half his army were archers. He dismounted his men-at-arms and posted his archers as advancing wings on each side of both "battles" of infantry. "From the day of Crécy," writes Green, "feudalism tottered slowly but surely to its grave. The churl had struck the noble." Yet, as has been well remarked, it is interesting to note how little Froissart knew of this when he was writing in the fourteenth century.

To Froissart, as to the princes and the lords and to Francis I in the early sixteenth century, chivalry and its emblazoned banners were more than the art of war, and they failed to realize that the destinies of war were passing. In some cases these had passed already, from the medieval warrior in armor to the brave archer and pikeman.

This rapid growth of archers in a feudal army is seen in the battles of the Wars of the Roses, which were chiefly fought by dismounted men-at-arms and innumerable archers, some of whom were raised by parliamentary vote, some hired, and some mustered, as those in the wars of Edward I against Scotland, as retainers of the great lords and knights.

Advancements in Weapons

The gun, or "fire stick," that is to say the arquebus, which was then called harquebus, with difficulty took the place of the bow, and, with still greater difficulty, that of the crossbow.

In 1481, Louis XI deprived his sergeants-at-arms of both the latter weapons, not to arm them with guns but in order to give them the pike, the halbert, and the broadsword, of which the Swiss in the recent wars had made such formidable use.

Louis XI, however, increased the number of his mounted archers, and later placed them under the orders of the colonel of a company of free lancers known as Albanais, or Scouts. These combined bodies formed the French national light cavalry until Francis I replaced them by the light horse,

Above: Seventeenth-century Italian armor.

a body chiefly composed of mercenaries of different nations.

In England, since the thirteenth century, the mounted archers formed a considerable portion of the national forces. An army of 1,500 complete lances, which represented a total of as many as 7,000 horsemen, required a complement of at least 5,000 mounted archers, who were all skillful marksmen. In the time of Henry VIII, an English bowman could discharge as many as 12 arrows in a minute, and he would have considered himself disgraced if he had let fly a single shaft which failed to kill, wound, or, at least, strike an enemy.

The desperate melee at Fornoue (July 6, 1495), which forced Charles VIII to retrace his steps after his successful Italian expedition, was nearly the last of the confused and bloody struggles of the Middle Ages.

The sword and the bow contributed more than the cannon and the fire stick to the terrible result of the day. From that time, the infantry regained its old preeminence over the cavalry, and cannons were employed preferably to all other projectile weapons. A complete revolution was also about to ensue, as well in the tactics of an army in the field as in the attack and defense of fortresses. Louis XII and Francis I, in their Italian campaigns, in which they wasted so much of the resources and treasures of France, had to contend with German and Spanish mercenaries, at that time the best soldiers in the world. They opposed to them bodies of foreign infantry, sometimes lansquenets (see top of this page), sometimes Swiss, who made a trade of war, and who, to earn their pay, did not hesitate to fight against their own countrymen. There was one drawback, however, to the acceptance of their services, and that was that they frequently changed sides on the eve of an engagement, or refused to fight on the slightest pretext. More than once, the knights of France saw themselves suddenly abandoned by the infantry whose duty it was to support them, and who allowed them to be cut to pieces before

ABOVE: SWISS LANSQUENETS, INFANTRY FOR HIRE.

their eyes without stirring to assist them. This happened at the fatal Battle of Pavia, when the king and his nobles struggled on foot in hand-to-hand desperation until they fell or were taken prisoners.

In the ordinary arrangement, at this period, of any army giving battle in the open field, the free archers, the men-at-arms, and the knights were posted either in the center or at the wings. The infantry, properly so called, divided into little groups of five, identified as cinquains, which were thrown forward to skirmish, sent behind to cover the rear guard, or detached at intervals on the flanks in order to harass the enemy and to protect the baggage. During the engagement, all the knights, clad entirely in armor, dismounted in order to fight, and left their horses to the care of the infantry.

At this time, horses were used only to carry their riders on the march, which the weight of their armor would not have allowed them to perform on foot. A horseman, when disabled by long service or age, was no longer employed in the cavalry, but retired into the infantry, where he served as an *anspessade* (from the Italian *spezzate*, meaning "broken").

Infantry Arms and Armor

The medieval foot soldiers were usually armed with a steel *chapelle de fer* (a steel

ABOVE: A KNIGHT WITH A BATTLE-AX.

cap with, often, a point in front, lined with padding). This covered a chain-mail coif which was part of a continuous hauberk, and the arms and hands were covered with mail of a similar description. Bands of leather round the neck afforded the protection of a gorget, fixed to a hauberk composed of leather scales of large size and leaf like shape showing the mid-rib, while a belt round the waist and pendant leaves about the waist completed a most effective bodily defense. The legs were enclosed in soft leather chausses protected by metal studs upon which was a cross-gartering of leather thongs. The usual weapon was the ax. The rank and file of a knightly army were armed with, and carried with them, a wide variety of weapons for the assaulting of both the enemy and hostile towns.

Eustache Deschamps wrote of "evil daggers from Bordeaux and Clermont swords, stone-throwers, and of knives of steel, which are made at Milan. The hammer-axe, crooks and iron lances, javelins that are cast and thrown, guichards, two-handled swords and guisarmes, cannon, stones and arbalests on wheels, Damascus maces, flails, pikes such as the Flemings use, crossbows which are swift, holy water sprinklers that disfigure the body, scythes which slice one beyond hope of cure, let him die and swoon away him and thee, whosoever thou art who dost arm thyself lost be thy honor and valiancy who calls on me to take up arms."

Among the first written evidence relating to the existence of the cannon is the Ordinances of Florence in the year 1326, wherein authority is given to the Priors Gonfalionieri to appoint persons to superintend the manufacture of the cannon and iron balls for the defense of the camp in the Republic. Barbour, the Scottish poet, quotes an authority for the use of the cannon by Edward III in his Scottish campaign in 1327, but the authority is doubtful and the date of the first appearance of cannons in the field is still debated. Some say they were used at Crecy in the year 1346. Certainly, in 1382, the men of Gent carried guns into the field against the Brugeois, and at the combat of Pont-de-Comines in the same year we read *bombardes portatives* were used.

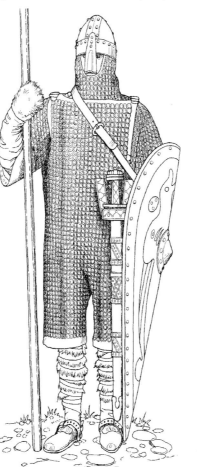

ABOVE: AN INFANTRYMAN WITH A PIKE.

The "hammer-axes" had a sharp edge on one side, and a hammer on the other, *croquepois* were sticks armed with an iron hook, and *guisarmes* were weapons shaped like scythes. This was a weapon dating from the Bronze Age and used as late as the seventeenth century. The guisarme usually terminated in a strong, sharp point, and the two sides were both sharpened to a razor like edge and various hooks and spikes added. The *fauchard* resembled a scythe in particular and was a species of guisarme. So deadly and so ghastly were the wounds inflicted by this weapon that an agitation for its abolition rose in the Middle Ages.

Espaphus espadon was a two-handed sword, *carreaulx* were "quarrels"—that is, great arrows or "bolts" usually discharged from a machine with the extremity armed with a piece of weighted lead. Quarrels and bolts were used by the arbalesters or crossbowmen. *Troyes* were machines dating from Roman times that were used for throwing stones, and also for affording shelter, when approaching a walled town. It could also be used as a battering ram. Such a machine seems also to have been used by the ancient Assyrians.

Espringales were machines like arbalests mounted on wheels, being huge steel bows which threw javelins, spears, and darts, and sometimes were adapted to throw two or more stones at a single discharge. These latter were vertical springs of steel which were pulled back by ropes and pulleys and, when released, would throw one missile from a sling at the extremity and another from a cup fixed to the steel. *Fuseaulx* were a kind of stick shaped like a spindle but very long and used for defensive purposes. It seems to have had no connection with fire or even rockets.

Plommees were great balls of lead or iron attached to the end of an iron chain. They were known popularly as "Holy Water Sprinklers." the military "flail" is allied to the weapon called "The Morning Star," a mace with a spiked head. It consisted of a shaft to which was affixed a staple having a chain depending, and to the end of which a ball of iron, usually covered with spikes, was attached.

Many of these weapons were carried by the rank and file of a feudal army from the earliest times. Some were adaptations of more primitive models, while two or three had their origin, as far as can be traced by specimens found, to the middle of the fourteenth century. Certainly, without the modern cannon and gunnery, the medieval soldier was not wanting in arms, and so, unlike the knight, his leader and overlord, armed only with lance, sword, and ax, sometimes with the misericord to despatch his fallen foe, he was provided with arms for every emergency on the field of battle or in a siege.

The Medieval Warhorse

The horses employed by the knights during the Middle Ages frequently entered into accounts of all the noble contests of arms. Perhaps no animal is so intimately mixed up with the history of mankind as the horse. Certainly this was the case in the age of medieval society.

In the old stories and poetry, the medieval warriors not in heavy armor are generally described as being mounted on Arab steeds, won in conquest of the Moslem Arabs (Saracens). In the thirteenth century, they were obtained from Turkey and Greece, and at a later period from North Africa. France also had its native breed, which had a high reputation, especially for its fierceness in battle. Gascony and, on the other side of the Spanish frontier, Castile and Aragon were much celebrated for their horses.

The Gascons prided themselves greatly on their horses, and they sometimes displayed this pride in a singular manner. In 1172, Raymond de Saint-Gilles, Count of Toulouse, held a grand *cour plénière* and, as a display of ostentation, caused 30 of his horses to be burned in the presence of his guests.

It may be mentioned that a male horse was ridden only by knights, and to ride a mare was looked upon as a degradation. French knights' horses were nearly always docked both in ears and tail. The kind of horses most

commonly in evidence in the age of medieval society were the destrier, the *roncin,* the *sommier* and the palfrey. The latter was a sober kind of hack used for distance riding.

When a medieval warrior was merely going for a ride or on a journey, he usually bestrode a palfrey. However, when he was going to take the field, one of his esquires led at his right hand (whence the name of destrier given to this sort of steed) a charger or high horse, which the knight mounted only at the last moment. Hence the expression "to ride the high horse," which has become proverbial. The destrier was the knight's heavy warhorse, the palfrey that on which he often rode when not in immediate warfare or engaged in a tournament, while his esquire or page bestrode the destrier carrying his helm and armor. The roncin belonged especially to his entourage or servants, while the sommier carried his luggage. Ladies usually rode the palfreys.

The Orkney Islands appear to have been celebrated for their destriers, and Brittany for her palfreys. England seems not to have been celebrated for its breed of horses in the Middle Ages, and those her kings and nobles possessed seem to have been imported from the Continent.

At this time, a horse was considered the most handsome present that could be made by a king or great lord, and horses were often given as bribes.

Thus, in 1227, the monks of the Abbey of Troarn obtained from Guillaume de Tille the ratification of a grant made to them by his father in consideration of a gift to him of a mark of silver and a palfrey. The monks of Saint-Evroul in 1165 purchased a like favor from the Earl of Gloucester by presenting to him two palfreys.

It has been said that the widow of Herbert de Mesnil gave King John a palfrey in order to obtain the wardship of her children. And one Geoffrey Fitz-Richard gave the same king a palfrey to obtain a concession in the forest of Beaulieu.

ABOVE: A WARRIOR AND A WARHORSE IN PARADE LIVERY.

Above: A sixteenth century English knight astride his armored war horse.

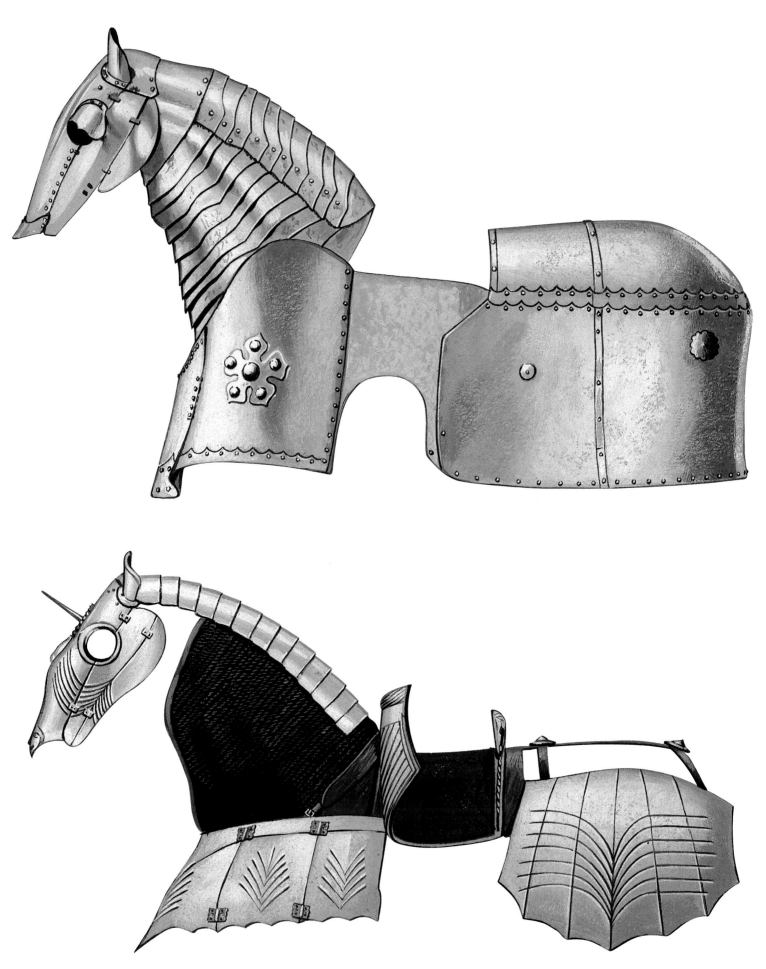

ABOVE: TWO EXAMPLES OF MEDIEVAL HORSE ARMOR. THE SET AT TOP WAS MORE COMPLETE (AND HEAVIER). PROTECTION FOR THE NECK WAS ALWAYS VITAL.

In 1172, Raymond, Count of Saint-Gilles, gave his overlord, the King of England, as tribute, 10 destriers.

As the color of horses in the Middle Ages, white seems to have been prized most highly, and after that, dapple-gray or chestnut. The same colors were in favor both in Europe and in the Middle East and Africa among the Moors.

To be a skillful rider was before all things necessary to a medieval warrior. From the time he had been taken as a page, until he rose to be a valet or squire, his daily exercises were for this end. One of the feats of horsemanship practiced ordinarily was to jump into the saddle in full armor. In *The Romance of Richard Coeur de Lion,* a messenger coming to King Richard has no less than 500 such bells suspended to his horse.

Fine horses were at this period, as now, much prized. In *The Romance of the Rose*, a youthful knight is portrayed as even preferring theft to having his stables without good steeds: "A youth of fairest goodness, he loved fine mansions, castles fair And jewels rich and vestments rare, Grand stables horses past all price, And sooner were he charred with vice. Of theft or murder than 'twere said His stables harbored crock or jade."

It was often the custom of a knight victorious in a tournament to offer his adversary's dearest possession, next to his sword — his destrier or warhorse — to his own lady-love. Thus, in *The Romance of Floire and Blanceflor,* Floire says: "But my love is fair and fine When he goes to the Tournament And lays low a knight He presents me with his war horse."

Often the knights who had conquered their opponents in the tournament, and whose armor and horses were by the laws of the tournament forfeited, presented them to those poor knights who otherwise could not be mounted. So a fair lady, seeing this generosity, remarks: "My champion gives to one a war horse, To another a palfrey, or a courser."

The custom of hanging small bells on the horses' harness, according to some old writers, is to be traced to the

origin of the heraldic term "vair," and so to the fur "vair and gris" which is permitted to be worn only by knights, is often used in the medieval stories to denote a certain person was knighted.

In the *Dictionaire de Ménage*, the word "vair" or "vaire" is derived from the verb "variar," meaning to change or variegate. "Vair" therefore was a fur of variegated colors. But this fur, by its very name, demonstrates it was not natural but made by the art of the furriers, and was composed chiefly of two skins, one white, the other gray, lapping over each other, figured over by small pieces in the shape of little bells arranged opposite each other, gray and white, in rows, so as to make one entire skin.

The origin of this ornamented fur is to be found in the custom of medieval society.

The explanation by Bénéton de Peyrins is extremely curious: "It is necessary," he writes, "to remember the way horses about to enter a battle or tournament were dressed. Over their caparisons — or coats of iron which they wore to shield them from blows — they wore a long caparison or cloth of rich material emblazoned with the armorial bearings of their knightly owners. If the knight's coat was of one color, so too was the horse's.

"The whole horse cloth was also garnished with little bells of two shapes, intermingled together. In imitation of the medieval knight's plumes on his helmet and on his horse's head, we find still in countries abroad where the mule is driven the feather still decking his often weary old head, while round his collar the bells still survive of another age."

These rows of little bells which ornamented the horse cloth of the medieval warrior were called belfries, like the veritable belfries that gave warning so often of the border or robber bands about to fall on some hapless village or town. After a time, however, these little rows of real bells were discontinued, and it became a custom to embroider them only in rows of two different shapes on the rich horse cloths.

ABOVE: A KNIGHT IN CHAIN MAIL RIDING AN UNARMORED WAR HORSE.

This gave the knights and the furriers the idea to imitate in fur — by, as we have shown, using two colors of skins, alternately facing each other — discarding literal bells, and they gave to the fur the celebrated name so associated with the knightly order, "vair," and which no one except of that degree was allowed to wear.

Thus, by an ordinance of the King of France in 1294, no burgher or his wife is to wear "vair," nor gray (fur) nor ermine, and if they have such they are to render them up at the approaching of the Easter season.

Though horses were seldom used except for war and travel, it may be of interest to mention, according to the old *Romance of Bevis of Hampton,* that the knights rode sometimes for wagers on them, as, in this romance over a three-mile course on steeds and palfreys, for "40 pounds of ready gold."

This was in the reign of Richard I. In the reign of John, "running horses" are frequently mentioned in the household expenditure, and Edward III had also a number of these "running" horses.

Referring again to the color of medieval horses, white or gray, which was called "Lyard" — were the favorite colors, but "Favel," a chestnut, was also held in great admiration. A bay horse was called "Bayard" — a dark roan or mulberry color, "Morel."

As to the Favel, a very old proverb has it: "He that will in Court dwell Must curry Favelle. And he that will in Court abide Must curry Favelle back and side."

To "curry Favel" meant at that time to be subservient to the caprices of a patron in hope of advantage to come. Nowadays we have forgotten what Favel meant, and have corrupted the phrase into "curry favor."

Nor must it be imagined, in that rough and ready age, that horses were neglected or their intelligence not rightly

ABOVE: KNIGHT AND WAR HORSE, BOTH WELL ARMORED.

esteemed. Indeed, a knight's feats at a tournament or in battle very greatly depended on these qualities of his destrier.

In a very interesting extant illumination of this period, a good knight is depicted resting in his tent — striped in gold, red, green, and blue — pitched in a meadow after a great tournament.

The tent door is open, so we see him in it waiting for his supper, with two candles set on the table. However, he is shown as a good chevalier and a humane one to his horse, for the latter is sharing the shelter of the tent and eating in it out of a trough. The good knight's armor laid aside, in his robes of peace and having just been to Vespers, he is awaiting from the hands of his young squire his well-earned supper.

That, too, these chevaliers and those to whom the jugglers recounted their tales appreciated the intelligence and faithfulness of their charges, we have evidenced in *The Ballad of Graelent.* Toward the end of the story, Graelent is borne away into the land of fairies, but we are told "his destrier grieved greatly for his master's loss. He sought again and again the mighty forest, yet never was at rest by night or day.

"No peace might he find, but ever he pawed with his hoofs upon the ground and neighed so loudly that the noise went all the country round. Many a man coveted so noble an animal and sought to put bit and bridle in his mouth, yet never might one set hands upon him, for he would not suffer another master. So each year in its season the forest was filled with the cry and the trouble of this noble horse, which might not find its lord."

A knight's destrier cost him 20 pounds in 1375, but, of course, at the present-day value of money this was a large sum. The palfrey cost 12 pounds in 1303. A bay one obtained for Queen Marguerite of France — second wife of Edward I — was bought for this sum, and a Ferrand, or bay one, for 6 pounds.

The sumpter horse or mule which carried the luggage cost an average of 6 pounds. Henry V expended "for a dapple-grey horse and a black horse 16 pounds 13 schillings, for a white one and a sorrel one 10 pounds, and for two white horses 10 pounds."

Horse Armor

As to horse armor, nothing is more constantly met with in the old chronicles than accounts of the destructive effects of missiles, whether from bow or crossbow, upon knights' horses in battle, yet excepting the poetic fancy of Wace in his *Roman de Rou,* who mounts Fitzosbert on an iron-clad horse at Senlac.

The first mention of horse armor, as far as England is concerned, is at the Battle of Gisors in 1198, when Richard I speaks of the capture of 140 sets in terms which plainly show that he then met with it for the first time. Indeed, no reference is made in English statutes of horse armor until 1298, so that it seems certain it was until then unknown.

In France, its introduction seems earlier, for at this time a man-at-arms received half as much pay if his horse was branded, and, in 1303, every man with an estate of 500 livres was bound to provide horse armor. A mailed horse appears in the effigy of Sir Robert de Shirland in Sheppey, and there is a fine figure of a destrier completely clad in mail among the figures of *The Painted Chamber* (published by the Society of Antiquarians). One reason that it was so late in its appearance was that the Norman knights, copying their predecessors, the Danes, during the civil wars of Henry I, Stephen, and Henry II, fought their battles dismounted, rendering horse armor of relatively minor importance.

Later, it rose in importance as knights ceased for a time to engage on foot. When Monstrelet wrote, it was the pride of the knight to make his destrier's head-front even blaze in jewels.

This head-front was called the *chaufron,* originally the *chevron.* The chaufron bore a spike, a custom dating to the time of Edward III.

In the ballad *Anturs of Arthur*, it is said: "Open his cheveronne before strode as a unicorn all scharpe as a thorn an nanlas of stele." The charger ridden by Lord Scales in his tournament with the Bastard of Burgundy had a "Schaffro with a large sharps pyke of steele," which penetrated the Bastard's horse and caused him to rear and dismount that good knight.

The oldest chaufron handed down is now in Warwick Castle. However, all this is getting beyond the age of chain mail, when barbed horses were never found — or, if any were, it was a new and, until then, an untried expedient.

Draft Horses

Of course, horses were important in the Middle Ages not alone for the knight as — to quote Chaucer — "foaming steeds on the golden bridle gnawing," but also for the lady and the baronic household. In medieval times, horses were indispensable, whether for battle, passengers, or baggage. In the fields, they shared the work with the mule.

Carriages were slowly formulated. The sledge type was the earliest. Then the cart. It took many a century to arrive at the Roman "biga," though that indeed was but a poor improvement on the original Assyrian chariot. Travel was irksome, dangerous, and lengthy.

To take one example: It took four days for Sir Thomas Swynford, the good knight, to reach London from Pontefract riding with his utmost speed, in the reign of Edward II. Of course, when a knight was encumbered with his entourage and large household gear (even to their beds) from one castle to another, the time taken — with no roads and constant water-courses flooding the track — was many a long day's journey.

No wonder, the journey taking so long and inns few and far between, hospitality at some country knight's house or sturdy yeoman's grange was so often sought by the medieval travelers, when in Chaucer's words they did not ask in vain: "His table dormant in the hall always stands ever covered, all the longe day."

Meanwhile, the numerous religious houses, which then were broadcast throughout England and France, took in, as a matter of course, these weary medieval travelers. Each such had its "hospitium," where those needing rest and refreshment asked for and obtained it. In this way, the monastery or abbey, originally founded in a wilderness, became a nucleus for news and traffic. The large estates, too, of such, brought artisans together, and so, round its walls, grew up a town, such as St. Albans or St. Edmundsbury. Of course, the wayside towns would not have come into being without horse traffic.

The Medieval Art of War

PERHAPS UNTIL AS LATE as the eighteenth century, the art of war had attained no higher degree of perfection than it had among the Romans, until, of course, the successive invasions of the barbarians began to burst like an overflowing river over the rich Roman colonies. These "barbarians," most of whom were natives of the Caucasus Mountains, were the Iberians, who never halted until they had reached Spain; the Cimbrians, who installed themselves among the Gauls; and the Sarmatians and the Scythians, who inhabited the vast forests of Germany before the great wars of Julius Caesar.

Medieval Warriors and Their Art

The system of government and administration established by Theodoric in Italy had the advantage of distributing 200,000 excellent troops in the midst of a population which, glad to find itself uncalled upon for military service, and but little taxed, allowed the work of the conquest to be consolidated.

Theodoric, for the defense of the country, required the millenaries (soldiers of a battalion numbering 1,000 men). They occupied, with their families, distinct portions of territory, which they were bound to hold under arms, and in defense of which they were always ready to march. Theodoric had also already recognized the utility

ABOVE: A ROMAN WARRIOR.

of urban garrisons. Italy's youths, organized in a military manner, flocked to the gymnasium of Ravenna, and the king himself presided over their exercises. His levies, in regard to their discipline, their instruction, and their equipment, resembled the ancient legions of Rome.

The iron cap, the shield, the broadsword, and the arrow of the Goths had been replaced by the spear, the javelin, the helmet, and the cuirass of the Romans.

As instructors, the old soldiers received from the royal treasury for their services a particular grant, which was annually paid to them until they retired altogether from the profession of arms. The provincial officers had to distribute arms, food, and hay on the different points of the road that the troops were expected to follow. The inhabitants had to provide lodging. This was the only military service expected of them, but none could escape it. The towns were at this time almost always fortified, and entrenched camps covered nearly all of Italy. The castles in the rural districts, constructed to protect the frontiers, were usually full of troops whose support was part of the duty of the pretorial prefect, and whose insubordination often necessitated severe measures of repression.

"Keep up a spirit of military discipline. It is often difficult to enforce it under civil rule," said Theodoric to Servatus, one of his generals. The peoples of northern Europe, whom

ABOVE: A MILESTONE OF MEDIEVAL WARFARE: WILLIAM OF NORMANDY DEFEATS THE ANGLO-SAXONS IN THE INVASION OF BRITAIN (1066).

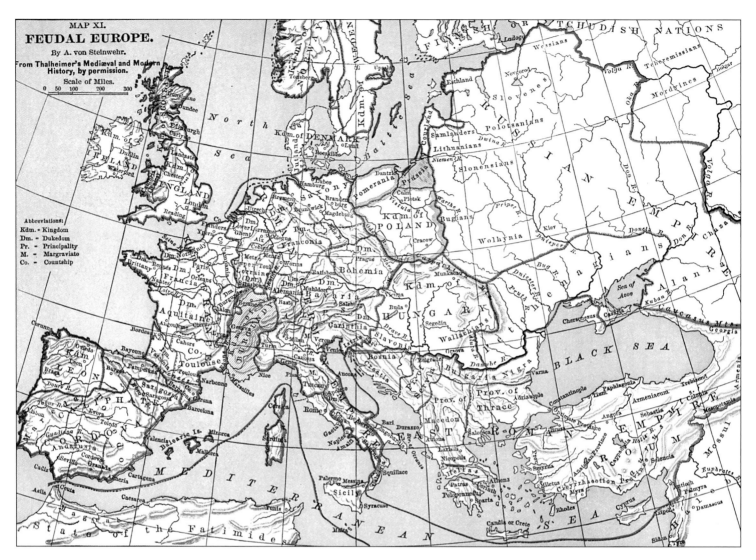

the Romans thought of as "barbarians," were clearly as adept at the military sciences as the Romans. In the wars which occurred in the early sixth century, other "barbarian" kings, namely Alaric, Clovis, Gondebaud, and Thierry, made use of and applied with skill the rules of Greco-Roman strategy — either in executing long military maneuvers or in displaying all the strategic science that sieges then required — in attacking or defending the fortified towns of Avignon, Carcassonne, and Arles.

In proportion, as the preponderance of the Goths, the Ostrogoths, and the Visigoths diminished in Europe, that of the Franks and the Lombards increased. The latter were the first to institute the feudal system, founded on the possession of conquered territory, in Italy.

The conquerors established their camp in the midst of the vanquished country, seized half the land, reduced to servitude a portion of the colonies, and imposed heavy taxes on those whom they had not despoiled.

After the king distributed the great fiefs among his principal officers, these great vassals then made a subdivision of the land granted them by their suzerains in favor of their own men-at-arms and satellites, and these latter, in their turn, ceded a portion of their lands to the common soldiers.

The obligation of personal service, the hierarchic subordination of vassalage, were the necessary consequence of feudal institutions. A century later, feudalism, which was beginning to establish itself in Gaul, as in Italy, as a consequence of the successful invasion of the Franks, was nearly stamped out by the Islamic invasion of the Spanish Moors. This great army had been led by their chief, Abderamus, as far as the banks of the Loire, where they were stopped by Charles Martel, who routed them with great slaughter.

After the brilliant victory by the Franks at Poitiers in the year 732, where the repulse of Arab civilization left the field open to the defenders of the Christian faith, and to the originators of the feudal regime, the victorious army underwent a sudden change.

The Frankish knights adopted the rich Moslem Arab armor as an inheritance of their victory. The feudal troopers donned a coat of mail, and, hereafter, a full suit of armor became a necessary accessory to a warrior of high rank. The bow, which had long been thrown aside, was once more taken into favor and became the special arm of the footmen.

The reign of Charlemagne, which was one long series of expeditions and conquests, was naturally favorable to the progress and development of this art.

Charlemagne, Emperor of the Franks and a man of genius, understood how to profit by the inventions and creations of his predecessors. Step by step, he added to the warlike traditions of Greece and Rome the improvements that were rendered necessary by the nature of the enemies with whom he had to contend — namely, the Lombards, the Saxons, and so forth. He kept up the feudal service of the ban; he established permanent orders of militia, composed of his own serfs and vassals. However, as soon as he undertook a distant expedition, his auxiliaries, 10 times as numerous as his vassals, rendered his army a German one, rather than a French one. He caused a number of fortresses to be constructed everywhere throughout his vast empire, but he never allowed his subjects to build ally on their own account. Yet he seems never to have attached any importance, as a protection to his territory, to the larger enclosed towns, in which he might have held in reserve considerable depots of troops.

Charlemagne himself usually resided in rural residences and in open and unprotected villages, barely guarded by a few military pickets. At the slightest signal, it is true, a whole army would have arisen as one man to defend him. However, under no circumstances would he have consented to await his enemy under the shelter of fortifications; he was always the true primeval German, seeking the open plain for his field of battle, rather than the hillside, preferring cavalry to infantry, and a direct struggle, a hand-to-hand fight, to encounters at a distance, waged and won by the missiles of the slinger and the shafts of the bowmen.

His principal victories were gained in the open country, where he was enabled to deploy his masses of mailed horsemen. He never willingly sat down before a stronghold, a circumstance which shows that he was aware of his want of skill in the conduct of a siege. Also, he was never fortunate in mountain warfare, as was evidenced in the disastrous day at Roncevaux in 778, which cast a shadow over the last years of his life.

Thirty years after the death of the great emperor, the treaty of Mersen (847) freed the great vassals from the obligation of answering the summonses of the sovereign, and of rushing to arms at his appeal, unless for the purpose of defending the state. It substituted the practice of furnishing armed contingents, whose services were to be rendered for a fixed period, settled beforehand. A kind of political and pecuniary contract, in virtue of which a fief was subdivided into several smaller ones, perpetuated the feudal regime. Each man became the man of another man, bound to place himself at his disposal in time of war, and to be ready to start on any expedition at his command, according to the wishes of his immediate seignior. During the tenth century, this regime grew stronger and stronger.

The oath of infeudation, or the act of homage, remained a sacred tie between the seignior and the vassal. This homage involved the rendering of numerous feudal services, such as those of the ban, and of the *arrière-ban*, those rendered by the servitors of different ranks, known as bachelors, clients, esquires, bannerets, men-at-arms, barons, and so forth; names already ancient, but whose rank and place in battle were only determined on the day they were all grouped and posted, each under his special banner, a distinction that implied a separate kind of equipment for each. Thus, the vassals were in the power of the seignior, who, having the right to dispose of their military services, enjoyed a right that gave him the power of assembling and leading to battle a certain number of feudal groups.

Wars Against the Huns and the Rise of the Goths

Suddenly, in the fourth century, a movement which commenced in the center of Asia caused an irruption of a race hitherto unknown in Europe. These were the Huns, before whom the terrified Goths retreated, but who at first made but a brief apparition in Europe. If Rome, at that time, was wanting in seasoned legions, she could rely, at least in the provinces of her empire, upon many numerous and powerful auxiliaries who were accustomed to fight under her standard, some for the sake of pay, and others to defend their own hearths.

In 451, in the reign of the Emperor Valentinian III, who had bribed the barbarians instead of repulsing them with the sword, Attila, the King of the Huns, bore down upon Europe at the head of an estimated 700,000 fighting men of various nationalities. In less than three months he had overrun and laid waste Moravia, Bohemia, Hesse, and Württemberg, crossed the Rhine below Strasbourg, the Moselle at Trèves (Trier) and at Metz, the Meuse at Tongres, and the Scheldt at Tournai. After two bloody raids into Burgundy and the county around Orléans, he pitched his tents on the plains of Champagne.

The tactics of Attila were to avoid pitched battles, and to give a wide berth to the fortresses, contenting himself with sacking and plundering their outskirts. He laid waste the open country, burned villages, put their inoffensive inhabitants to the sword, and made it his chief object to divide and isolate the Roman legions, finally crushing them by the weight of numbers.

Europe was stirred up at the tidings of this terrible invasion. Aetius, the Roman leader among the Gauls, had called to his aid the Franks, whose leader was Merovius, the Burgundians, the Saxons, and the southern Visigoths, whose king was Theodoric. This numerous army, composed of excellent troops under the orders of Aetius, marched to meet the barbarians, and encountered them in the neighborhood of Châlons-sur-Marne. The battle lasted three days, and the defeat of the Huns was complete.

The ferocious Attila, who had called himself the Scourge of God, had run his course like some fatal meteor, leaving in his track nothing but conflagrations and ruins, expiring in the midst of an orgy in 455. A truceless, unceasing war was still being waged over Europe.

Political chaos, a chaos that Christianity alone was destined to regenerate, was at its height in the Old World. Toward the close of the sixth century, Theodoric, King of the Eastern Goths, who had protected Byzantium when threatened by the Bulgarians, and who had remained in the pay of the Emperor Zeno, was determined to find an occupation for his warlike and restless subjects by leading them against Odoacer. He was the sovereign of the Herulians, who at that time united under his sway Sicily and the Italian peninsula, but whose subjects were at best but a ferocious and turbulent mob.

The young King of the Goths (he was only 34 years of age) started from the depths of Serbia, with the consent of the chief of the empire, at the head of an entire warlike population, to whom he promised the conquest of Italy. He easily overcame the King of the Herulians. And, having conquered Italy, he posted

ABOVE: ATTILA THE HUN.

his soldiers in the various provinces of the peninsula in such a manner that their pay and their rations might continue to be supplied to them as regularly in peace as in war.

Feudal Warfare

"Obey my summons, or I will burn you!" were the words of the seignior in the bait published by the crier, and, at the second summons, the sound of the trumpet rang out in the crossroads, in the streets, and in the country places, calling the men to arms. To fail to answer the call of the ban was to commit a crime of the worst character.

In the Norman Conquest, that great expedition of William, Duke of Normandy, against the Anglo-Saxons in 1066 (see illustration on page 85), William had no other auxiliaries than his Norman vassals and subjects. He conquered Harold and took possession of England with a numerous and trained army, furnished with terrible warlike machines and engines.

The Norman Conquest was, to a certain extent, a prelude to the Crusades, for those raids across the seas, repeated from time to time for more than two centuries, bore no resemblance to the barbarian invasions, either Moslem Arab or Norman, which had previously been recorded in history.

New measures, inspired by the circumstances of the times, were the consequence of the general crumbling to pieces of all the Eastern nations. Among these may be mentioned the establishment of the communal militia which set out for a campaign accompanied by its spiritual pastors, and received the last offices of religion at their hands on the field of battle. The regular pay was allowed to those who were destitute of private resources. A knight received, at first, the equivalent of 10 francs a day, and a squire received 5. The chartering of ships was intended for the transport of troops. The system of commissariat was for armies in the field, and for the supply of military equipment and arms.

This communal militia, sprung from the freeing of the communes and the detachments of paid troops, soon grew into a standing army, which was formally incorporated for the first time by Louis le Jeune in about 1140, and increased by Philip Augustus, who added to it the affiliated knights. Under the latter sovereign, an army in the field presented three ranks of combatants-bannerets, knights, and squires, to whom were added the men-at-arms. A motley crew on foot, without officers or discipline, followed the troops and hovered about them during an engagement, picking up the spoils of the conquered, and killing the wounded with clubs or battle-axes, called glaives de mercy.

The disasters of the crusaders in the East, after two centuries of useless heroism and tremendous efforts, were principally due to the defects in their military administration, which foresaw nothing. It was incapable of adjusting to the difficulties inherent in a war in a distant and almost unknown land, whither the enthusiastic crowds who wore the Cross bent their adventurous steps. Famine, plague, leprosy, and fever destroyed the Christian armies on their journey to Palestine and during their stay there. These evils would have been greater still had it not been for the creation of the different military orders which sprang into existence under the pressure of these almost inevitable calamities, and which supplied hospital attendants, chaplains, and soldiers.

The continuation of the feudal wars in Europe dealt the last blow to the disorganization of the Christian military societies. While Philippe le Bel was destroying the Knights Templars, whom he held to be obstacles to his political plans, he was simultaneously seeking in every way the means of restraining a haughty aristocracy, always under arms, whose systematic want of discipline was a danger both to the throne and to the country. When he had obtained from the representatives of the nation, assembled together in States-General, the right to impose taxes according to the requirements of the sovereign, he set to work on the definitive organization of a permanent, paid army. He set the age of military service at 18, and decreed that none of his subjects, except the old and the sick, should be exempt from it, unless they paid a certain sum to the royal treasury, and supplied, according to their rank and means, one or more substitutes (by decrees of 1302, 1303, and 1306) to serve under the flag of the army in the field of the king.

ABOVE: A TURKISH WARRIOR.

Until that time, military service had been obligatory for only 40 consecutive days, or, at the most, for three months. This service was, indeed, often of less duration, according to the different degrees of infeudation of any particular fief, and was hedged about, with so many privileges and so many exemptions, that if a feudal army did not succeed in bringing a short campaign to a prosperous issue, it generally met with a fatal collapse.

In accordance with this design, Philippe le Bel, at the opening of the Flemish campaign, summoned "for four months to his standards, archbishops, bishops, abbots, dukes, counts, barons, and other nobles, all liable to the ban," each of whom could claim pay at the rate of 12 deniers (about 4 francs) a day, besides a sum of 30 sous (about 30 francs) for their equipment. Philippe le Long (1314) and Philippe de Valois (1337–1340) continued and improved the work of Philippe le Eel. Thereafter, the army of the king was regularly established. The crossbowmen and the men-at-arms were the first corps who received a permanent organization and a fixed rate of pay.

In the fourteenth century, the French infantry, composed merely of more or less badly armed archers, inspired its leaders with no great confidence. Its want of skill and its cowardice were too often compromised. It was necessary, in order to support those combatants always ready to take to flight, to employ English, Italian, or German mercenaries, who fought well when they were liberally paid. These professional soldiers, who were more practiced in war and more courageous than the regular soldiers, were entrusted with the cannons, which at this time were carried by the camp followers.

The imperfections of the earliest cannons, the difficulty which attended their use, and the danger incurred by those who discharged them, caused the old arms to be long preferred to these new ones. In fact, long after the new artillery had made considerable progress, it was employed simultaneously with the medieval style of projectiles. The period, during which this important transition in projectile weapons was slowly taking place, was one of the most wretched in the annals of military art.

The great battles of the fourteenth century present us with striking examples of an entire absence of skill in tactics: Mons-en-Puelle (1304), where King Philippe le Bel was all but surprised in his camp; Cassel (1328), where Philippe de Valois escaped half-naked from his enemies' hands; Crecy (1346), where the English used cannons for the first time; Poitiers (1356), where King John was taken prisoner on the battlefield; Nicopolis (1393), where knighthood covered itself with disgrace; Agincourt (1415), where the flower of the French nobility perished. These are all examples of the most shameful confusion during the struggle, and of the most disgraceful butchery after the defeat.

During the whole of this long epoch of bloody contests, true knights and staunch soldiers were very rare, and good leaders were rarer still. In Italy, the condottieri, whose principal commander was the Englishman John Hawkwood, and in France, the free companies, commanded by the renowned Armand de Cervoles, and even those bands of *routiers,* who pillaged and plundered the realm to such an extent, says an old chronicler, "that not even a cock was heard to crow in it," were the only troops who showed any acquaintance with the resources of military warfare or the slightest knowledge of strategic science. It was among the ranks of these indefatigable soldiers that the celebrated Bertrand du Guesclin made his first campaign in September 1364. He was, of course, captured in the Battle of Auray (between John de Montford and Charles de Blois) on September 29 (as illustrated on this page).

The paid gendarmerie, a mixture of heavy and light cavalry, committed, in the reign of Charles VI, many breaches of discipline, without atoning for them by lending any really efficacious aid to French medieval society, which was almost entirely cut to pieces in the bloody disaster of Agincourt (October 25, 1415). Charles VII, replaced on the throne of his ancestors by his nobles after he

ABOVE: THE BATTLE OF AURAY, SEPTEMBER 29, 1364.

had driven out the English, "by the help of God and Joan the Virgin," determined therefore to disband the gendarmerie. He formed, from picked men numbering 9,000 combatants, the framework of 15 new companies of artillery. These, in turn, augmented the regular cavalry of the kingdom.

Each gendarme, thoroughly equipped, was attended by two archers and two followers on horseback. This group of five mounted men was called a lance fully equipped. In 1447, a sixth man and horse were added to it.

A little later, Charles VII raised several paid bands, recruited by voluntary enlistment and commanded by responsible captains, who were paid by the war treasurers, according to the number of men on the monthly muster roll. This creation of mercenary troops diminished still further the importance of the ban, which was no longer anything but a badly equipped secondary militia, though still armed with bows and pikes and still obliged to wear a uniform. On the actual field of battle, the pikemen were always posted in the van; behind them came the foot archers, wearing *salades,* or helmets without out visors, the brigantine or short coat of mail, and armed with crossbows. But this reorganization had no invigorating effect on the infantry of the communes, and the franc-archer remained the type of the cowardly soldier.

The death of Charles the Bold, Duke of Burgundy, slain in the Battle of Nancy (1477), completed the downfall of the feudal medieval society, whose last and most martial representative he was. Louis XI, who had gathered around him a devoted army, composed of mercenaries from all countries, and who could entirely rely upon the fidelity of his Scottish guard, began attacking the great fiefs, which were, in reality, the rivals of his throne, and succeeded in destroying them, having no further need of them and their haughty vassalage. Little by little, the seignorial standards dis-

ABOVE: THE BATTLE OF SAN ROMANO (1432) BETWEEN FLORENCE AND SIENNA, AS DEPICTED BY ITALIAN RENAISSANCE MASTER PAOLO UCCELLO.

appeared, and their war cries ceased to resound. A fief held under the obligation to carry arms no longer forced the vassal, its occupier, under the pain of felony and bodily confiscation, to equip and arm himself at the first appeal of his suzerain, and to follow the royal example with a definite number of fighting men.

The principle of purchasing exemption from military service being hereafter admitted, all, whether nobles or villains, were at liberty either to serve or to purchase their exemption. Some few feudal gendarmes still remained, but most were free. Of the squires-at-arms, some were feudal, others free or even plain pages. Canons, abbots, and prelates, whom feudal laws had forced to contribute their personal military service, had long since found substitutes in the persons of the attorneys or bailiffs, who superintended the ban and *arrière-ban* of the land owning nobles.

Some of the clergy, however, preferred to be individually present with the armies of their sovereign; many a prelate or abbot was delighted to add to his coat of arms a cuirass, a sword, a helmet, or some other warlike emblem.

In 1356, the bishops of Châlons, of Sens, and of Melun distinguished themselves by feats of personal bravery at the bloody engagement of Poitiers. In 1359, the Bishop of Rheims, by a few vigorous sorties, was the means of saving that city when the English besieged it. The Archbishop of Sens, William of Montagu, fell, sword in hand, on the field of Agincourt. In 1455, a simple monk successfully defended Belgrade; while at the siege of Plaisance, Philip of Savoy, Bishop of Valence, was knighted for his prowess in the breach itself.

It is true that many of these ecclesiastical dignitaries had never been solemnly invested. However, the example they followed was a lofty one, for several popes, John X, Leo IX, Urban II, Innocent II, and Julius II (who had first distinguished himself as an able leader under the name of Julien de la Rovere) had personally commanded the troops of the Holy See.

INSIGNIA

No troops, until the time of the Crusades, had any distinguishing mark among themselves, except the difference of their arms, and the idea of a military uniform had not then arisen.

However, with the emblazoned arms, the standards, and the pennants, there came into use scarves, worn as sashes, over the cuirass and of which the color, which generally matched that of the standard of the feudal seignior of the wearer, became as much a rallying signal as the standards themselves.

The necessity of distinguishing friends from foes at a distance naturally also brought about more or less marked distinctions of dress.

Order Within the Ranks

The administration and internal regulation of an army, which had been one of the principal cares of the Gothic and earlier Frankish kings, were entirely neglected, like everything pertaining to the art of war, for many centuries. For instance, at the beginning of the fourteenth century, the captains of the different companies were allowed to distribute the pay to their men as they pleased after each muster, and were solely and entirely entrusted with the administration of their companies. They were thus entirely irresponsible and did not concern themselves to see that the regulations prescribed by superior authority, concerning the general discipline of the army, were carried into effect.

In 1355, during the captivity of King John in England, special commissioners were appointed, with the title of controllers, whose duty it was to superintend the internal economy of the army generally and to put a stop to the numerous abuses that existed. However, the disturbed and unfortunate period at which this attempt was made rendered it almost necessarily a barren one. When the dauphin came to the throne as Charles V in 1364, he returned to this project, which he had indeed himself originated, but at his death anarchy again reigned for more than a century.

Civil and foreign wars laid waste and exhausted France without bringing to the surface a single creative mind, with the exception perhaps of Jean Bureau, the grand master of artillery under Charles VIII. It is by no means going beyond the mark to state that the reverses sustained in Italy, in the reigns of Charles VIII and Louis XII, were owing less to the chivalrous recklessness of the nobility and their ignorance of the first principles of warfare, than to the gross faults of the military administration of the country.

Even in Francis I's time, the public service was in such a miserable condition that he was never really properly informed of the actual effective strength of his army. His captains, in whose interest it was to exaggerate the number of the rank and file under their standards, habitually deceived the generals and their superiors. To such a degree was this carried that, on the eve of the Battle of Pavia, Francis I was led to believe that his army was a third stronger than it really was.

At last, however, in 1517, there issued from this chaotic confusion the first germ of a proper system of supervision and control of all matters relating to war. If the tacticians of Italy were the first to fathom theoretically the science of war, it was the Swiss, under Marshal Trivulce, the Spaniards, under Gonzalvez of Cordoba, and finally the Flemish, under the Duke of Alba, who successfully restored the military combinations of ancient Greece. They were the first to maneuver in dense masses and battalions, and they were the first to successfully employ the column formation of troops.

The pikemen of France followed their example, while the troops armed with projectile weapons fought as skirmishers in the van, or in lines two or three deep. It was not, however, until Henry IV's time that any considerable body of troops was seen capable of advancing in close column without breaking its formation, and it was not until Louis XIII's time that the regiment, first introduced in the preceding reign, became a recognized, permanent military unit. Toward the close of the fifteenth century, the French native cavalry still consisted entirely of heavy troopers.

Enlistment

The legal age at which the enlistment of soldiers could be made, the manner in which it was effected, and the length of service, varied considerably throughout the Middle Ages and the period of the Renaissance.

In Henry II's time (1154–1189), it was the custom to hire soldiers for three months. Henry IV

FREE-LANCERS

From the constant wars, particularly those of the Hundred Years, the knights-bachelors, landless and impoverished, had often been tempted to lawless courses. The frequent prohibitions of tournaments, by both the Church and the more peaceful sovereigns, had also its necessary effect in impoverishing these medieval warriors of the free lance to whom tournaments afforded one principal means of subsistence: "Joust and tournament were forbid, all his means of living gone."

The license and vices imported by those who had returned from the Crusades, and who had been, from long years of warfare, completely weaned from any peaceful avocations, became the rogues. The poverty to which noble families, particularly the younger sons, had been reduced by these fatal expeditions, all made a mass of disintegrated "swords," wandering about without leaders, or, if they had leaders, they were little better than themselves.

The class, therefore, of able, wise, and valiant men such as the bannerets, to enlist these free-lances, was of immense value. Their institution at this unsettled period, when old feudal chains were broken and the sterner discipline of a past age decayed, was not only a necessity but a blessing to the overlord and the sovereign.

(1399–1415) increased this period, but not without difficulty, for, to quote the words of Sully, "Our soldiers can now only be enlisted by force, and can only be persuaded to march by the use of the stick and the threat of the gibbet."

To this picture we must add the significant fact that the system of drill was a very insufficient one. It was by no means unusual to find soldiers, whose stay with the standards was after all but a very temporary one, entirely incapable of handling the arms they were entrusted with. The urban militia were, however, far superior to these recruits, for, since the reign of France's Charles V (1364–1380), it was customary to drill the citizen every Sunday with pike, bow, and crossbow, particularly in the frontier towns. It was not until Coligny's time, in the middle of the sixteenth century, that traces can be found of any regulations imposing on commanding officers the duties of teaching and drilling soldiers.

Banners

Distinctive marks in war have, from the earliest history that has come down to us, been used by men engaged in such, and in the battles of the Middle Ages when contending knights were enveloped in mail and their faces covered by laced helmets. This armorial cognizance, pennons and banners, were not simply used as adornments but as necessities. It was useful as a rallying point, for in a medieval battle, when all about the field companies of men were scattered, the banner recalled them to the main body when necessary. Banners marked the companies of different leaders — the glittering danced in the sun in its rising and setting. Further, the banner of knights-bannerets was not merely decoration but an emblem of authority and order.

However, not every knight was entitled to a banner, though all were entitled to pennons. At first, those who were qualified to display a banner were great feudal knights who could muster so many men to that banner. Such a knight would apply formally to the commander in the field for the status of banneret. If granted, the heralds cut the tails from his knightly pennon

ABOVE: A FREE-LANCE WARRIOR.

and so squared it into a banner, or the commander himself, as a special honor, might do this.

Thus, it happened to the celebrated English knight Chandos. Though he had served valiantly at Poitiers, and in 1365 was the hero and counselor of the Count de Montfort in his war with the Count of Blois, this had not seemed to justify his claiming to display his banner. However, before the Battle of Navaret in Spain, whither he had accompanied his lord the Black Prince, he took the title of knight-banneret. He advanced, in front of the armies drawn up opposite each other for battle, with his banner unfolded in his hand. He presented it to the Prince, saying, "Sir, behold here is my banner. I require you to display it abroad, and give me leave this today to raise it, for, Sir, I thank God and you, I possess land and heritage sufficient to maintain it withal."

The prince and King Peter took the banner between their hands, which was blazoned *"argent a pile gules,"* and after cutting off the end to make it square, they spread it. And the prince delivered it to Chandos, saying, "Sir John, behold your banner, and God send you joy, honor and strength to preserve it."

Chandos bowed and, after thanking the prince, he went back to his own company and said, "Sir knights, behold my banner and yours. Keep it as your own."

However, the distinction between a knight-banneret and the knight-bachelor was merely in military rank and precedence, and the former may be considered an institution more of policy than of chivalry.

The knight-bachelor displayed, or was entitled to display, a pennon or forked ensign; the banneret, which as in the case of Chandos, had a flag square on all sides, was the proper emblem of the baron. A knight-banneret was expected to bring into the field at least 30 men-at-arms; that is, knights or squires mounted, and in complete order, at his own expense. Each man-at-arms, besides his attendants on foot, ought to have a mounted crossbowman and a horseman armed with a bow and an ax.

Therefore, the number of horsemen alone who assembled under a banner was at least 300 and, counting followers on foot, might amount to 1,000 men.

The banneret might indeed, if he had remained a simple knight, have arrayed the same force under a pennon, but his accepting a banner bound him to bring out that number at least. So strict was this obligation on bannerets that in the reign of Charles VII of France (1422–1461), his nobles told him that their estates had been so wasted by the long wars with England that they could no longer support the number of men attached to the dignity of banneret. From that time, as far as France is concerned, these great companies of men-at-arms, which had hitherto been led by knights-bannerets, became a discarded custom. If an ordinary knight, by his prowess and skill, was at hand, he led the companies himself. While the custom lasted, it had an excellent effect.

Demanding a Banner

The lands which carried with them the right of levying men and enlisting them to a knight's service in war, and so giving him the power to demand a banner, were described as *terres à bannière*, where the banner flew from one of the turrets on the castle or the knight's dwelling.

There were small banners which knights carried in wartime, and the little *banderoles*, which they held in their hands in entering a tournament. With these, they made the sign of the Cross before commencing the joust, and also those other tiny flags they often carried on their helmets afford the origin of those little weathercocks made in the form of a flag so often seen on their dwellings. Immediately, when a knight acquired such a dwelling, up went his banner, fluttering from a lofty staff (*arbore le lien le plus éminent*).

The Church also gave the right of banners to those of her knightly servants who led the men of her various wide-spreading lands and abbeys for defense or war. Such a banner was usually kept in a church and, on its return at the head of the ecclesiastical retainers, was received with great ceremony by the chiefs of the community. In the cathedral of Chartres, there is a representation in one of the windows of

WAYS OF ACQUIRING A BANNER

1. *Entre en bannière:*
The transition of a knight-bachelor into the status of a banneret.
2. *Lever bannière:*
When a knight acquired a fief which carried with it a right of banner.
3. *Porter bannière:*
To march with it to war.
4. *Relever bannière:*
To succeed by inheritance to a property of extinct bannerets.
5. *Développer bannière:*
To be made a banneret (as Chandos was) by a prince or general (on the field of battle) because the rolled banner was displayed by the prince or general for the petitioning knight.

the knight who was about to lead the Church's men to battle receiving the banner and belt at the hands of the presiding prelate. The knight is clothed in blue, with a cap of scarlet. Many towns also had their banners for the use of those who of knightly rank they had nominated as their leaders and defenders in war.

Attacking Fortifications

Until the invention of gunpowder, or, rather, until that of artillery, the whole art of fortification, says the learned Prosper Mérimée, consisted in following more or less exactly the traditions handed down by the Romans. The stronghold of the Middle Ages had precisely the same characteristic as the ancient castellum. The methods of attack against which the engineers had to guard were the assault by escalade, either by surprise or by force of numbers, and the breach, caused by sapping, mining, or by the battering rams of the besiegers.

The employment of machines or mechanized weapons of this description was much less frequent after than before the fall of the Roman Empire, when the art of war knew no higher flight than to lay siege to a place or sustain a siege.

The first operation of the besiegers was to destroy the outworks of the besieged place, such as the posterns, the barbicans, the barriers, and so forth. As most of these outworks were built of wood, attempts were generally made to cut them to pieces with hatchets, or to set them on fire with arrows to which were fastened pieces of burning tow steeped in sulfur, or some other incendiary composition. If the main body of the place was not so strongly fortified as to render a successful assault by force impossible, it was usual to attempt an escalade.

With this end in view, the moat, which was generally literally strewn with caltrops, was filled up with fascines, on which ladders were reared against the ramparts. Archers on the brink of the ditch, protected by mantlets stuck in the ground, drove away with their arrows any of the defenders who attempted to show themselves above the parapets or at the loopholes.

If the siege, in spite of the efforts of the besiegers, promised to be a long one, a blockade was the sole remaining means of reduction. This was difficult to carry out with forces which were not permanent, and which were generally far from numerous. It therefore became necessary for the besiegers to protect their approaches by wooden, earthen, or even stoneworks, constructed under cover of night, and solid and lofty enough to enable archers to aim right onto the battlements of the besieged place.

Wooden towers, several stories high, were also frequently resorted to. These were assembled, piece by piece, at the edge of the moat, or constructed out of bowshot, and subsequently rolled on wheels to the foot of the walls. At the siege of Toulouse, in 1218, a machine of this kind was built by the order of Simon de Montfort, capable of accommodating, according to the ballad of the "Albigeois," 500 men.

When the missiles hurled from the higher stories of these towers, called *chattes* in the south *(chats, chateaux,* or *bretesches* in the north), had driven the besieged from their ramparts and battlements, a movable bridge was lowered across the moat, and a hand-to-hand struggle then took place.

The besieged, to prevent or retard the approach of these dreaded towers, were accustomed to hurl immense stones and lighted darts against them, or to undermine or inundate the ground on which they stood, so that their own weight might cause them to topple over.

Besides the means we have just described, there still remained the sap and the mine. Miners, equipped with pickaxes, were sent into the ditch under the protection of a body of archers. A sloping roof, covered with mantlets, sheltered them from the missiles of the besieged. They then pierced the wall, stone by stone, until they had made a hole large enough to allow the passage of several soldiers at once, while the sappers put the finishing stroke to the aperture.

The besieged, observing in what direction the enemy was pursuing his operations, strove to concentrate all his means of defense at this point. Sometimes he attempted to crush the miners with immense stones or pieces of wood, or he poured molten lead or boiling oil over them. Sometimes, by hastily constructing a fresh wall in the rear of the one the miners

ABOVE: GOING OVER THE TOP OF A FORTRESS WALL BY MEANS OF LADDERS.

were breaking through, he gave the latter the trouble of beginning their work all over again just as they thought it was complete. The mine had this advantage over the sap—that the besieger, being out of sight while engaged in the former method of subterranean work, had every chance of surprising the besieged. In order to effect this, an underground gallery was dug as noiselessly as possible and carried beneath the foundations of the ramparts.

When the mine had reached the walls, these were propped up with pieces of timber, and the earth was dug away until they were supported entirely by this artificial method. Dry vine wood and other inflammable materials were then piled round the props and set on fire, so that when the timber was consumed, the walls crumbled down and opened a large breach to the besiegers. Nothing then was left for the garrison but to surrender in order to avoid the horrors of an assault and the sack of the town.

ABOVE: MEDIEVAL WARRIORS USING A CATAPULT TO BOMBARD THE WALLS OF A FORTIFIED CITY.

The only remedy possessed by a garrison against this last method of attack was to keep a good watch and to endeavor to discover the whereabouts of the mine, neutralizing it by a countermine. At the siege of Rennes in 1356, the governor of the town ordered basins of copper, each containing several globes of the same metal, to be placed all about the ramparts; when these globes were seen to vibrate and tremble at each stroke of the hidden pickaxe, it was easy to guess that the mine was not far off. There was also a body of night watchmen who carefully noted the enemy's movements, and who rang the alarm bell at the slightest noise. These watchmen were often replaced by dogs, whose barks, in case of a surprise, gave notice to the garrison.

The slow and laborious work of the miner was often advantageously replaced by the more powerful action of certain machines, which may be divided into two distinct classes.

The first, intended to be used at close quarters and to make a breach in the wall, comprised several varieties of the medieval battering ram. The second, employed at a distance, were identified as *pierriers, mangonneaux, espringales,* and so forth.

The battering ram, which was probably well known from the remotest periods, is described, in the documents of the Middle Ages, pretty much as we see it figured on the monuments of Nineveh. "On Easter day," says the anonymous author of the chronicle of the "Albigeois," "the bosson [the southern name of the battering ram] was placed in position. It is long, iron-headed, straight, and pointed, and it so hammered, and pierced, and smashed, that the wall was broken through. However, they [the besieged] lowered a loop of rope suspended from a machine, and in this noose, the bosson was caught and retained."

Generally speaking, the battering ram was a long, heavy beam, suspended in the center from a kind of massive trestle. The end which battered the wall was either covered with an iron hood or pointed with brass. The beam was swung backward and forward by the besiegers, and by dint of striking a wall always in the same spot it often succeeded in shattering or overthrowing it. At other times the ram, instead of being suspended in an oscillating manner, was mounted on wheels, and run forward with great rapidity against the wall to be battered.

The chronicle of the "Albigeois," just quoted, alludes to the head of the ram being caught in a noose; besides this maneuver, the garrison would hurl stones and pieces of timber upon it, in order to break it or put it out of trim; or else they would strive to deaden its blows by interposing a thick mattress of wool covered with leather between it and the stonework of their stronghold.

The machines which they employed to hurl their projectiles seem to have corresponded in nearly every respect with the catapults of the ancients. It was often merely a species of gigantic sling, worked by several men, and throwing pieces of rock and round masses of stone.

The *mangonneau, bricole, or trabuch,* was a kind of square wooden platform made of thick planks laid crosswise. A long beam, fastened at its lower end by a revolving axis to the platform, was supported at an angle of about 45 degrees by an elevated crosspiece resting on two uprights.

The distance between the revolving axis and the point of support was about one-half the length of the beam. The latter was then secured in this position by long cords fastened to the front of the platform.

The men who managed the bricole then lowered the beam backward by a windlass fixed in the rear, until it (the beam) formed an obtuse instead of an acute angle with the platform, and until the cord securing it in front was stretched to its utmost tension. While it was in this position, the projectile they wished to cast was placed in the spoon-shaped extremity of the beam. A spring then released the tension of the windlass and the beam, obeying that of the cord fastened to the front of the platform, swung rapidly forward, and hurled the projectile to great distances and to some considerable height.

These bricoles were sometimes employed to throw into besieged strongholds the dead bodies of horses and other animals, fireballs, and cases of inflammable matter. However, they were generally used to shatter the roofs of the buildings inside the walls, and to crush the protecting wooden sheds constructed on the ramparts. Their use was still continued long after the invention of gunpowder.

In the wars of the fourteenth century, particularly in the sieges of Tarazonia, Barcelona, and Burgos, bricoles were made use of side by side with cannons discharged with gunpowder. It was not until the close of the fifteenth century that the rapid progress of the new artillery, which enabled besiegers to breach a wall from a considerable distance with a smaller expenditure both of time and men, caused the whole paraphernalia of the old-fashioned ballistic machines to fall into disuse. Thereafter, a new era commenced in the science of attack and defense — an era whose immense results do not belong only to the period of the Renaissance.

Tournaments and Jousts

HOUGH THE MIDDLE AGES were an era which bristled with feuds and wars, at certain times peace reigned in the disturbed countries of Europe. It was then, having no foes to fight, that the ever restless lance of the knight urged him to those mimic representations of war, the tournaments. Many theories are entertained as to the precise origin of these grand and chivalric exhibitions. Classical tradition abounds in notices of military games and contests instituted for the purpose of displaying in noble rivalship the valor and address of distinguished soldiers. However, wide distinctions exist between these and the tournaments of chivalry, and a totally new origin is, without much necessity, sought for the latter.

One of the earliest historical instances that has been recorded is written by Nithard, a contemporary and grandson of Charlemagne. He writes of Charles the Bad and Louis the Pious meeting at Strasbourg when the vassals of both princes engaged in contests on horseback. Whether Germany, therefore, or France was the birthplace of these chivalrous amusements seems a doubtful point. Geoffrey de Preuilli, a Breton lord, is, however, generally credited with the invention of them in France in

1036, and was probably the first to draw up rules for how they were to be conducted. In France, therefore, tournaments seem first in regular use, and Matthew Paris calls them *conflictus gallici*. They probably traveled from France to England, and as early as the reign of Stephen, who is accused of softness because he could not, or would not, hinder them.

Matthew Paris, however, says that Richard I introduced tournaments into England in order that the French knights might not scoff at the English knights as being unskilled and awkward. Prohibitions of tournaments constantly occur in English history, and are to some extent an indication of the condition of the country. Edward II (1307–1327) issued a great number of letters forbidding them. The reason given is fear of breach of the peace and of terrifying quiet people. So, too, in France, Philip IV (1285–1314) forbade all to engage with the spear or joust under forfeiture of their arms.

That the tournament became a great institution in England, it will be sufficient to cite a passage from the English chronicler Roger de Hoveden: "A knight cannot shine in war if he has not prepared

ABOVE: A LADY OF THE FRENCH COURT PRESENTS THE PRIZE TO THE WINNER OF A FIFTEENTH CENTURY JOUST.

for it in tournaments. He must have seen his own blood flow, have had his teeth crackle under the blow of his adversary, have been dashed to the earth with such force as to feel the weight of his foe, and disarmed 20 times; he must 20 times have retrieved his failures, more set than ever upon the combat. Then will he be able to confront actual war with the hope of being victorious."

What Were Tournaments?

The tournament, indeed, was looked upon as a veritable military school, for by these voluntary and regulated combats a warrior exercised and trained himself for that offensive and defensive strife which entirely filled the life of the medieval warrior. Here, too, he learned that subtlety and "finesse" in fighting which made the knights so victorious in other lands, for it was not so much brute force as a dexterity in wielding his arms that made those arms bring him victory.

We may cite the Normans in their conquests of England and Sicily to prove this. Far from being the colossal height of the heroes of romance, they were small men. The Germans, who opposed the Normans in Italy, derided their shortness of stature, but the Normans possessed a compound of audacity and stratagem which constant trials in jousts and tournaments strengthened and made perfect.

The scribes — arguably the most learned class in Europe — shaved, like priests, carried their lances victorious through Europe, and by such skill and training raised their hero, Robert Guiscard, to the ducal throne of Apulia and Calabria. They were apt exemplars, in later days of medieval society, of how each medieval warrior should cultivate like qualities, even in the mimic wars of the tournament.

In tournaments, too, the training of younger knights was accomplished. They were well called, therefore, Schools of Prowess.

The elder knights, who often took the role of instructors to the younger ones, got to know the fighting capacity of these youths of the younger generation. They trained them to the word of command, taught them to reflect well before making a charge, to group and move themselves together to the best advantage before engaging — lessons they themselves had learned the expediency of, on many a

RIGHT: A TOURNAMENT IN THE GERMAN CITY OF NUREMBERG.

rear battlefield, and encouraged them also to invent new ways, in the lists, to circumvent their opponents.

Thus it was that contemporaries justified the tournament when it was attacked, and why both in England and in France it was so flourishing.

In the latter country, in the historical ballad *Guillaume le Maréchal*, the recital of tournaments occupies 3,000 of the 20,000 verses. The author describes fifteen tournaments which followed one another within a few years in the lands of Normandy, Chartres, and Perche. He says: "I cannot keep up with all the tournaments that take place. It would take great trouble to do so, for almost every fortnight there is a tournament in some place or other."

Gilbert of Mons, in the ballad *Garin le Lorraine*, informs us that every creation of new knights, every great marriage, had almost necessarily to be accompanied by a tournament in which the young barons could exhibit their strength and bear their first arms.

Proclaiming a Tournament

A tournament was proclaimed far and wide by the heralds-at-arms for a king, lord, noble, knight, or lady who designed to give one. These went forth on horseback to castle and town, and sometimes from court to court of foreign countries, clad in their festive insignia of office, attended by a trumpeter. In every castle yard and market cross they came to, first the trumpeter blew his blast, and then the herald-at-arms made his proclamation of the coming warlike festival.

Preparing for a Tournament

The preparations for a tournament afforded an animated and interesting picture. The tournament venues — known as "lists" — were at first of a round shape, like the theaters of antiquity, but were later constructed in a square and, later still, in an oblong form. The interiors were very elaborate, and were often gilded. They were usually painted with emblems and heraldic devices and ornamented with rich hangings and historical tapestries.

While the lists were being prepared, the knights who were to take part in the tournament, as well as those who were to be only its spectators, had their armorial banners hung out from the windows of the houses they were lodg-

ing in, and affixed their coats of arms to the outer walls of the monasteries, castles, and cloisters in the neighborhood.

When this was done, the nobles and the ladies went round and inspected them, and a herald or pursuivant-at-arms named their owners. If a lady recognized any knight against whom she had any ground for complaint, she touched his banner or his shield, in order to bring him under the notice of the judges of the camp. If, after inquiry, he was found guilty, he was forbidden to appear in the tournament.

For some time before the tournament, which occurred three weeks after it had been proclaimed, the prince who may have summoned it opened his hall to the throng of knights and squires who intended to take part in it. However, as the appointed time approached, strict regulations forbade the presence of the party who accepted the challenge.

If they wished to visit any friend or lady within the walls of the city, they were permitted to do so only in disguise, and even that was prohibited on the eve of the festival. On the eve of the tournament, the youthful esquires practiced among themselves in the lists with less weighty and less dangerous weapons than those wielded by the knights. These preludes, which were often graced by the presence of the ladies, were identified as *épreuves* (trials), *vépres du tournoi* (tournament vespers), or *escrimes* (fencing bouts). The esquires who distinguished themselves the most in these trials were frequently immediately admitted to knighthood and allowed to take part in the ensuing feats.

Stands, usually roofed and closed in, were erected at the ends of the lists to afford shelter to persons of distinction in the event of bad weather. These stands, sometimes built in the shape of a tower, were divided into boxes, and more or less magnificently decorated with tapestry, hangings, pennons, shields of arms, and banners. Kings, queens, princes, dames, and damsels sat here, along with the older knights whom the judges of the combats had determined were too old to take a personal role. The kings-at-arms, the heralds, and pursuivants-at-arms, who had proclaimed the tournament up and down the country, now stood within the arena or just without it, and were expected to narrowly observe the combatants and to draw up a faithful report of the different incidents of the combat without forgetting a single blow. These officers had to particularly see that the blows given did not transgress the laws of chivalry regarding the tournament.

ABOVE: A SIXTEENTH-CENTURY KNIGHT AND WARHORSE IN TOURNAMENT LIVERY. FOR JOUSTING, THE HORSE WOULD BE MORE HEAVILY ARMORED.

The Laws of Chivalry Regarding the Tournament

The highly respected laws of chivalry regarding the tournament can be summarized in the four principal admonitions which are delineated herewith:

1. A knight should take care not to bear arms in this sport which can strike with the point (in fencing *à l'estoc*), but everyone may carry his sword, his shield, and his lance for jousting. He must beware not to strike a knight from behind, nor should either combatant maliciously injure the other when he happens to be unhelmed.

2. According to medieval custom, the knight who rides outside his course shall be held recreant or overthrown (*recréant ou assole*).

3. It is against the usages of chivalry to strike an adversary's horse when jousting.

4. No blow should be delivered too high or too low. If the blows are aimed too low, it is against the laws laid down for tournaments.

In *The Ballad of Perceforest*, a knight is depicted who was so infuriated with his adversary, that he aimed a blow at him when he had lost his helmet. This was, and is, considered infamous and treasonable. In the ardor of the melee, many faults were unwittingly made and many intriguing incidents arose.

So ardent was one unknown knight in a tournament, he was named "The Knight of the Smoke." Another, having lost his helmet, forgetting in the onset what he did, snatched off a damsel's hat and, in this strange covering, met his adversaries, much to the amusement of those who looked on.

The Night Before

The night before a tournament, squires stood at their knights' tents, holding their shields. If those warriors had been admitted to former tournaments, they held the shields not upright but slantwise. At all events, these same squires were often, for that purpose, fantastically arrayed, sometimes masquerading in the furs of animals. A good squire was almost as important to a knight in a tournament as was a good horse. On the knight's squire often depended the knight's life, because it was so important that his armor be adjusted properly and securely. On his celerity depended his master's having a fresh lance when his was shattered; on him depended recovery of the warrior's helmet if it was thrown off by his adversary's skill, or, if it was loosened, its replacement before he engaged his opponent. That squires were good, quick, and smart was imperative, and no doubt when the knight was about to attend a tournament, he chose the best from the numerous noble lads in his castle who had, by then, attained the rank of squire.

ABOVE: PRACTICING FOR THE TOURNAMENT BY TILTING AT A "QUINTAIN," A REVOLVING EFFIGY OF A KNIGHT.

The Tournament

In the halcyon period of medieval society, its courteous tournaments and its warlike exhibitions occasioned many an accident and brought about many a fatal result. History mentions a tournament in Germany where 60 persons perished in a struggle waged with weapons deprived of edge and point. No question of mere gallantry, and no point of honor, was involved in the oldest tournaments on record. These were the tournaments first alluded to in the chronicles of the reign of Charles the Bald (840–877). No pomp of draper and and no brilliancy of banner adorned them then. No princesses and no noble ladies showed themselves in all their pride of beauty and of dress around those ancient lists.

The tournament (in old French, *tournoiment*) of those days was merely a violent athletic pastime, in which the iron men of that period measured their strength one against the other with sword strokes, lance thrusts, and mace blows. However, as the customs of medieval society gradually softened the manners of the nobility, so the primitive coarseness and roughness of these trials of strength became somewhat modified and regulated.

Tradition declares that the tournament properly so called was first inaugurated in Brittany, in the tenth century, by Geoffrey, the Sire de Preuilli. As a rule, tournaments were proclaimed, when a promotion of knights, or a royal marriage, or a solemn entry of a sovereign into a town took place. The character of these chivalrous festivals changed according to the time and place at which they occurred.

The arms used on these occasions varied in a similar manner. In France, the tournament lance was made of the lightest and the straightest wood, either fir, aspen, or sycamore, pointed with steel, and with a pennant floating from the end; while in Germany and Scotland they were made of the heaviest and the toughest wood, with a long, iron, pear-shaped point. The tournament must not be confounded with the tilt or joust (from the Latin *juxta*), which was a single hand-to-hand combat, nor with the passage of arms, in which several combatants, both on foot and on horseback, were engaged, and imitated the attack and defense of some military position, some pass, or some narrow, mountainous defile. Tilts usually formed part of a tournament, and marked its close. However, there were also more complicated tilts, open to all comers, which lasted for several days, and were identified as *joutes plénieres*.

As the ladies were the life and soul of the tilts, the knights always terminated the proceedings by a special passage of arms which was identified as *lance des dames*. They were always ready to pay this homage to the charms of the fair sex, and frequently fought for them with sword, ax, dagger, and, of course, lance.

Coats of arms, which were striking characteristics of chivalry, and which were adopted by the nobility as one of its most notable attributes, had no doubt a contemporaneous origin with the institution whose emblem they became. It is supposed to have been in the eleventh century, at the time of the First Crusade, that the necessity of distinguishing among the multitude of nobles and knights who flocked to the Holy Land led to the invention of the different heraldic colors and devices.

Each crusader chose and kept his own particular emblem. These emblems became the external marks of nobility, and were to be seen everywhere — on the war tents, on the banners, on the liveries, on the clothes, and on every object belonging to a noble family. Hence the language of her-

---

THE TOURNAMENT LANCE

In France, the tournament lance was made of the lightest and the straightest wood, either fir, aspen, or sycamore, pointed with steel and with a pennon floating from the end; while in Germany and Scotland they were made of the heaviest and the toughest wood, with a long, iron, pear-shaped point. England followed the French fashion.

ABOVE: A MOUNTED KNIGHT WITH HIS TOURNAMENT LANCE.

CHEERING AT THE TOURNAMENT

It is said that the heralds should cry out to the youthful knights not "on ye brave" but "ye sons of the brave."

In the chronicle of the monk of Vigeoise, he says: "It was also the custom to salute at the tournaments the elder knights with the cry of 'Heroes,' while the younger were 'Sons of Heroes.' These cries filled the heralds' pockets with money. Largesse was lavishly scattered, not only by the medieval warriors about to enter the fray, but by their ladies in the galleries around."

aldry, that figurative and hieroglyphic jargon, incomprehensible to everybody at that period except professional heralds-at-arms.

The camp marshals and the seconds or counselors of the knights, whose duty it was to enforce the laws of Christian chivalry, and to give their advice and assistance to all who might require it, had also their respective posts. The kings-at-arms, the heralds-at-arms, and the pursuivants-at-arms, as noted previously, stood within the arena or just outside to observe the combatants, and to draw up a faithful and minute report of the different incidents of the combat, without forgetting a single blow.

Every now and then, they lifted up their voices to encourage the younger knights who were making their first appearance in the lists. "Recollect whose son you are! Be worthy of your ancestry!" they cried out in loud voices.

Besides these, there were the pages and sergeants, who were specially entrusted with the duty of keeping order, of picking up and replacing broken weapons, and of raising unhorsed knights. These men and boys were posted everywhere in and about the lists. Musicians on separate stands held themselves ready to celebrate with noisy flourishes every great feat of arms and every fortunate and brilliant stroke.

The sound of their clarions announced the entry of the medieval warriors into the lists, stepping with slow and solemn cadence, magnificently armed and equipped, and followed by their esquires on horseback. Sometimes the ladies were the first to enter the lists. Then came the knights, leading slaves by golden or silver chains, whom they set at liberty only when the signal was given for the combat to commence.

The ladies almost always bestowed a favor on their favorite knight or servitor — generally a scarf, a veil, a headdress, a mantle, a bracelet, or even a plain bow of ribbon which had formed part of their own dress. This was identified as an *enseigne* or *nobloy* (distinguishing mark), and was placed on a knight's shield, lance, or helmet, so that his lady might be able to recognize him in the melee, particularly when his weapons were broken, or when he had lost some essential portion of his armor.

While the combat lasted, the heralds uttered loud cries of encouragement, and the musicians sounded loud flourishes, at

Left: A sixteenth-century French knight whose warhorse has been properly armored for the tournament.

each decisive blow of lance or sword. Between each tilt, the nobles and the ladies distributed a quantity of small coins among the crowd, who received it with loud and joyous cries of *"Largesse!"*

The combat being over and the victor being declared, according to the reports of the heralds and pursuivants, the prize was given away with all proper solemnity by the elder knights, and sometimes by the ladies. The latter conducted the conqueror with great pomp and triumph to the splendid banquet which followed the tournament.

The place of honor occupied by the successful knight, the resplendent clothes in which he was dressed, the kiss that he had the privilege of giving to the most beautiful ladies, the poems and the songs in which his prowess was celebrated, were the last items in this knightly pageant, which was generally accompanied by bloodshed, and frequently by the death of some of its actors.

As we have already stated, the usages of the tournament often varied. Nothing, for example, could be more unlike the warlike sports of Germany in the thirteenth century, as related in the *Nibelungenlied*. Nothing could be more unlike those bloody and ferocious struggles than the Provencal and Sicilian tournaments of the fifteenth century, described in such glowing language by good King Rene in the magnificent manuscript which he spent his leisure in illuminating with miniatures.

This poet-king, refined in manners, generous in disposition, and cultivated in his tastes, attempted, under the influence of the romantic and religious charm which still pervaded the chivalric sports of this epoch, to perpetuate with pen and pencil, in prose and in verse, the memory of a magnificent festival over which he presided, and which may be considered an unsurpassed example of the ceremonies of the time. All who take an interest in the subject should read this intriguing manuscript, which describes, among other things, the famous struggle between the Duke of Brittany and the Duke of Bourbon.

In this may be found related to its smallest details the whole ceremony of a grand tournament, its forms, its progress, and its incidents. In it appear careful comments upon every trifle that increased the brilliancy or added to the

ABOVE: A TOURNAMENT KNIGHT.

effect of this courtly festival, as well as everything that threw a light upon the spirit in which it was carried out, or the usages that regulated every detail, from the armor of the knights to the smallest incidents of the ceremonial.

In its pages, illustrations reproduce with exact truthfulness the helmets of the knights with barred visors and leather shields, their maces, their swords, and their armor, intended to protect the croup and the hind legs of their chargers. Its text, written with great care and in an elegant hand, records the rules to be observed, in accordance with knighthood's truest spirit, at the different stages of the combat and the tournament, and minutely describes all their preliminaries and accessories. It records the giving and the accepting of a challenge, the mutual exchange of gages, the presentation of warrants of nobility by the kings-at-arms, the distribution of the coats of arms or insignia of the two parties to the strife, the entry of the nobles, and the bestowal of the prizes upon the conquerors by the queen of the tournament.

King Rene's book is a document all the more valuable to a historian of the customs of chivalry, in that it was written at a time when they still existed in all their splendor. Although signs of their decline had already showed themselves, that punctilious sovereign, Philippe le Bel (1285–1314), with his court of lawyers and usurers, had already dealt chivalry a crushing blow by the regulations he drew up for the better government of single combats and gages of battle. Between his reign and that of Charles VII (1422–1461), this decline became more marked. Commerce had made much progress, the wealth of the middle classes had much increased, and the monarchy had acquired a preponderating influence, to the detriment both of feudalism and of medieval society, which began simultaneously to decline. The reign of Louis XI (1461–1483), a reign of espionage and cunning, was fatal to them. Thereafter, their little remaining prestige rapidly waned and soon entirely expired. Francis I (1515–1547) made several fruitless attempts to rekindle the dying embers of chivalry, and, at a later period, Henri IV (1589–1610) and Louis XIV (1643–1715), vainly essayed, with brilliant pageantry and passages of arms, to quicken once more the phantom of the noble institution which came into existence with the Middle Ages, and with them had passed away.

Pas d'Armes and Jousts

Somewhat similar to knights-errant were those who, not so much sharing in the wandering propensities of the former, still sought adventures. Unlike the knight-errant, who, as a rule, rode forth attended only by a single squire, and engaged singly in the contests he provoked or found, these others sought such with brother knights. The medieval writers called such combats *pas d'armes*.

Some of these adventures were almost similar — except in the number of those engaged — to the knight-errant's. These challengers fixed their shields on bridges, on trees, and on palings, with the notice they would contest the passage with all who passed (hence *pas d'armes*), who should touch their shield with sword or lance, and, if victorious, they claimed a guerdon from the conquered. Differing, however, from the knight-errant, who generally — except he entered a joust or a tournament — had no one witnessing his combat, except his henchmen, these knights often met in public and, before a full court, ran a course. Princes, too, provided these opportunities and, as was the case in tournaments, proclaimed beforehand that a passage of arms would take place. It was in such a "passage" that Henry II of France received his mortal wound from the lance of Montgomery during the fetes held to celebrate the marriage of Elizabeth of France to Philip II of Spain, for in this *pas d'armes* the king and his nobles all displayed their skill.

The Joust

The jousts were to have been held most frequently when no tournaments had been proclaimed and the warlike spirit of the medieval warriors, not resting in idleness at home, promoted them to these contests in which they challenged all competitors. From an abridged account of the *pas d'armes* called the "Juste of Saint-Inglebert" is gathered the following:

The emprise was sustained by three gallant knights of France — Boucicaut, Reynold de Ruy, and de Sampi. Their articles bound them to abide 30 days at Saint-Inglebert, near Calais, and there to undertake the encounter of all knights and squires, Frenchmen, or strangers who should come hither for the breaking of five spears, sharp or with rochets (blunted with caps on) at their pleasure. In their tents they hung two shields, called "Peace" and "War," with their armorial blazons on each. The stranger desiring to joust was invited to come or send and touch which shield he would.

The weapons of courtesy were to be employed if he chose the shield of peace. If that of war, the defenders were to give him the desired encounter with sharp weapons.

The stranger medieval warriors were invited to bring some nobles with them to assist in judging the field, and the proclamation concludes with an entreaty to knights, squires, and strangers, that they will not hold this offer as made for any pride, hatred or ill-will. However, only that the challengers do it to have their honorable company and acquaintance, which with their whole heart they desire.

They are assured of a fair field, without fraud or advantage. It was provided that the shields used should not be covered with iron or steel.

The French king was extremely pleased by this gallant challenge, and exhorted the challengers to regard the honor of their prince and realm and spare no cost, for which he was willing to contribute 10,000 francs. A number of knights and squires came from England to Calais to accept this gallant invitation, and, at the entrance of the "fresh and jolly month of May," the challengers pitched their green pavilions on a fair plain between Calais and the Abbey of Saint-Inglebert.

Two shields hung before each tent with the arms of the owners. On May 21, as had been proclaimed, the three knights were properly saddled according to the laws of a tournament. On the same day, those knights who were at Calais sailed forth, either as spectators or as tilters.

The place of the jousting was smooth and green with grass. Sir John Holland was the first who sent his squire to touch the shield of Sir Boucicaut, who instantly issued forth from his tent completely armed. Having mounted his horse and grasped his spear, which was solid and well steeled, they took their distance. When the two knights had eyed each other for a short time, they spurred their horses and met full gallop with such a force that Sir Boucicaut pierced the shield of the Earl of Huntingdon and the point of his lance slipped along his arm, but without wounding him. The two knights, having passed, continued their gallop to the end of the list. This course was much praised. At the second course, they hit each other slightly, but no harm was done. Their horses refused to complete the third.

The Earl of Huntingdon, who wished to continue the tilt and was heated, returned to his place, expecting that Sir Boucicaut would call for his lance. However, he did not, and showed plainly he would not that day tilt more with the Earl.

Sir John Holland, seeing this, sent his squire to touch the shield of the Lord de Sampi. They couched their lances and pointed them at each other. At the onset, their horses crossed, notwithstanding which, they met. However, by this crossing, which was blamed, the Earl was without a helmet. He returned to his squires, who soon rehelmed him, and, having resumed their lances, they met full gallop and hit each other with such a force in the middle of their shields, they would have been unhorsed had they not kept tight seats by the pressure of their legs against their horses' sides. They went back to their proper places, where they refreshed themselves and took breath.

Sir John Holland, who had a great desire to shine at this combat, had his helmet braced and re-grasped his spear. The Lord de Sampi saw him advance at the gallop, and did not decline meeting, but spurred his horse on instantly. They gave blows to their helmets that luckily were of well-tempered steel, which made sparks of fire fly from them. At this course, the Lord de Sampi lost his helmet, but the two knights continued their career and returned to their places.

This tilt was much praised, and the English and French said that the Earl of Huntingdon and the Lord de Sampi had excellently well jousted without sparing or doing themselves any injury.

The Earl wished to break another lance in honor of his lady, but it was refused him. He then quitted the lists to make room for others, for he had run his six lances with such ability and courage as gained him praise from all sides.

The other jousts were accomplished with similar spirit, and the whole was regarded as one of the most gallant enterprises which had been fulfilled for some time.

This account given of the passage of arms at Saint-Inglebert was in contradiction to a tournament — a joust.

In the tournament, a great many more knights were engaged in the general melee — in a joust, two knights at a time. While it took place, the squires saw to their master's arms and horses and stood in readiness to help him in every way short of joining in the contest, which was allowed only in the melee.

The knights, after mounting, set their lances in "the rest" (a half ring attached to the saddlebow). The object in a tournament was to strike an opponent, either on the head — the more effectual but more difficult aim — or on the body. The shock of heavy armed men often dismounted both opponents. If both sat firm, the lances were generally shivered, but often it happened that both man and horse fell together. If the horses did not swerve and the lances did not break and either knight aimed true and held his lance firm, mortal wounds were often given.

If both knights, as in the above incident at Saint-Inglebert, were unhurt and kept their seats, they wheeled their horses round and charged again with fresh lances until one or both were unhorsed. Often then, the victor dismounted and the combat was continued on foot with swords. Two men completely armed in mail might slash at each other with swords for a long time without much injury being done.

The combats of such portrayed in the *Morte d'Arthur* and other stories lasted for hours, and the knights paused at intervals, to drink and get cool. Then they began again. They always seemed ready, so slight were their wounds, to attend the feast in the evening of a tournament.

THE LADIES' DAY

The last day of a tournament was devoted to the ladies. As the knights-bannerets in actual warfare shouted their individual *crie de guerre*, so on this occasion the gallantry of the knights entering the lists raised their ladies' names as an incentive in the onset. *Lances des Dames* was on this day the name given to the final tournament.

A combat on horseback, armed with the lance, was considered the most noble in jousting, so it was rightly used in the ladies' tournament. It was an old axiom in considering the relative honorable position that lance had to sword. A lance, being the longer weapon, could disengage a sword — whereas a sword could, only with difficulty, parry or disengage the lance. The lance, therefore, was the superior weapon.

It was in this final tournament, more even than the preceding days, when the ladies' insignias adorned each faithful cavalier's helm or armor. At the end of the *Lances des Dames*, rightly, it was the ladies' hands that were given to the victors as the prize. It was then, we are told, a kiss was given them by the honored knight, and we are told this was the usual thing to do.

Possibly, it was then, at the feet of his lady, a young knight would uncover his shield for her to see his nobility and paternity; otherwise, it was the practice for all medieval warriors entering a tournament for the first time to carry their shields whitened over.

This custom may have been to show that, up to that time, their careers had been a blank, and that the shield was waiting until their enterprises should blazon it in the glowing colors of a chivalrous life.

In Lieu of Battle

The tournaments and *pas d'armes* embraced, as has been said, challenges in lieu of battles. As early as Saxon times, Edmund Ironside proposed to Canute to claim the kingdom by eight champions. William of Normandy challenged Harold and accepted a challenge from Geoffrey of Anjou. John sent a cartel to Louis VII; Edward III to Philip of Valois; Richard II to Charles VI; Francis I to Charles V.

These challenges, as Cornish Well says in his work on medieval society, were partly the natural outcome of the military spirit delighting in personal distinction, and partly of the nature of an ordeal (like the judicial ordeal before treated of), on the principle that God would defend the right. Who does not remember the jongleur, or troubadour, riding on Senlac's bloody field before the Norman host, throwing his lance into the air, and catching it while he sang the "Song of Roland" and challenged the opposing Saxons? At the Siege of Jerusalem in 1097, one of Robert of Normandy's men attacked the city wall alone and was killed. No man followed him.

Peter the Hermit summoned the Moslem Arab lord of Antioch to send him forth three of his knights to fight against three Christian knights. Another knight at Cherbourg (1379) invited three champions, the most amorous knights of the enemy, to fight with three amorous knights on his side for the love of their ladies. At the Battle of Cockerel (1384) an English knight, Rowland du Boy, left the ranks, presented himself, and won. At Bannockburn, De Bohun burned before his monarch's eye to do some deed of chivalry, and pricked forth alone against Robert Bruce as he rode along the Scot lines.

The Lord of the Castle of Josselin in Brittany in 1351 called upon the captain of the town and Castle of Ploermel to send him forth one, two, or three champions, to joust with swords against another three for the love of their ladies.

Their Captain Brandenburg replied, "Our ladies will not that we adventure ourselves for the passing chance of a single joust, but, if you will, choose you out 20 or 30 of your companions and let them fight in a fair field."

So the 60 champions heard them, put on their harness, and went forth to the place of arms, 25 on foot and another five on horseback. Then they fought and many were killed on their side and the other, and, at last, the English had the worst of it. All who were not slain were made prisoners and courteously ransomed when healed of their wounds.

Froissart recounts that he saw, sitting at King Charles' table after, one of these Breton knights called Yvain Charnelz, and his face was so cut and slashed that he showed how hard the fight had been.

In the War of the Disinherited, in 1266, the barons at Kenilworth disdained to wait behind their defenses and kept the castle gates open in defiance of Prince Edward for 10 months, thinking chivalry more glorious than warfare — that is to say from the morrow of St. John the Baptist to the morrow of St. Thomas.

For the Ladies

These jousts or *pas d'armes* served in times of peace to keep alive a medieval warrior's spirits when tranquillity might gradually have subdued them. They furnished him with opportunities of comparing himself with the most celebrated of his companions. If he had unwillingly contracted a habit of pride, they often afforded him a lesson and a remedy. Above all, the women seem to have favored the jousts even more than the tournaments. The jousts seem to have enabled them to judge with their own eyes the merits of their cavaliers, and to comprehend what their lovers or husbands meant when they told them tales of battle and of chivalry. The women were able to appreciate the value of knightly fame, as they often saw, in such a combat that ended fatally both its glory and its mortality.

It was no wonder, therefore, when a *pas d'armes* was announced, that valorous medieval warriors jousted in them, until one was declared the victor, and that the countryside, and often a city, the court, and its fairest dames, gathered to the lists.

Weapons of the Joust

As to the weapons used in jousting, if only a friendly trial of skill was contemplated, the lances were headed with a small coronal instead of a sharp point. If the sword was used at all, it was with the edge only, which would inflict no wound on a well-armed man, or, at most, a flesh wound. However, the sword was never used with a point which might penetrate the opening of the helmet or the joints of the armor and inflict a fatal wound. This was the *joute à plaisance*. If the combatants were allowed to use sharp weapons and to put forth all their force and skill against each other, this was the *joute à l'outrance* and was of common occurrence.

In a manuscript in the Egerton Collection in the British Museum, there is a colorful account of how the knights were rewarded after a successful joust. "When the heralds cry *à l'ostel! à l'ostel!* then shall the gentlemen within unhelm them before the said ladies and make their obeisance and go home into their lodgings and change them, the gentlemen without coming into the presence of the ladies.

"Then comes forth a lady by the advice of all the ladies and gentlewomen and gives the diamond unto the best jouster without, saying in this wise, 'Sir, these ladies and gentlewomen thank you for your disporte and great labor that ye have this day in their presence — and the said ladies and gentlewomen say that ye have best joust this day. Therefore the said ladies and gentlewomen give you this diamond, and send you much joy and worship of your lady.' Thus, shall be done with the ruble and with the squire unto the other two next the best jousters.

"This done, then shall the herald of armies stands up all on high, and shall say withall in high voice — John hath well jousted, Ric hath jousted better, and Thomas hath jousted best of all.' Then shall he that the diamond is given unto take a lady by the hand and bygone the dance, and when the ladies have danced as long as they liketh, then spyce wyne and drynk and then avoid."

We have mentioned above that though blunted weapons were generally used at tournaments and so few deaths happened, when these weapons were unblunted, accidents often took place.

Thus, in the manuscript *Life and Acts of Richard Beauchamp, Earl of Warwick*, it states "how a mighty duke challenged Earl Richard for his lady's sake and, in jousting, slew the duke and, thereupon, the Empress took the Earl's staff and wear from a medieval warrior shoulder, and for great love and favor she set it on her shoulder. Then Earl Richard made one of pearl and precious stones and offered her that and she gladly and lovingly received it."

The duke perished by his adversary's driving his lance half a yard through his breast. However, seldom was the termination of a joust fatal, particularly if it

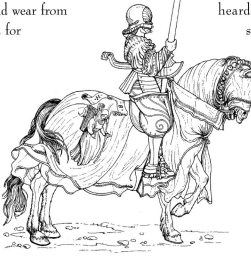

Above: A knight with tournament lance.

was a *joute à plaisance*, such as that which took place in Windsor Park in 1048, the sixth year of the reign of Edward I. According to a document in the Record Office of the Tower of London, it appears that the medieval warriors were armed in a tunic and surcoat, a helmet of leather gilt or silvered, with crests of parchment, a wooden shield, and a sword of parchment, silvered and strengthened with whalebone, with a gilded hilt.

Even if real weapons — as was generally the case — were actually used in tournaments or single combats, little damage was usually done.

The Scale and Violence of Tournaments

In these encounters, it was not, like those in jousts of *pas d'armes*, a question of individual tilts between picked knights, but often entire small armies entered the lists to charge eagerly on one another.

In the tournament at Lagny-sur-Marne, more than 3,000 medieval warriors were engaged, composed of French, Flemings, Normans, and Burgundians. Considering the number of combatants, a tournament like that of Lagny, which was fought in the open field, exactly represented a decisive action of real war.

According to the biographer of William Marshall, who recounts this engagement, the knights who were taken prisoner mattered more than those, many though they were, who were killed in it or grievously wounded. "Banners," he writes, "were unfurled. The field was so full of them that the sun was concealed. There was great noise and din.

"All strove to strike well. Then you would have heard such a crash of lances that the earth was strewn with fragments, and that the horses could not advance further. Great was the tumult upon the field. Each corps of the army cheered its ensign. The medieval warriors seized each other's bridles and went to each other's aid."

Soon, the account goes on, the young King of England, the eldest son of Henry II, gave the signal for the grand melee. Then began a desperate strife in the vineyards, ditches, and across the thick forests of vine-stocks. One could see the horses falling and men sinking, trampled underfoot, wounded, and beaten to death. Always, William the Marshal distinguished himself; everything he struck with his sword was cloven and cut to pieces; he pierced bucklers and dented shields. William was associated with a daring companion called Roger of Gaugi, and the two made their clerks prove in writing "that between Pentecost and Lent, they took 300 knights prisoner without counting horses and harness."

The two armies, having come face-to-face, slowly approached each other until they were not separated further than the range of a bow. Who would make the first attack? Who would be the first to make a sortie from the lines?

ABOVE: KING HENRI II OF FRANCE, WOUNDED IN A TOURNAMENT BY MONTGOMERY (1559).

It was the young Fromondin. His shield hard against his breast, he encountered a knight and, unhorsing him, hurled himself on another, whom he likewise overthrew. His lance was shattered, but, with a fragment, he still thrust and threatened. Already order in two armies was gone, and the melee became general. Each lance crossed another, and the earth was covered with their debris. The vassals were thrown, and their terrified horses fled. The wounded uttered horrible cries, and it was not in one place but in as many as 40 that they thrust at each other.

Five times Fromondin fell and remounted another horse. With one blow, he cut down the Flemish knight Baldwin, with a second Bernard of Naisil; finally, covered with sweat, he went to a place where no one could follow him. There, he was able to unfasten his helmet and refresh himself for an instant. In these combats, *armes courtoises* were never used in the melee. They were often the occasion of much bloodshed.

When Edward I was on his way from the Holy Land in 1274, he spent some time in France and was present at a great tournament at Chalons. He was assailed by a knight who tried to drag him from his horse. The king was the stronger of the two, so he lifted the man off his saddle and rode away with him. His party tried to rescue him, and the fight became so fierce on both sides that the melee was called "the Little Battle of Chalons," so much did it resemble one.

Indeed, the melee often was a combat for life and death, closed only by the defeat of one party, or by the heralds, or the prince, giving the word to cease. "The king hath thrown his warder (truncheon) down" was the signal to stop the battle in the lists at Coventry, when Mowbray and Bolingbroke met.

A Tournament on Magdalene's Day

Eustache Deschamps gives, in one of his poems, a good description of the proclamation of a tournament. He writes of one held at Saint-Denis. "All stranger knights and squires and all others who seek renown dark, hark to the honor and the praise and of arms the very great festival. It is by order of the knight of the golden eagle, with him 30 on horseback all garbed alike, tilting in his company, and ready to [run a course] with any of their profession on the morrow of the Day of Magdalene, in the noble city, so it is understood which bears the name of Paris as its right.

"There will be the queen adorned like an angel, 30 ladies dressed after the same habit and fashion as for the secret isle, the herald will give you its name; on Sunday dancing, and on Monday tilting for splendid prizes, as many lances as one likes to use, on the morrow of the Day of Magdalene, he who jousts best of all without any substitution [i.e., another taking his place] shall have for a prize a chaplet of gold, fine and good with a diamond set lozenge-shaped therein, which the queen will present and give, and strangers

RIGHT: A SIXTEENTH-CENTURY
ITALIAN KNIGHT AND WARHORSE
IN TOURNAMENT FINERY.

shall have 15 [days] to come and 15 to return. Safe conduct without villainous treason, thus doth the golden eagle make proclamation for the morrow of Magdalene's Day.

"After the day, all squires may present themselves. For on Tuesday, other tilts will be arranged by a squire and with him 30 in his array, equipped alike will be the comrades so that the ranks may be formed and dressed, and a damsel with fair lightsome body. Shall there be with her 30 of the same habit and bearing, to watch and counsel the jousters on the morrow of Magdalene's Day, the best jouster of all shall not have a woolen scarf but of fine silver a chaplet for his diadem, and within it a clasp of gold without alloy, the damsel will give it them, so it is said, the golden eagle will give a dinner on Monday evening, and will keep festival.

"The noble king of France will hold full court on Tuesday evening. The festival has been proclaimed for the morrow of Magdalene's Day, envoy prince, who wishes to exploit great deeds to such festivities thou should counsel the knights; for it is time that then should be understood great deeds by those who have gone to war for this cause be pleased to advise concerning these matters on the morrow of Magdalene's Day."

The Duel

The Church, while approving the generous protection which chivalry extended to the weak and the oppressed, always endeavored to destroy the savage doctrine of paganism which confounded might with right. However, it was in vain that she opposed all her influence and authority to the custom of dueling; she was obliged to restrict herself to lessening the evil effects of the opinions that generally prevailed, without hoping to destroy the opinions themselves.

The point of honor had no existence in the breasts of the warriors of antiquity. They sacrificed themselves to their country and to the commonwealth, and they loved glory — a sentiment which, with them, was collective and not individual, for with them society, as a whole, was everything.

The nineteenth-century duel, whether it be considered a brutal and speedy method of settling private quarrels or a proper act of submission to the divine will which cannot fail to crown right with success, springs from the strong individuality of barbarism and from the personal tendency of savage dignity and independence.

This strange confusion of ideas relative to victory and innocence, to might and right, first gave rise to trial by ordeal, or the judgment of God, which included ordeal by fire, by boiling water, by the Cross, and by the sword, to which women, and even princesses, were subjected. Mankind, in the simplicity of its belief,

ABOVE: TWO WARRIORS PREPARE TO DUEL FOR THE HONOR OF A LADY.

appealed to God, the sovereign judge, and implored Him to grant strength and victory to the just cause. Trial by ordeal fell into discredit at about the time of Charlemagne, and was superseded, toward the latter half of the twelfth century, by the judicial duel.

The institution of chivalry favored this hasty method of decision, which was in accordance with the manners and ideas of the period. Questions which otherwise would have been difficult to solve were thus abruptly settled and, from these bloody decisions there was no appeal.

In some countries, indeed, the judge who had decided between two antagonists had himself to submit to the judgment of God, as represented by the judicial duel. He was forced to come down from his judgment seat and contend in arms against the criminal he had just condemned. On the other hand, however, it must be said that the judge, in his turn, possessed the privilege of challenging a prisoner who refused to bow to his decision. If the principle of this rough combatant justice he once admitted, it must be acknowledged that a spirit of wisdom dictated every possible precaution to render its inconveniences as few as possible.

The duel, in fact, took place only when a crime punishable by death had been committed, and then only when there were no witnesses to the crime, but merely grave suspicions against the supposed criminal. All persons less than 21 or

more than 60 years of age — priests, invalids, and women — were dispensed from taking part in these combats and were allowed to be represented by champions. If the two parties to a dispute were of a different rank in life, certain regulations were drawn up in favor of the plaintiff. A knight who challenged a serf was forced to fight with a serf's weapons — that is to say, with a shield and a staff — and to wear a leathern jerkin. If, on the contrary, the challenge came from the serf, the knight was allowed to fight as a knight; that is to say, on horseback and in armor.

It was customary for the two parties in a judicial duel to appear before their count or lord. After reciting his wrongs, the plaintiff threw down his gage, generally a glove or gauntlet, which his adversary then exchanged for his own as a sign that he accepted the challenge. Both were then led to the seignorial prison, where they were detained until the day fixed for the combat, unless they could obtain substantial sureties who would make themselves responsible for their safe custody, and bind themselves, in case their bailee failed to appear at the appointed time to undergo the penalties attached to the committal of the act that had necessitated the appeal to arms.

This was identified as the vice prison. On the day filled for the combat, the two adversaries, accompanied by heir seconds and by a priest, appeared in the lists mounted and armed at all points, their weapons in their hands, their swords and daggers girded on. They knelt down opposite one another with their hands clasped, each in his turn solemnly swearing upon the Cross and upon Holy Writ that he alone was in the right and that his antagonist was false and disloyal. He added, moreover, that he carried no charm or talisman about his person. A herald-at-arms then gave public notice, at each of the four corners of the lists, to the spectators of the combat to remain perfectly passive, to make no movement, and to utter no cry that could either encourage or annoy the combatants, under pain of losing a limb, or even life itself.

The seconds then withdrew and the camp marshal, after seeing that both antagonists were fairly placed, and had their proper share of the wind and the sun, called out three times, *"Laissez-les aller!"* and the fight began. This moment is illustrated in the engraving on this page, which is taken from a fifteenth-century manuscript entitled *Cérémonies des Gages de Bataille*, which is in the collection of the Bibliothèque Nationale in Paris.

The judicial duel never commenced before noon and was allowed to last only until the stars appeared in the sky. If the defendant held out until then, he was considered to have gained his cause.

The knight who was beaten, whether killed or merely wounded, was dragged off the ground by his feet, the fastenings of his breastplate were cut, his armor was thrown, piece by piece, into the lists, and his steed and his weapons were divided between the marshal and the judges of the duel. Indeed sometimes, as, for instance, in Normandy and Scandinavia, according to medieval usage, the vanquished champion was hanged or burned alive, according to the nature of the crime, while if he had fought as the champion of another person, that person was usually put to death with him.

The Church, although she allowed a priest to be present in the lists, never granted even a tacit approval to these judicial duels; she excommunicated the successful duelist, and refused the rites of burial to his victim; nor was she alone in condemning this barbarous custom. The lay authorities did all in their power, but without very much success, to restrict the number of these bloody appeals. St. Louis, in a celebrated decree of 1260, substituted trial by evidence in place of the judicial duel, but he found himself able to enforce this reform only within the area of his own dominions, and imperfectly even there. Long after his reign, it is on record that the Parliament of Paris ordered certain criminal eases to be decided by personal combat. When at last, in the fifteenth century, the custom of the judicial duel fell into disuse, the nobility still retained and practiced single combat. A personal affront, often an extremely slight one, a quarrel, a slight to be avenged, was enough to bring two rivals or two enemies to blows.

This combative custom, which made a man's strength and personal skill the guardians of his honor, was sustained and encouraged by the spirit of chivalry and by that of German feudalism. Sometimes, however, the practice was considered justifiable on other grounds. History, for instance, has honorably recorded "The Battle of the Thirty," which took place in 1351, between 30 knights of Brittany, under the Sire de Beaumanoir, and 30 English knights, and another equally bloody struggle of the same kind between Bayard and 10 other French knights, and 11 Spaniards, before the walls of Trani.

The national honor alone was the motive of these two celebrated duels. However, they were only the exceptions to the rule. It almost seems as if the members of the nobility, in

ABOVE: A MOUNTED KNIGHT, READY FOR THE JOUST.

their efforts to cling to the memory of the rapidly expiring traditions of medieval society, became more inveterate in their adherence to the cruel system of dueling.

In the sixteenth century, under the last monarchs of the House of Valois, the Place Royale and the Pre aux Clercs were often watered with the blood of the best families of France. In vain did Henry IV and Louis XIII issue the most stringent edicts against this barbarous custom. In vain did the decree, called the Decree of Blois, render nugatory all letters of pardon granted to duelists, "even if they were signed by the king himself."

In spite of everything, the nobles, upon whose privileges the monarchy daily made fresh encroachments, had recourse to dueling as if to assert their connection with a chivalric and adventurous past. The most trivial, ridiculous, and shameful motives served as pretexts for a renewal of the bloody struggles, which originally had been inspired by a generous courage and a loyal sympathy with justice. However, we must go back to the time of the zenith of the Middle Ages to see its tournaments, its tilts, and its passages of arms.

The Mystique of Chivalry

THE INSTITUTION OF CHIVALRY, a system of honor and duty, was that by which the medieval European knight sought to distinguish himself from other warriors of the Middle Ages. Derived from the French *cheval* and the Latin *caballus*, chivalry had three aspects — the military, the social, and the religious. In the military sense, chivalry was the heavy cavalry of the Middle Ages which constituted the chief and most effective warlike force. The knight, or chevalier, was the professional soldier of the time. In medieval Latin, the ordinary word *miles* (soldier) was equivalent to "knight." The rise of cavalry related to the decline of infantry on the battlefield.

From a social point of view, knighthood was a great honor reserved for the warrior class. Knighthood was not hereditary, though only the sons of a knight were eligible for its ranks. In boyhood, the candidates were sent to the court of some noble, where they were trained in the use of horses and weapons and were taught lessons of courtesy. From the thirteenth century, the candidates, after they had attained the rank of squire, were allowed to take part in battles. However, it was only when they had come of age, commonly 21 years, that they

ABOVE: A WARRIOR MAKES A PLEDGE TO A LADY.

were admitted to the rank of knight by means of a peculiar ceremonial called "dubbing." In the ceremonial in which knighthood was conferred, through the Church's blessing of the sword, and by the virtue of this blessing, chivalry assumed a religious character.

In early Christianity, although Tertullian's teaching that Christianity and the profession of arms were incompatible and condemned as heretical, the military career was regarded with little favor. In chivalry, religion and the profession of arms were reconciled. This change in attitude on the part of the Church dates, according to some, from the Crusades, when Christian armies were for the first time devoted to a sacred purpose. Even prior to the Crusades, however, an anticipation of this attitude is found in the custom called the "Truce of God."

The word *chivalry*, according to Philarete Charles, whose ingenious opinions we often borrow, expresses a mixture of manners, ideas, and customs peculiar to the Middle Ages of Europe, and to which no analogy is to be traced in the annals of the human people.

The Eddas, Tacitus, and the Dano-Anglo-Saxon poems of Beowulf contain the only positive

ABOVE: IN A CONTEST ALLEGORICAL OF A TOURNAMENT, AND COMMANDED BY THE EMPEROR, TWO CHEVALIERS DEBATE THEOLOGICAL QUESTIONS.

documents concerning the origin of chivalry. It reached its apogee rapidly after its birth and gradually declined toward the close of the thirteenth century.

During that period, ladies took a very prominent position. They armed the knights, conferred the order of knighthood, and bestowed the prizes of honor. It was under the influence of the ideas peculiar to this epoch that Dante wrote his great poem *The Divine Comedy*, "for the sole purpose," he said, "of glorifying Beatrice Portinari," a child of 11 years of age whom he had accidentally seen in a church.

It was at this time that the Swabian knights, invaded by the "barbarous" Hungarians, who were in the habit of slaying their enemies with their enormous bows and arrows, implored them, "in the name of the ladies," to take sword in hand, in order to fight in "a more civilized manner."

However, chivalry soon began to decline, both as an institution and as a doctrine. Froissart characterizes and describes with picturesque liveliness this tendency to decay, which, as time advanced, gradually resulted in a complete transformation, so that the chivalric ideal was lost. As a result, the independence of the soldier, once the slave only of his God and of his lady, gave way to the obsequiousness of the courtier, and he finally became a selfish and pitiful servant. At these different epochs of organic transformation, chivalry was constantly modifying itself according to each nation's particular tendency.

Above: Two knights, one lady.

When Chivalry Was in Flower

The age in which chivalry was in flower was one in which force was paramount, and the sword, and not the courts, was the chief arbiter of justice. The extinction of the ancient Roman civilization by the inroads of the barbarians had been effected by the sword. That tradition had not died out.

The reign of Charlemagne introduced a certain revival of letters, in those lands nearest to his court, but by bringing in the feudal system, he again, by its obligations of military service, made the sword paramount.

In these northern lands in which chivalry chiefly flowered most brightly, though Christianity had greatly taken the place of ancient heathendom, many of its rites and beliefs were still kept alive. All those manifestations which we now know are due to nature were then ascribed to the supernatural.

The rise of comets, the eclipses of the sun and the moon, the Black Death that often ravaged Europe, the storms that swept over the great forests were all the work of the supernatural, or of an offended God, who was to be propitiated by offerings vowed and prayers made to the many saints who filled the places of the ancient gods. It is no wonder, therefore, that the sword was supernaturally supposed to be an effective element in the courts of justice. Trials by battle between conflicting suitors were common, so force — the strongest sword, the strongest arm, and the strongest horse — decided the issue.

Notwithstanding all this, we have to acknowledge that the age of chivalry was essentially one of faith, a faith that hallowed all the smallest vocations of life, and it is no wonder, therefore, that the free and individual chivalry which now arose was impregnated with it, and knighthood was essentially Christian.

In this, it differed from men previously banded together for military purposes, and whose life was the sword, both in the ages before its appearance, and after its decline. The Roman world had its Equestrian order, but it was not a religious body. The ancient Teutons had their warrior class, admitted by certain rites to take their places in its ranks, but it was not a religious class. The earlier chivalry had an admission of members, in order to hold fiefs and take upon them all the obligations of feudalism, but such was not for religious purposes. In later times, up to our own, men were raised in armies to higher rank for valor and experience in their profession, but never for religion's sake, pure and simple.

Even the modern conference of knighthood in Britain is given for secular, and not for religious, reasons, but the knighthood we are considering in this chapter differed essentially from all these. It was the "flower of the ages of faith," and its very life blood was drawn from the Cross. It was the temporal and earthly image of the *Church Militant*.

Emblematic and numerous as were the observances of the latter, they were equaled by those adopted by these new Christian knights. Thus, the sword was made in the form of a cross, in token of the cause in which it was to be used, and, as it was always to be employed in the defense of justice, it was to be cutting on both sides.

The spear was straight and even, because truth is so, and its iron head was significant of strength. The pennon, which must be seen afar, was the sign of courage which wished not to be hidden. The steel helmet was symbolic of modesty. The hauberk was a castle or a fortification against the powers of evil. The leg armor was to keep the feet free from the peril of evil ways. The spurs were tokens of diligence and swiftness in all honorable designs. The gorget signified obedience, and, as it encompassed the neck, so should the commands of his lord encompass the knight. The mace represented strength or courage, and the knife (or misericord) with which the combatant dispatched his enemy was used when other arms failed.

The shield was typical of the knights, standing between the prince and the people, or between the prince and his enemies, as the safeguard of the former. The gauntlets, with which the knight lifted up his hand on high, were to remind him of prayer to God, and that he was not to be guilty of putting his hand to a false oath.

The saddle of his horse betokened surety of courage, and the great charger which pertained to chivalry, an emblem of courage and readiness in daring.

ABOVE: DUEL OVER THE HONOR OF LADIES FROM THE *HISTOIRE DE GERARD DE NEVERS*.

Despite, therefore, many shortcomings in its high ideals, as is ever the case in all the fallible conceptions of men, knighthood, when in its glory, was essentially religious; not perhaps in the sense in which we should apply it when speaking of it in modern times, but when it signified the presence of a strong devotional spirit, the influence of awe, hope, and the mysterious interpositions of aid from the supernatural.

In this light, the period of which we are speaking was more distinguished for its religious character than any other of which the history of the world makes mention. This feature, which belonged to the Middle Ages society in general, was the property of almost all its individual knights. It infused into the light love-strain of the minstrel a deeper pathos, giving a soft and solemn beauty to many of the customs of domestic life, and blending the soldier's splendid dream of glory with one of immortality and paradise.

So it was that in all the medieval poets of this age, the aim of every knight seems to have been to obtain the guerdon of a rest in heaven. To these hardy men who traversed countless roads, suffered toils innumerable under different climates — cold and heat, sunshine and snow — and passed whole days without unlacing their helmets and easing themselves of their hauberks, the idea of eternal rest held an unfailing appeal. To rest on a good bed may not be a very spiritual or a very elevated idea, but it was alluring to the tired warrior.

The Origins of Chivalry

There can be little doubt that the original of chivalric forms and institutions may be discovered in the military customs prevalent among nations after the Middle Ages.

The Roman Equites formed, in the earliest ages of the republic, the great ornament of its army. They were distinguished by a gold ring, which was presented by the state, and provided with horses at a public charge.

In the rude ceremonial of the Germans, youths were admitted into the assembly of warriors, when we observe a still nearer approach to the observance of a knightly institution. They were endowed with the spear and the shield, and, from that time forth, attached themselves with devoted constancy to some particular chieftain.

"The noblest youths," says Tacitus, "were not ashamed to be numbered among the faithful companies of celebrated leaders, to whom they devoted their arms and service. A noble emulation prevailed among the leaders to acquire the greatest number of bold companions. In the hour of danger it was shameful for the chief to be surpassed in valor by his companions, shameful for the companions not to equal the valor of their chief. To survive him if he fell was irretrievable disgrace. To protect his person, to increase his glory by their own triumphs, were the most holy of their duties."

A military caste existed among all these peoples that then populated Europe before the time even of Charlemagne, to whom must be credited the introduction into his vast dominions of the feudal system. Even in our own country, King Alfred is said to have admitted Athelstan to the military dignity, by clothing him in a purple vest with a belt set with gems and a sword sheathed in gold. However, despite any religious rites, which the Anglo-Saxons grouped round the giving of knighthood, it soon became corrupt.

The chronicler John of Salisbury observed that a knight, to be a good one, should inure himself to labor, to run, carry weights, bear the sun and the dust, and be content with hard living and coarse food. Said John, "Some think that military glory consists in this, that they shine in elegant dress, that they make their clothes tight to their bodies, and so bind on their linen and silken garments as to seem a skin color, like their flesh. Each is boldest in the banquet hall, but in the battle everyone desires to do the least. They would rather shoot arrows at the enemy than come to close fighting — if they return home without a scar, they sing triumphantly of their battles and boast of a thousand deaths."

From these few proofs it seems certain that, from the age of Charlemagne and even earlier, the sons of chiefs and kings and the higher nobility assumed manly arms with some sort of investiture, and were a class apart from the ordinary soldier. However, these ceremonies which began to surround the entrance into military life of a young soldier would have done little perhaps in themselves toward forming that intrinsic principle which characterized the later and more genuine chivalry.

In the reign of Charlemagne, however, we find a military distinction that appears in fact, as well as in name, to have given birth to that institution. Under the Carolingian dynasty, property was of two kinds.

The holders of Allodial lands enjoyed them absolutely and independently; on the other hand, benefices or fiefs (from the Anglo-Saxon word *feof,* cattle or money) were granted by a lord to a person who, in return for that grant, and for the protection the lord afforded him, obliged himself to do some military service.

In its early days, therefore, chivalry was founded on feudal obligations and was closely bound up with the military service of fiefs. Land thus held in England was called "a knight's fee," and in Normandy "fiefs de haubert," from the

IN SERVICE OF THE IDEAL WOMAN

The youth training for knighthood was bidden to choose an ideal sovereign from among the noble and beautiful ladies of the aristocratic world that he frequented, a sort of terrestrial divinity whom he was to swear to serve, and to whom he was henceforth to recount all his thoughts and actions, treating her at the same time with all the delicacy and devotion which the example of those around him had shown him to be her due.

He was taught, above all, to revere the august character of chivalry, and to respect, in the persons of the knights who composed this institution, the dignity to which he himself aspired.

coat of mail which it entitled, and required, every tenant to wear. Military tenure was said to be "by service and chivalry."

To serve as a soldier, mounted and equipped, was the common duty of vassals from the highest to the lowest. It implied no personal merit and it gave, of itself, no claim to civil privileges. It was, before everything, obligatory and dependent on the will of another. For as long as the lord and his descendants held the fief, those duties were demanded. There were various ceremonies which characterized these relations between the lord and the vassal. The latter, when doing homage to the former, knelt before him and, placing his hand in that of his future lord, declared that he would become his man and as such acknowledged himself bound to defend his life and his honor. He

ABOVE: A LADY WATCHES THE WARRIORS RETURN FROM THE WARS.

then took the oath of fidelity, having previously removed his sword and spurs. Called *hommage-lige*, it bound the vassal to military service for an unlimited time and wherever the lord thought fit to lead his dependents.

When war was permanent, or nearly so, the hommage-lige prevailed. Thus, the code of laws known as "The Assises de Jerusalem," drawn up after the taking of the Holy City by the Crusaders in 1099, is regarded as the rule, even though at that time the obligations of feudal service were becoming obsolete and free knighthood was becoming prevalent.

The Nature of Chivalry

The chief of all these obligations in the oldest form of chivalry (called by French writers on the subject *"l'ancienne Chevalerie"*) was military service. However, other services were also called upon on certain occasions from the holder of a fief — i.e., to help to ransom his overlord if taken prisoner; to help in dowering the lord's daughter in marriage; to do the same when that chief's elder son was made a knight, or he himself was about to start on the Crusades.

Estates might, and often did, change hands; others were confiscated, or left without owners on account of the death of the heir. Hence ensued fresh and heavy duties paid over to the lord. If the vassal was a minor, the suzerain became his guardian, and as such received the income.

The daughters of the vassal were obliged to receive husbands at the hands of the lord, unless they paid forfeit.

Even in England, where the feudal system was dying out, the obligations of those holding manors — which represented somewhat the Norman fief and was left by them untouched — were obtained.

The above obligations of the feudal system — besides those, such as the lord's right to make his tenants bake their bread in his feudal oven, to grind their corn in his mill, to make wine in his press — show how hardly all feudal service fell upon the vassal, and, if in these common details of ordinary life they were so, much more in the constant military services as a soldier that the vassal was called upon to render.

This feudal service, as long as the fief remained in a family, was passed on from father to son. For this reason, some of the French writers call it *"une chevalerie de naissance,"* which often, to the casual reader of their works, might lead him into the belief that knighthood was hereditary. As we have said, the fief itself, unless forfeited for not complying with the obligations it carried, or for treason in the holder of it, was hereditary, but the dignity of knighthood was never so — it was not transferable and simply personal. There are numerous instances extant of youths of noble and even royal birth who, if they had possessed knighthood by right of birth, would never afterward have sought it; whereas they constantly did. Thus, Henry, King of England, sent his son Edward to the court of Alfonso of Castile, to receive the

ABOVE: LADIES AWAIT THE RETURN OF THEIR NOBLE WARRIORS.

tensions, but from their wealth. These same territorial knights became, by degrees, ashamed of assuming the title of knights, until they could challenge it by real desert. This class of noble and gallant cavaliers, serving commonly for pay, but on the most honorable footing, became, far more numerous through the Crusades.

Chivalry During the Collapse of Feudalism

While the cities in Western Europe were throwing off their feudal chains, they did not gain individual freedom. They only exchanged them for the collective and communal freedom. As societies they were free, but as individuals they were not yet emancipated.

The peasantry also on the seignorial estates were still chained to the wheel of labor, even though they were ceasing to be serfs. The craftsman was ruled by his guild, by the parish in which he worshiped, and the quarter of the city in which he dwelt; none of these had individual freedom. The only outcome for this rising spirit of individual freedom was that to be found, therefore, in the new knighthood.

The medieval knighthood or chivalry was the embodiment of the feudal system. It now had its place taken by this nobler chivalry founded on individual freedom and religion. Being free, and being religious, it differed from the earlier form of obligatory knight service. However, it was strictly enforced under this newer and freer phase of knighthood, that none should receive the accolade unless tracing their parentage or descent from these feudal families — in other words, from the military and ruling class.

Thus, Charles II of France, by his ordinance of 1294, declared "*quod nullus possit accipere militare cingulum nisi ex parte patris saltem sit miles*" (here the order of knighthood is allowed to a man, if he can prove on one side that he comes of a feudal family).

Meanwhile, the Emperor Frederic, by an ordinance decreed at Naples, declared "*ad militarem honorem nullus accedat qui non sit de genere militum,*" and this obligation, for a neophyte in knighthood, of showing he was of the old feudal military caste, remained intact from the decaying force of chivalry. A sovereign, or prince, often permitted the citizen class to receive the accolade.

order of knighthood at his hands in the city of Burgos (Walsingham).

From these brief remarks on the medieval feudal obligations attached to knighthood, it can easily be understood how cramped and fettered a brave man's soul became by such restrictions, and how, though he longed for military glory, he longed to gain it where, and how, he willed, and not at the beck and call of an overlord. The vast upheaval that the First Crusade in 1095 made in the Christian countries of Western Christendom fostered and helped the growing spirit in chivalry of freedom from feudal restraint.

The cry that went forth to the military caste was not made by the feudal lord, or, if it was so made to his vassal, it was left to the latter's individual decision to obey it or not — for, it was considered in that age, this cry came from God Himself.

Again the multiplication of fiefs, by their subdivision, helped to swell the ranks of knighthood at this period. This subdivision greatly impoverished the owner's family, and the younger members eagerly sought a knighthood which was not dependent on a fief.

A younger brother, leaving the paternal estate in which he took a slender share, might well look to wealth and dignity in the service of a powerful lord. Knighthood, which he could not claim, as not holding a fief as his legal right, became the object of his chief ambition. It raised him in the scale of society, equaling him in dress, arms, and title to the rich fief-holders. As it was bestowed only for his merit, it did much more than make him equal to those who had no pre-

Chivalry During the Crusades

During the Crusades, all feudal service was in abeyance, so it was necessary for the richer barons to take into their pay as many medieval warriors as they could afford to maintain. During this time, we find chivalry therefore acquired its full vigor as an order of personal nobility. Its original connection with feudal tenure, if not altogether effaced, became, in great measure, forgotten in the splendor of the form which it now wore. Again it was during this period — the Crusading period — that the Church stepped forward and, as these warriors were about to engage in what she considered a holy warfare, freed them, while engaged in it, from the feudal obligations of that of their respective fiefs.

In these holy wars, the warriors were the free agents of the Cross, and so it was now we find coming into universal practice, at the making of a knight, those more religious and complicated ceremonies, henceforth bound up with chivalry or knighthood.

The "new chivalry" of a freer sort arose during the period of the First Crusade at the end of the eleventh century. That Crusade and the subsequent ones, by familiarizing the European warriors with the civilization of the Moslem Arabs and the Moors, brought with it an amelioration of their living and education, but it also brought with it a great laxity of manners between the two sexes.

Women, as they were in the Moslem world, became the object of knightly vows, but they lost much of that older and simpler life of the past generations. Women were no longer kept in seclusion within the walls of home life, but were present at festivals, and at tournaments, and they sat in the halls of their husbands' castles.

The Ballad of Perceforest tells us of a feast where 800 knights had each of them a lady eating off his plate. In *The Ballad of Lancelot du Lac*, a lady, who was troubled with a jealous husband, complains that it had been a long time since a knight ate off her plate.

ABOVE: STRUCK BY CUPID'S ARROW, AN AGED KNIGHT COMES TO HIS QUEEN.

This phase of the chivalric age was every day exhibited by its Church men as well as its laymen. If the former could discover the method of reconciling the apparent discrepancy, an adventurous soldier was not the most unlikely person to take advantage of the invention. Nor does it seem to have entered into the minds of the venerable chroniclers, who have recorded the deeds of their favorite knights, that they might tarnish the brightness of their fame by telling the errors they committed.

The same pride and seeming consciousness of noble truths appear to have dictated the anecdotes of licentiousness at which we nowadays blush, as well as those which incline us toward admiration. The tales from the famous history of *The Knights of the Round Table*, while they are glowing with the praises of their devotion, record with the greatest particularity, in the same tone, the violation of the principles of morality. "While their heroes are sent in the most devout spirit to search for the Holy Grail," the book states, "we find them recreating themselves from their toils by the most depraved pleasures, and the medieval warriors whose characters seemed to have been portrayed in the manner best calculated to fill us with respect, suddenly rise before us as the worst of hypocrites."

ABOVE: IN ACCORDANCE WITH CHIVALROUS DOCTRINE, THIRTEENTH-CENTURY LADIES AWARD PRIZES TO KNIGHTS WHO JOUST FOR THE SAKE OF THEIR HONOR.

Women in the World of the Medieval Warrior

O PREPARE THE NOBLE LADIES for the role they were destined to play in the world of medieval society, they were taught from their childhood to practice every virtue, to cherish every noble feeling, and generally to emulate the dignity demanded by the social privileges of their rank. They were profuse in their acts of kindness and civility to the knights, whether friends or strangers, who entered the gates of their castles.

On a medieval warrior's return from a tournament or battle, they unbuckled his armor with their own hands. They prepared perfumes and spotless linen for his wear. They dressed him in gala clothes, in mantle and scarf that they had themselves embroidered, they prepared his bath, and waited on him at the table.

Destined to become the wives of these same knights who frequented their homes as girls, they did their utmost to bring themselves under the knights' notice by their modest demeanor, and to make themselves beloved by the courtesy and the attentions which they lavished upon them. It was theirs to respond, with admiration and tenderness, to the boldness and the bravery of the medieval warriors who sought glory only to lay it at their mistresses' feet, and who asked for nothing more than to be subject to the gentle sway of beauty, grace, and virtue.

ABOVE: KNIGHT AND LADY.

Courts of Love

It was thus, for instance, that in Provence, from the eleventh to the fourteenth centuries, the most powerful nobles humbly obeyed, in everything that concerned the heart, the decrees issued by the courts or tribunals of love. A kind of feminine Olympus was held with great ceremony on certain days, and at which the ladies most distinguished by birth, beauty, intelligence, and knowledge, met to deliberate, publicly or with closed doors, with proper gravity and solemnity, on delicate questions of gallantry, which in those days were considered highly important. These courts of love, which appear to have been regular and permanent institutions in the twelfth century, had a special code, in accordance with which the sentences pronounced were more or less rigorously in conformity. However, this code has not been handed down to our day, and we possess only its outline conveyed in the commentaries of the legal writers of the fifteenth century. Causes in these courts were sometimes decided on written evidence, and sometimes the parties themselves were allowed to appear in person.

The celebrated women who at different epochs and in different places presided over these romantic assizes included the beautiful Eleanor of Aquitaine, Queen of France, and

ABOVE: ANNE OF BRITTANY AND HER PATRON SAINTS. SHE CREATED THE ORDER OF CORDELIERS, A SOCIETY OF WIDOWS OF KNIGHTS.

afterward of England; Sibyl of Anjou, who married Thierry, Count of Flanders. There were also the Countess of Die, known as the Sappho of France; and the famous Laura or Lauretta of Sade, whom Petrarch — who chose her for the lady of his lore — has immortalized in his verse.

Damsels in the Service of the Warrior

It was often considered a great privilege of the ladies to do the arming of the knight. He mounted his horse with an easy bound, and the damsels gave him a shield emblazoned with a lion. The young daughter of a knight was trained to do this and many other things to help the young cavaliers. If he came to her father's castle, it was she who was told to greet him and disarm him, with making ready his chamber and his bed, with preparing his bath, and even (we have on this point many unquestionable texts, especially in *The Ballad of Girart de Roussillon*) with massaging him in order to help him to go to sleep.

One gathers from the *Chansons de Gestes* that it was these young women who made all the advances in love to knights when thus entertaining them. Maidens thought these youths handsome, and they told them so without the least embarrassment. So to arm a newly made knight came easily to a young maiden.

In *The Ballad of Don Flores de Grèece*, a knight preparing to go to battle is armed by a young damsel, who also unbuckled the knight's armor with her own hands, and prepared perfumes and spotless linen for his wear (on return from warfare or a tournament). She clothed him in mantle and scarf that she herself had embroidered, prepared his bath, and waited on him at his table. No doubt arming a knight to go into danger gave the ladies a deep interest.

ABOVE: A KNIGHT AND LADY OF THE FOURTEENTH CENTURY.

In the Battle of Agincourt, four such knights, having been armed by their damsels, went into the fight. One, we are told, was killed, one was made prisoner, another was missing after the battle, and the fourth saved his life by dishonorable flight. The lady in whom this last one had wakened an interest felt so much his disgrace, and for having placed her regard on a knight who had dishonored his order, that she declared that she preferred death to longer living.

Women Warriors

Not all medieval warriors were men. Not by any means. During the later Middle Ages, women were admitted as members of certain orders of chivalry, albeit not often specifically as knights. They were certainly more than mere "honorary members," and as such had certain privileges of rank and service. They were admitted into the Spanish Order of St. James of Compostella and so into the Order of St. John of Jerusalem. An order called "The Servants of Virtue" was instituted for them in Italy by Eleanora de Guzman, but only to such of the highest rank. Anne, last Duchess of Brittany, instituted for widows the Order of Cordeliers, the Cord of St. Francis indicating their profession.

Florine, the daughter of the Duke of Burgundy, fought bravely in the Crusades at the side of her lover, the son of Denmark's king. Certainly, too, there is Joan of Arc, France's greatest heroine, whose bravery is legendary.

In 1158, King Sancho III of Castile founded the Order of Calatrava, and women were admitted to such under the name of "chevalières de Calatrava." It seems extremely possible that the rank they thus acquired was more than honorary. In many cases they were designated as "equitissa" or "chevalierè." In a Charter of the year 1379, Mary de Bethune is called "chevaliere." A seignior of Yvaroux named Breton had six sons, all knights, and two daughters who are described as "chevalières."

Loyalty, courtesy, liberality, and justice were the virtues essential to the character of a woman warrior in the days of chivalry. A more splendid virtue than all others demanded of the young aspirant for woman warriorhood, both before and after initiation, was the pursuit of good, the detestation of evil, not alone when found in her own soul but in that of the world.

Hemericourt, cited by Honoré de St. Marie, says that women who were not married and yet inherited fiefs were created knights in order to perform the obligations those fiefs carried with them to the overlords. However, often, whenever a fief thus fell into the hands of a female, the overlord claimed the right of wardship, and her future marriage was always arranged so that her husband should fulfill the military obligations that her lands carried. If she, in the very rare event remained unmarried, the lord usually kept the lands as his own.

Certainly, a pastime of the noble girls, like the noble lads, was riding. Like the lads, the young damsels might gallop around the castle yard. Like her brother, a noble girl might boast that she could speak in French, German, Italian, Spanish, and Norman, and that she had a proficiency in letters that equaled or surpassed his. Like the male children, it was often in their eagerness to arm themselves like their elders, that the girls wanted armor such as even girls could don.

The duties of these girls were those found generally in domestic service of their lord and lady. Like the male pages, they accompanied the lord and lady on the hunt, in their travels, in their visits to neighboring castles, in their walks, and often carried messages.

From a social point of view, woman warriorhood was a great honor reserved for a noble class, although far less is known of these women than of their male counterparts. Indeed, there were far fewer of them than there were

ABOVE: FLORINE OF BURGUNDY, A WOMAN CRUSADER.

knights. The dresses worn by the woman warrior and her friends were of the richest fabric. Precious gems and pearls were also lavishly used.

It was a romantic and glorious career, if opened up to her, though it opened up to but a select few. It was, and has always been held, that every woman warrior, like a male knight, had in herself, whatever her social circumstances, the inherent power of creating others to her order. The question of women being able to confer knighthood seems only to have been when knighthood itself was not in its pristine glory, at a time when its sacramental character was gradually being forgotten. In those cases when women achieved knighthood, many were rulers, and of sovereign rank, notably queens and princesses.

The Medieval Warrior at Home

EDIEVAL SOCIETY PROGRESSED, not only in manners but in the standard of living. As it did so, a greater refinement crept in. Those drafty gray castles became better adorned, their chambers with greater comforts, and the household they sheltered not, as earlier, a mere throng of rough and mailed men, but servants under the knights, and squires, each apportioned to their domestic duties.

The household of a knight was called his "menie," or entourage, and later his "family." This latter did not consist solely, as in the modern sense, of his wife and children or relations, but of his whole household of servants and retainers. A great part of the duties which are not relegated to the lower orders of domestics were then performed by pages, damsels, and young squires of gentle, and often noble, degree. Such considered it in the Middle Ages no disgrace to do many services in a brave knight's household which their posterity today would utterly refuse to do.

We must suppose from numerous hints and descriptions that an elaborate system of manners and customs prevailed long before they were codified in any treatise such as this. For instance, the Bayeux Tapestry of the eleventh century shows a feast, with a page or server kneeling, his napkin round his neck, long before *The Book of Courtesy* (circa 1460). The earl's son attended the duke, the knight's second son was the earl's servant, the esquire's son wore the knight's livery, and the gentleman's son was the esquire's servant. Indeed, under the system of entail and devolution of feudal estates, this was, in time of peace, the only possible livelihood for a gentleman's younger son. Few knights' sons ever went into the Church or had any aptitude to study law. Debarred from trade, a lad could only, at his family's bidding, offer his services to some good knight or lord who, by his estate, kept up a large household.

The Medieval Hall and Table

The hall was lighted by torches or candles, so the squire who dealt out and looked after the candles therefore held an important post. These were made of the poorer sort of tallow, but the rich had them made of wax, "of wax thereto if ye take tent."

"To Candlemas, as I you say of candles delivery squires shall have so long if it is that man will crave." Said a medieval household manual: "Of bread and ale also the butler shall make delivery throughout the year to squires, and also wine to knight or else he doth not his office right."

The chief article on the knight's table was the silver ship which formed the salt cellar, for as no salt was used in cooking until late in the Middle Ages, it was to be added at the table. This cellar was called "the Nef." It constituted the gradation of rank, for the host, his relatives, and guests sat above it, while his ordinary household was below it.

There were no forks and no instruments for helping from the dishes. Each person had a knife and spoon which he licked or wiped upon his bread before using them in the common dish. The bowl of water which preceded and followed became a necessity.

ABOVE: THE LORD AND LADY OUT ON A PROMENADE, ATTENDED BY PAGES, HERALDS, KNIGHTS, AND LADIES-IN-WAITING.

In some rich households, in addition to the chief meal, there was one which consisted of wines, spices, and dried fruits. Many of the latter were brought to Europe by crusaders. These included plums from Syria, as well as imported and locally made jellies, gingerbread, and pickles. Cucumbers and melons were extensively eaten during the Middle Ages, and lemon juice (after the lemon had been introduced from the south of Europe) was very popular with fish and meat. Beer, more than wine, was an essential staple. The brewers were generally always women, and known in England as "brewsters."

Another peculiarity in regard to food was that not only by the chairs people sat on, but also by the dishes they were served in, was rank marked. The way the meat was apportioned, a whole animal, whether meat, fish, or fowl, was only for a lord or knight of high degree. When the master of the house and his guests were commoners, everything down to a lark must be "hewed on gobbets"; namely, cut into small pieces. The meat was always underdone, as over cooked meat was thought to provoke the tempers of those who ate it.

Bread and butter dates from the reign of Edward IV (1461–1483), before which drippings were used. Bread was of many kinds. "Simnel" or "manchet" was the finest, "wassel" was the best common quality, and "cocket" was the inferior. "Muslin" was made of barley, wheat, and oats mixed. Christmas bread was made of fine flour, eggs, and milk. There was also spice bread, and griddle cakes were then peculiar to Wales. Merchants in those days dealt in sweetmeats and spices.

At feasts, pheasants and peacocks were the favorite dishes. Both are mentioned as such in the kitchen accounts used in the eleventh century in the abbey on Lake Constance. Foreign foods and ingredients were also imported by the monks. At Hirschau, under the Abbot William (1069–1091), a number of foreign fruits, fishes, lemons and figs, and spices, such as pepper and ginger, were known and used by the monks at their abbey. Also at Cluny in 1180, the abbot, desiring a stricter enforcement of the rule, complained of all these luxuries then rife in his abbey.

In France, the art of cooking was a well-known science in the year 1300. After 1400, the cooks of the famous cooking school of Charles VII and his "cordon-bleu," aimed to make the simplest food attractive and to disguise its nature. The peacocks were brought in to the sound of drum beats and clapping of hands.

In England, it was the same. During the reign of Richard II, it was a time of luxurious feeding. The ordinary dinner of a lord or wealthy knight at the end of the fourteenth century consisted in three courses of 7, 5, and 6 dishes each, and 5 on feast days, 11 or 12. When George Neville was raised to the See of York, 4,000 cold game pies, 104 peacocks, and 200 pheasants were provided.

The "largesse" and profusion of Italian luxury at feasts, circa 1400 and onwards, may be illustrated by a description given in *Roman Life and Manners* by Ludwig Friedlander, of the one given by Benedetti Salutati on February 16, 1476, to the sons of King Ferrante of Naples. The staircase was decked with embroidered carpets and wreaths of yew. The great hall was decorated with tapestries. From the canopy, which was in cloth with the colors of Aragon, two candelabras of carved and gilded wood hung down. Opposite the main entrance, on a gilded platform covered with carpets, stood the dining table, spread with the finest linen over a worked cover. One side of the hall was taken up by a huge sideboard — the shelves in their number proclaiming, as was the custom, the rank of the owner. On the shelves were set 80 ornamental pieces of plate, mostly of silver, some of gold, and bowls, dishes, and plates of richest workmanship.

The "hors d'oeuvre" consisted of a little majolica bowl, passed round, of milk pudding. Eight silver dishes of capon-breast jelly followed, decorated with coats of arms and mottoes. The principal guest — the Duke of Calabria — received a dish with a fountain in the middle, spraying forth a shower of orange-flower water. The finest part of the banquet consisted of 12 courses of various game, veal, ham, pheasants, partridges, capons, fowls, and "blancmange." At the end, a large silver dish was set before the duke, who took off the cover and released a number of birds. (This will remind the reader of the old nursery song about "Four-and-twenty black-birds baked in a pie.") On two magnificent salvers, there were two peacocks with tails spread, bearing essence in their beaks and the duke's arms attached to silk ribbon on their breasts.

The second part of the feast consisted of nine courses of various sweets — tarts, marzipan, and light and delicate pastry with hippocras as a drink. The wines, indeed, mostly Italian and Sicilian, were chosen by the guest, who studied a list of 15 brands to choose from. At the end of the banquet, every guest was handed, by the pages, fragrant water to wash his hands. Then the cloth was removed and a large dish was placed on the table containing a mountain of green twigs and blossoms, which gave forth a fragrance to the whole hall. During the meal and after, the guests were entertained by the jugglers with music and a play in dumb-show. About an hour later, dessert was served — spices and sugar designs in silver vessels with covers of wax sugar on which were emblazoned coats of arms. The feast lasted four hours. Barons and knights who were owners of lands sought the fame of possessing a spirit of "largesse" and open profuseness, often in strange ways.

In 1174, Henry II of England, as Duke of Aquitaine, summoned to Beaucaire an assembly of his knights and squires. For their honor, Bertram Rambaut, the celebrated troubadour-knight, had a piece of land plowed and sown with 30,000 "sols" in pennies. Guillaume de Martel, who had a following of 300 knights, had all the provisions in his kitchens cooked, not on wood-bundles of branches but on lighted wax-torches. Raimond de Venous showed a cruel prodigality in his boastfulness of being a knight full of the spirit of "largesse," for he had 30 of his horses burned alive (as fuel). It was, needless to say, after these prodigal feasts, that the attendants, particularly the wandering jugglers, after celebrating in their songs the profuse hospitality of the knight who provided it, cried out, "Largesse, largesse!" and received rich presents of money and often splendid wearing apparel.

The latter was particularly a gift to the troubadour-knight, their master, who, refusing money, never disdained a rich robe, a good warhorse, or a suit of armor for his skill. Thus, in *The Ballad of Richard Coeur de Lion*, we read that after the capture of Acre, he distributed among the heralds and laborers who accompanied him a great part of his largesse in money, jewels, horses, and fine robes, which had fallen to his share. It was not only out of a natural liberality that princes and knights gave largesse, it was that as these men skilled in song and versification were — with the exception of the monkish chroniclers — the only medium to keep alive and hand on their deeds of prowess to another age, so they might be encouraged by rich gifts to do so.

It will be seen by the above that the heralds and minstrels are often coupled in the same category. Froissart tells us that at a Christmas entertainment given by the Count of Foix, there were many minstrels as well as his own, as strangers, and he gave to the heralds and minstrels "the sum of 500 franks," and gave to the Duke of Tourayne's minstrels "gowns of green cloth of gold, furred with ermine, valued at 200 franks." A sword as "largesse," though often given with harness to a troubadour, was never given to these jugglers or minstrels, and these latter — unlike the former — were forbidden to carry arms; so in the Statute of Arms for Tournaments, passed in the reign of Edward I, 1295, it is laid down *"E qui nul Roy de Harrarunz ne minestrals portent privez armez."* Largesse, therefore, it can be seen from the foregoing, was a virtue extremely popular. The debts it brought with it were not considered a disgrace but a sign of nobility.

Self-Sufficiency

As to the food that maintained a wealthy knight's house, the household was self-supporting and independent of external help to a degree which is difficult to conceive in these days of easy supplies and rapid communication. A castle or large manor house had its own cornfields and pastures, stacks of corn and hay granaries, and storehouses of all kinds.

The owner had mills, slaughterhouses, brewhouses, and salting houses. If the cloth which the household wore was not woven at home, at least the sheep were shorn there and the wool went to be sold or exchanged for cloth at the nearest staple town. Whatever was not of home manufacture was conveyed from the wood, the quarry, or the town by packhorses and barges. It may also have been bought from itinerant peddlers at the fairs held periodically throughout the land. In these castles and manors, too, great stores, particularly if the owners were rich, of gold and silver plate, jewels and furs and precious raiment were found. At a time when interaction with foreign countries was difficult, much capital remained in England.

The word *livery* constantly appears in the household expenses. *Livery (liberatura)* properly means "allowance." It did not necessarily mean "uniform" but "deliveries," i.e., of rations or fuel for their rooms. However, it did also carry with it the modern idea of "cloth," generally the mark of the owner's color or arms. Nearly the earliest entry found in the "rolls" on the subject of male livery is an order of King John to provide, for his natural son Geoffrey, six hoods and tunicles and a cape of russet furred with lambskin, two robes of russet with a lambskin cloak, 30 yards of woolen cloth, stockings, and two pairs of boots.

At Home in the Castle

The bed chamber that the squire was carefully to prepare for the knight was invariably of the form called a "tester bed." The squire slept in a pellet bed either at the foot of his master's bed or across the doorway outside as protection. The hangings often were of velvet, silk, or worsted. "A green velvet bed embroidered in gold of Cyprus with the arms of England and Hainaut" was provided for Queen Phillipa in 1335.

Another of "embroidered baldekyn with the same arms with three curtains of red sendal [a kind of silk] and 10 carpets of red tapestry" were described as the property of John, late Duke of Exeter, in 1401. Two silk beds with a furred covering of miniver were granted in 1400 to the king's sister Elizabeth, widow of the Earl of Exeter.

The sheets of the richer knights and their ladies were made of cloth from Champagne, Flanders, or Rennes. It was usually linen or linsey-woolsey. For the higher classes they were also set with jewels, principally jacinths, which were supposed to have the power of sending people to sleep. The blankets themselves were of wool or fustian, the latter most prized. The bedstead, which was a mere box without bottom or lid, was filled with straw, and, on this, the mattress and bed were laid. Titled persons slept on the bed uppermost, and commoners on the mattress. Despite the meanness of the straw that these box bedsteads contained, the quilts covering them were generally works of art, frequently of velvet and silk, and embroidered with great care and beauty.

Important items in every bedroom were the "standard and coffer," two chests large and small. The former held the articles in everyday use, while the latter contained such things as were too valuable to be trusted out of the owner's sight. The cost of a standard in 1388 was 30 shillings. The coffer, which was more ornamented, cost 50 shillings. Around the walls were hangings called "arras" from the great factory at the city of Arras in northern France. As these hangings projected from the wall, "behind the arras" was the convenient station for eavesdroppers.

Bathing and washing were performed with the help of articles brought for the occasion and never left in the bed chamber. Princes and nobles washed in silver basins and the lower classes in wooden tubs. These latter, too, were utilized when the ritual bath was given to the neophyte for knighthood. Such, too, were used when the medieval warrior returned from a battle or tournament and, casting off his armor, took his bath, often given by some industrious maiden.

In the ballads and stories, we find many references to the young medieval warriors bathing in the rivers and streams when they were in the field. It seems, therefore, that the medieval knight was far cleaner than a later generation, when in Louis XIV's court, the ladies and the aristocratic fops of the period never washed, but greased their faces.

That the medieval knight despised the unwashed is borne out in the ballad of Garin le Lorraine, the typical war poem of the period, where the serf Rigaud is contrasted with his master, with "his hair bristling, and his face as black as coal. He went for six months without bathing; none but rain water ever touched his face."

The windows of the castles and manors, originally simple open slits — hence it is said the narrow apertures in the earliest Norman churches — were after a time fitted with wooden shutters, and afterward of skin. As for glass, the Earl of Northumberland is recorded to have removed it from his castle windows when he left home and carefully laid it away until his return. In 1252, we find Henry III commanding the manufacture of "white glass" for the great hall of Northampton Castle and for glass windows in the chamber of his queen in Nottingham Castle. Medieval drinking cups of glass were in existence, but surviving examples are very rare.

Splendor in the Castle

The baron or knight could not reign as king in his castle, but he could make his castle as strong and as splendid as he chose; he could not demand the military service of his vassals for his private war, but he could, if he chose to pay for it, support a vast household of armed and liveried servants, a retinue of pomp and splendor, ready beneath their mail and liveries for any opportunity of disturbance. Much can be said of the care and planting of gardens by the medieval warriors and their ladies. Originally, the castle was a plain, grim, feudal keep, but as years rolled on, and the returning crusader had learned a greater skill in architecture from mixing with more architecturally sophisticated nations, soon it was surrounded by other buildings, and the simple yard expanded into gardens that extended to the outer walls of the compound.

The Household of Gaston, Count of Foix

Housekeeping in the family of Gaston, Count of Foix, a prince whose court was at Nemours, was considered not only of a noble but of a knightly preeminence. The writer Froissart lived in his house about 12 weeks, much recommended to Gaston on account of having brought with him a book containing all the songs, ballads, and virelays which Wenceslaus of Bohemia, the gentle Duke of Brabant, had made and the historian himself had compiled or transcribed.

"Every night after supper," says Froissart, "I read therein to him, and while I read there was none durst speak anything to interrupt me, so much did the Count delight in listening. I have in my time seen many knights, kings, princes, and others, but I never saw anyone like him in person. His countenance sanguine, fair, and smiling, his eyes grey and amorous whenever he chose to cast them. In every way he was so perfect he could not be praised too much. He loved that which ought to be loved, he hated that which ought to be hated. He was a very wise knight, also of high enterprise and of right good counsel. He never had a bad person about him. He said many orisons every day, a nocturne of the Psalter, and matins of Our Lady, and of the Holy Ghost and of the Cross, and a dirge every day. He gave five florins, in small coins every day to the poor about his gate for the love of God. He was generous and courteous in his gifts.

"He loved hounds above all animals, for winter and summer, he loved the hunt. Every month he took account what he spent. He changed in rotation (to escape fraud) those who received his monies every two months. He had certain coffers in his own chamber out of which often he would himself take money to give to lords, knights, and others who came to him, for he would have none depart without gifts. . . . At midnight when he came out of his chamber into the hall to supper, he had ever borne before him 12 torches burning, carried by 12 young pages or squires standing before his table all supper time. They gave a great light, and the hall was ever full of knights and squires, and many other tables set for those who wished to sup. But none were allowed to address him at his own table unless he was called upon to do so. His meat was a little wild fowl composed of the wings and legs only, and during each day he ate and drank sparsely.

"He had great pleasure in musical instruments, on which he himself was a performer, and that right well. So he had songs sung before him, and other musical things as he sat at table. None rejoiced more in brave deeds of arms than he did, so there was seen in his hall and courtyard knights and squires of prowess going up and down and conversing."

The Chapel and Churches

When Mass was said every day, and attended by the knight as regularly as he pursued the hunt or the tournament, chapels and oratories were found in each of his dwellings and the domestic chaplain was one of his household. In royal houses and those of great nobles, this private establishment was not infrequently collegiate, with a dean, canons, clerks, and singing men and boys.

The royal chapel at Windsor is perhaps the best remaining example in England, but small chapels and ecclesiastically designed buildings may be found in nearly every old castle and manor house which still exists — such as the chapel of the Colchester Castle from the twelfth century; of Ormsbro Castle from the late twelfth century. Also of note are that of Igtham Moat in Kent, and that of Haddon Hall.

In a wealthy medieval warrior's house, beside the general chapel, there was often a small oratory for the use of himself and his wife, in later times called "a closet." These chapels were thoroughly furnished with vessels, books, and vestments, according to the means of the owner. From the household book of the then Earl of Northumberland, we gather that his chapel had three altars. Every morning throughout the land, the bell sounded for Mass, and in the evening for Vespers. The priest who served these chapels was, in his spare time, usually employed, more or less, in secular duties; some engaged in their employer's service, some, if unattached, in those of lords and on royal missions, for, as they were the most learned in that age and most skilled in the diplomacy then known, their services were much sought.

These chapels and ecclesiastical establishments in the more wealthy knights' and lords' houses were the scenes of many offerings at the time of the great Church festivals. Miracle plays took place in them, and all who joined in them had their rewards.

If it seems a wonder that every knight's castle or manor contained a chapel or at least an oratory, let it be remembered how essential chivalry, in its later development, had been fostered by the Church, and on what a high ideal had been set the virtues pertaining to chivalry. The medieval warriors, too, never forgot their brothers-in-arms who had passed away, hence the many said Masses for them. The knightly edifices of the medieval Church were constructed, not alone for worship but for instruction, and that instruction conveyed by visible objects. To the eyes of a medieval person, the churches blazed with Biblical history and were a living language. These churches then, to such, were stories in stone. So John Gerson wrote: "Images are made for us for no other reason than to show to simple folk what they are unable to know from Holy Scripture, and yet what they ought to believe."

The very arrangement of the churches conveyed to the unlearned knight a spiritual lesson. They faced toward the east, since such recalled the birthplace of his Savior. They were generally built on an elevated spot of ground, symbolic of the superiority of divine things over terrestrial. The porch, the choir, and the sanctuary were emblems to him of the way of penitence, of the Christian life, and of the saintly and heavenly beyond. Or, possibly, he had been taught the mystical interpretation of the portions of his church. The door was the earth; the nave, the sea; the sanctuary, heaven; and the great rose window, the air or ether with its rosy light. The figures of angels and archangels represented themselves.

High above the principal door was the figure of God the Father, and over His head, the Dove of the Paraclete, while the Christ on his Cross, the Father held on his knee; below an innumerable number of saints and angels, the latter often playing on musical instruments. Perhaps instead of these august figures over the entrance was carved the scene of the Last Judgment, this latter being extremely frequent in the twelfth century. This was to combat the unbelief of the people who needed a reminder that the words and prophecy pointed to the Last Judgment, rather than that the world would come to an end when the millennium from the birth of Christ had been accomplished.

It was perhaps this teaching power of carved stone, painted glass, soaring pillars, and wondrous doors, in an illiterate age, which made knights and serfs contribute to rear these magnificent cathedrals and churches in France and England, not alone for the glory of God but because they found within their mystic walls, and outside their portals, that education alone in spiritual things they could only learn by the eye conveying it to their souls.

The Hunt

Hunting had a similarity to actual warfare, and shared with the tournament, therefore, an inexpressible fascination for the medieval warriors. From earliest childhood, its orders, its duties, and its delights they had been encouraged to pursue. The wide-spreading forests that then covered Europe, including Britain, the lair of the wolf, the wild boar, and the deer, had an inexpressible fascination for all of noble and knightly birth in the days of medieval society, which we at this distance of time can hardly realize.

This ardor in the hunt — also known as "the chase" — was extreme. In England, William the Conqueror devastated whole villages to form a new forest and whence he was said to love the deer as if he had been their father. Penal laws against depredations in the forests were punishable with loss of limbs and severe fines. In France, Louis XI, when laid up in his last illness in 1483 and unable to hunt, made a mimic hunt in his chamber and ordered an enormous number of rats to be let loose in it, with an equal number of cats, so the pursuit of his favorite pastime might still go on.

By 1189, Henry II of England had restored all the forest laws of his predecessors, which provided that any man found guilty of hunting in the royal forests, without a license, should have his eyes put out and his limbs mutilated. William of Newburgh, a chronicler of the time, said that Henry II punished the killing of a deer as severely as the murder of a man.

Even in books of devotion or religion, terms used in the hunt were employed. An Abbe Michel, living in the reign of Francis I, thus begins his book: "I commence with the Forest of Conscience, which contains the hunt of spiritual princes and pastors," and so, under the form of hunting he portrays the soul contending against the wild beasts which represent the sins and evils of life. "The fear of God, Holy love, confession, penitence, satisfaction, retreats, etc., are the Hounds the Christian is to employ in this spiritual chase."

The hunt was not merely a way for medieval warriors to escape inactivity. It was a passion, often even such a mania that the Church was obliged to condemn it, and this for many reasons. First, because the noble knight, preoccupied with roving the forest, forgot even religious services. Second, because the harshness of the laws which regulated the exercise of the hunt and the forests and game, things sacred and inviolable, became, in many respects, an intolerable scourge to the peasantry and his crops. For one noble who relaxed the forest laws, far more maintained them with untold cruelty and greed.

The fox, the deer, the boar, and the wolf were the chief animals of larger breeds hunted by the medieval warriors in England. By the early twentieth century, the fox was still present, the red deer still left for a time in diminished numbers on Exmoor, but the wild boar and wolf were already extinct. Boars were last reported in Chartley Park, Staffordshire, in 1688. In Edward II's reign, the Peak in Derbyshire is mentioned as infested with them, and so it was down until the reign of Henry VII (1485–1509), when wolves seem to have become very rare, if not extinct, in England.

In the wild hills and glens of the neighboring kingdom of Scotland, they existed much longer, and it is said that the last wolf was killed here by Sir Evan Cameron of Lochiel in 1680. In France, the land preeminently of chivalry and its kindred sport — the hunt — all these beasts were even more numerous than in Britain. In Brittany, the cry of the wolf was often heard at night as late as 1920.

The pursuit of the boar was esteemed by the medieval warriors the noblest in the hunt; minute directions in medieval books are devoted to the subject. The hunt should be at moonlight, so as to give the dogs opportunity to find him, and these dogs should also be chosen young and strong to seize him by the throat. We are told a boar should be attacked on horseback, preferably to on foot — that the spear should be long, broad, and sharp. Attacking him is a greater feat than attacking an armed man, and what joy, an old writer says, to sup afterward off him and to hand round the delicious morsels. At dinner after a hunt, if the king was present and if the quarry had been the wild boar, the hunters presented the delicacy to him and recited the memorable events of the day, particularly anything marvelous, omitting anything in their tale which was not laughable or joyous.

The Dogs

The chief dogs employed by the medieval warriors and nobles in the hunt includes the breed called the lymer (from the old French word *liamen*, a "strap"), because these hounds were held on leashes. They were a heavy smooth-haired black and tan hound, standing about 27 inches high, resembling a blood-hound. The man who held the lymer was called "harborer," and it was his business to go out early in the morning on his ring-walks and to find, by this hound, where a hart or other beast had gone into the wood. He then informed the huntsman.

Another breed of dog was the "braches," mostly black and tan, standing about 17 or 18 inches in height. They were hunted in packs. Sometimes called "ratches," they were dogs that had a sharp scent of the quarry and were much used in hunting the hare.

Then there was the greyhound, also called the "gaze-hound," because it is said "the beams of his sight are so stead-fastly settled." The word *greyhound* seems to have had no connection with the color; by some it is thought to have come from the Celtic *gre* — large or noble. In old illuminations, they are always depicted wearing collars, and, in the old Welsh laws, all greyhounds without their collars lost their privileges. They also were chiefly employed chasing the smaller animals.

Alaunts, or wolfhounds, were another breed that was swift and could hunt by scent alone. In consequence of their ferocity, they were used for bears and boars and were commonly muzzled when not at work. Their best color was white, with black spots about their eyes. The Lord Dacre of Fynnys bore a wolfhound on his standard. In late peerages, Lord Dacre's "supporter" is erroneously stated to be a wolf.

During his imprisonment by the Moslem Arabs (Saracens) in Egypt, France's St. Louis met with a fine breed of dogs said to have come from Tartary. On his release and return to France, he brought some of these dogs with him, and they formed the fine breed of hunting dogs that, until the French Revolution, filled the royal kennels at Saint-Palaye.

The huntsman in the thirteenth and fourteenth centuries kept the hounds and was allowed a halfpenny a day for each dog of all breeds. In the *Book of Courtesy*, written about 1460 to instruct young pages in a knight's household, it is said: "A ha'penny the hunt takes on the day for every hound, the sooth to say two east [handfuls] of bread has the fewterer [keeper] if two leash greyhounds there are, to each a bone that is to tell if I the sooth to you shall spell besides his vantage [profit] that may befall of skins and other things withal. That hunters better can tell than I and therefore I leave it utterly."

Le Livre de la Chace, by Gaston Comte de Foix, and *The Master of Game*, written between the years 1406 and 1413 by Edward II, Duke of York, who fell at the Battle of Agincourt in 1415, were full descriptions of the hounds' kennel. The lodging room was to be 10 fathoms long and 5 broad, with one door in front and one behind into a green court of the same size, facing the sun. It was to be paved and had a fire-place.The bench and room were to be cleaned every day and fresh straw brought in. There was to be a loft over the room to prevent extremes of heat and cold, and a young lad was to live in the lodging room "to prevent quarrels."

Constantly we find in the old manor rolls the obligation of the holder to contribute toward the pleasure of the overlord, by lending his hawks or his hounds. Thus, William Eugaine holds Pightesley and Laxton under William the Conqueror by the sergeantry of hunting wolves, foxes, and other vermin. During the reign of Henry III (1216–1272), Humphrey de Monte held the Manor of Whitfield by sergeantry of providing a *brache* (hound) for the king whenever he should come to the forest of Whittlebury to hunt the hart, hind, buck, or doe.

Falconry

Falconry, one branch of the hunt, was indulged in by both the knights and the wealthy clergy, and an extraordinary importance was attributed to the possession, and the use, of these little birds of prey. They were inseparably connected with the aristocratic and personal privileges of their owner and could not be alienated, even with his consent, to make up the ransom of their master if he had haply been taken prisoner. Persons of plebeian station were not permitted to purchase or to keep them.

They were usually recognized symbols of superiority. For this, kings, bishops, and noble ladies never went abroad without their birds on their fists. Knights even carried them into battle. Prelates deposited them in the chancel while they recited the service of the altar. A bishop of the fourteenth century excommunicated for sacrilege the thieves who stole a falcon from her perch in the cloister of the Abbey of Bermondsey, "the falcon being the bishop's own," and the theft being committed while a service in the church was going on.

While no one under knightly rank was allowed to possess or fly a falcon, there were birds of a different species for each rank. For the priest, there was the sparrow hawk, for a knave (squire) the kestrel, and for a yeoman the goshawk. However, even these sometimes were used by those of knightly rank for the hunt. Sir Thomas carried a goshawk.

Such an etiquette was preserved toward the noblest and lower-estimated birds of all sorts, so that there is a story of Louis IX that, when he was out hawking with one of his birds, a beautiful and strong bird, it dared to attack an eagle. The courtiers praised its valiance, but the king, seeing it had attacked the noblest of birds — the eagle — ordered it to be killed.

The regulations of falconry constituted a science to be mastered only after months of assiduous study. The education of these birds required the exertion of great skill. Each falcon was carried on a glove which could not be used for any other purpose. It bore the arms of the knight or lord and was often embroidered with gold and precious stones.

In many kingdoms, the office of Grand Falconer was one of the highest of distinctions. In France, the emoluments of this dignity were 80,000 francs a year. Even on entering on the long and arduous war between his own country and France, Edward III of England could not do without a hunt with his falcons.

LADIES AND CHESS

The skill of many ladies exceeded that of men in this favorite game. In *Les Echez Armoreux*, there is a lady whose skill is thus described in the poet Lydgate's translation: "And this maid of which I tell had a name and did excel at this noble game. She passed all, nay, was an expert and knew full well at the manner of every detail. There was not fond to reckon all, that was in craft to her equal, for she surmounted everyone."

In the *Clef d'Amors* and other handbooks on the festive science, it was declared no other diversion afforded such opportunities of dalliance and platonic love as chess. So the medieval stories give many examples of the value as a means to bring lovers together, for it was permissible to visit a lady in her chamber, or "bower," to play chess with her.

Thus, in *Raoul de Cambrai*, Beatrix falls in love with the young Bernier, but he is too shy to accept her advances, so she invites him to play chess or tables with her in her chamber in order to give him a chance of declaring himself, which he did, and was rewarded with many proofs of her love. So, too, in the Arthurian romance, Lancelot visited Guinevere in her bower, just as Tristram visited Yseult under the pretense of playing chess.

Indoor Amusements: Chess and Dice

From the tenth to the twelfth century, the chief characteristics of the life of the knight — when not at the tournament or battle — were his isolation, his lack of regular occupation, and the bleak monotony of everyday existence. The traditions of his order cut him off from the companionship of all save the members of his own family. When he was not fighting or hunting, time hung heavily on his hands. He had no daily duties and no daily responsibilities.

If jousts, tournaments, and martial games were the occupations of medieval warriors when not at war, they also, when these were not held, had milder pursuits in their castles and manors. In the enclosures and pits about the latter, they had animals, especially boars and bears, with which they amused themselves by making them fight. If it was warm, they sought the orchard to play at dice, chess, or even a sort of backgammon, often called "tables." Chess, one of the most ancient of games, was in high favor with knights and their ladies — with the former, because its tactics somewhat resembled their own in many a real battlefield. Its popularity among men more distinguished for physical than intellectual powers seems little short of incredible.

The longer winter evenings must have been tedious in the extreme. Dense forests often intervened between a knight and his nearest friend. No wonder the troubadour or juggler, with his budget of song, romance, and tricks, was everywhere warmly welcomed, and that the war game of chess, with its hierarchy of pieces which he brought with him, was eagerly studied. Chess had no great rivals to contend with at the time. It became the favorite indoor game of the knights. From 1100 onward, literary references to its popularity became more and more numerous, and by the middle of the thirteenth century — when the early prejudices of the Church against an invention of "heathenness" (for it was introduced from the Moslem East) had weakened — ignorance of chess was regarded as a social disability. The ballads and stories of the age are full of allusions to what was "the game of kings." Among the knights and ladies, skill in its mimic warfare was looked upon as a sufficient proof of noble descent. From the communities of religious centers of all medieval society as they were, chess reached the wealthy merchants of the towns. It was also essential that the troubadour should be a chess player, and he generally carried a board and men with him wherever he went.

Generally speaking, however, chess was confined to the castles. In the stories, it is mentioned as a matter which no merchant or mechanic could properly understand or appreciate. The fact that a menial knew anything of chess at once aroused suspicion. When Huon of Bordeaux was disguised as the servitor of a traveling minstrel, he found his word doubted when he boasted of his skill at chess. In Gautier de Coincy's *Nouvelles de la Sainte Vierge*, written about the year 1230, there is a story of how the devil, who had disguised himself as a servant, was discovered because he could play chess, and therefore could be no servant.

Still, chess appears to have been played at taverns, for Wycliff attacks the clergy of his time for going to inns to play "tables and chess," until "they had lost their wit."

Dice games were second only to chess as a favorite with the knights. Both dicing schools (*scolaedeciorum*) and dicers' guilds existed. In France, both knights and their ladies were very prone to dicing. Though St. Louis attempted a prohibition of dice games in 1251, he did so vainly.

Some have traced the origin of dice to knucklebones or else to small pebbles played in the old game of "odd and

Above: A Medieval knight, attended by squires, hunting with his falcons.

even." Many of the dice of the Middle Ages were curiously carved in the images of men and beasts.

That the game had a long ancestry is certain. Virgil, in a poem attributed to him, says: "What ho! Bring dice and good wine, who cares for tomorrow?"

Dice were forbidden by councils and the clergy — yet still they played. The tale *Du Prêtre at des Deux Ribauds* tells of a priest who lost his money, and even his horse, while playing dice with two fiddlers whom he chanced to meet on his way. The highwaymen had cheated. The dice was loaded, and it was with no little trouble that the priest kept his horse, but not his money. Adam of Perseigne, a preacher of the period, among other charges against his brother clergy, says, "They play at dice, instead of administering sacraments. Churches instead of being holy places, have become market places and haunts of brigands."

The Crusades

Jacques de Vitoy, Bishop of Ptolemais in the thirteenth century, said: "Jerusalem is the city of cities, the saint of saints, the queen of nations, and the princess of provinces. She is situated in the center of the world, in the middle of the Earth, so that all men may turn their steps to her; she is the patrimony of the patriarchs, the muse of the prophets, the mistress of the apostles, the cradle of our salvation, the home of our Lord and the mother of the faith."

In many ways, the Crusades were the defining moment for the medieval warrior — both the Christian and the Moslem — on every level: military, religious, political, and symbolic. The basic reason that the Crusades took place at all was to preserve Christian access to the Holy City of Jerusalem.

From the time of the triumph of Christianity over the paganism of the Roman world in the fourth century, it had been a custom among the people of Christian Europe to make pilgrimages to Jerusalem for the purpose of expiating a sinful life, praying at the Holy Sepulcher, and exhibiting gratitude for heavenly mercies. As long as Syria and Palestine formed a part of the Byzantine, Greek, or Eastern Roman Empire, access to the Holy City was secured to these pilgrims.

Above: A crusader of the Knights Templars.

After the fall of the Western Roman Empire in A.D. 475, the Eastern Roman Empire continued to control access to Christian holy places in Jerusalem and Bethlehem. In A.D. 610, however, Jerusalem was captured by the Persians, who ruled there until A.D. 630. At the same time, Muhammad had begun to preach his philosophy of spreading Islam by a force of arms, and his followers seized Jerusalem in A.D. 638. By the early eighth century, they had conquered the shores of the Mediterranean, from Spain to Constantinople. They did however continue to tolerate Christian pilgrims who wanted to visit the holy places, and Charlemagne would even form an alliance with the caliph Haroun al-Rashid.

While the Holy Land remained under the dominion of the Moslem Arabs (Saracens), the Christian pilgrim was also unmolested in his journey to and from the Holy Sepulcher. But when the Seljuk Turks, a fierce people from the plains of Tartary, took Jerusalem in 1076, and obtained full possession of the Holy Land in 1094, the native Christians and the pilgrims from Europe were ill-treated, and many of them became martyrs to their religion.

Meanwhile, in 1071, the Eastern Roman emperor Romanus Diogenes declared war on the Turks and lost. This

Above: Godfrey of Bouillon, Duke of Lorraine, leads the victorious crusaders into Jerusalem in July 1099.

led to a collapse of the Eastern Empire and general chaos throughout the Middle East as rival Arab caliphs and Turkish sultans jockeyed for jurisdiction of the remnants.

In 1094, the Seljuk Turks effectively cut off access to the Holy Land by European Christians. In 1095, at the Council of Clermont, Pope Urban II called upon the knights of Christendom — such as those in France, England, and the Germanic states of the Holy Roman Empire — to raise an army that could reclaim the Holy Land.

The first attempt, in 1096, was poorly organized and a disastrous failure. Undaunted, the crusaders returned in 1097, and two years later they recaptured Jerusalem. A kingdom of Jerusalem would be declared in 1099, and the First Crusade was deemed a success.

The kingdom of Jerusalem would endure for 45 years, but in 1144 it was overrun by the Turks. The Second Crusade failed in 1145, as did the Third Crusade in 1189. The Fourth Crusade, from 1200 to 1204, did not succeed in securing Jerusalem, but the French medieval warriors did capture Orthodox Constantinople and establish a Roman Christian kingdom there that survived until 1262.

None of the next four Crusades, which took place between 1212 and 1270, succeeded as the First Crusade had and were, for the most part, utter failures. The most tragic crusade was probably the Children's Crusade of 1212. Only about 200 of the estimated 50,000 children who went to the Holy Land survived to return home.

Depending on one's point of view, the Crusades were either an extraordinary show of valor or an exercise in profound futility. Yet their impact was not totally negative. The historic importance of the Crusades to Europe was not that they represented a series of military defeats but the fact that they brought Europe into contact with the East. Although they failed to permanently liberate Jerusalem from Turkish control, the Crusades did succeed in opening a new world and providing a widened perspective for Europeans. In fact, many believe that the Crusades were the catalyst that ultimately led to the Renaissance.

Pilgrimages

The Crusades would perhaps not have taken place, or, at least, would not have been attempted, had the order of knighthood not existed, or had military saintship not become a fashion. However, they would *certainly* never have taken place, if, long before their era, pilgrimages had not been practiced. The objective of the first of the Crusades was to free the holy places for the use and safety of Christian pilgrims. That land, hallowed by the presence of the divine founder of Christianity, had very early been the object of pilgrimage. Narratives of such have come down to us: one of a Christian of Bordeaux as early as A.D. 338, that of St. Paula and her daughter in about A.D. 586, given by St. Jerome; that of Bishop Arculf in A.D. 700; and of Willebad in A.D. 725.

In Britain, even as early as Saxon times, kings made treaties to secure the safe conduct of their subjects through foreign lands. There was, in the latter part of this Saxon period, a great rage for foreign pilgrimages. Thousands were continually going and coming between England and the principal shrines of Europe, especially the threshold of the Apostles at Rome. They were the subject of a letter from Charlemagne to King Offa, "concerning the strangers, who for the love of God and the salvation of their souls, wish to repair to the thresholds of the Blessed Apostles, let them travel in peace without any trouble."

Even before the Crusades, the pilgrim to the Holy Land had this distinction above all others — that he wore a special sign from the very hour that he took the vow upon him to make that most honorable pilgrimage. This sign was a cross made of two strips of colored cloth sewn on the shoulder of his robe. The English wore the Cross of white, the French of red, and the Flemish of green. Some, in their enthusiasm, had the Cross cut into their flesh.

The First Crusade

In 1094, those who returned to Europe from their pilgrimages gave a melancholy account of the cruelties and oppression suffered by the Christians in Palestine at the hands of the Seljuk Turks, and thus excited the greatest indignation in Christian Europe.

Among others who had been witnesses of the cruelties and oppression suffered by the Christians in Palestine was the zealous and fanatical monk Peter the Hermit, of Amiens, in the French province of Picardy. On his return to Europe from a pilgrimage to the Holy Land, Peter the Hermit resolved to arouse the Christian nations of Europe to a gigantic effort to wrest the Holy Land from the hands of the Moslems. Peter went from town to town, and from castle to castle, preaching of the duty of Christian Europe to expel the barbarian Turks from the Holy City. Wherever he went, numerous crowds assembled to hear him. Very

ABOVE: MOUNTED TURKISH CAVALRY ATTACKS A PHALANX OF CRUSADER INFANTRY. THE BATTLES OF THE CRUSADES WERE INCREDIBLY BLOODY.

soon all France and Italy had been roused to the wildest enthusiasm for an expedition against the Moslem desecrators of the shrine of the Savior.

Pope Urban II, who zealously abetted the design for an expedition for the redemption of the Holy Land, assembled the Council of the Church at Clermont, in southern France. This council was attended by numerous bishops and an immense concourse of people. When the pope, addressing the clergy and the multitude, said, "It is the duty of everyone to deny himself and take up the cross, that he may win Christ," there arose a simultaneous shout, "It is the will of God!" and great numbers demanded to be enlisted in the sacred army. As the symbol of enlistment in the cause of God was a red cross, to be worn on the right shoulder, the expedition was called a Crusade, and those who engaged in it were called crusaders. All who engaged in the enterprise received from the Church the promise of a remission of sins and an eternal heavenly reward after death.

Enthusiasm for the Crusade was so great throughout Christian Europe that many became impatient at what they considered the slowness of the preparations of princes. And, accordingly, in 1096, numerous bands, consisting of thousands of the lowest classes of society, set out for the Holy Land without order or discipline.

They were led by Peter the Hermit and a French knight called Walter the Penniless. They proceeded through Germany and Hungary toward Constantinople, but very few of them ever reached the Middle East. Having attempted to obtain the necessaries of life by forcible means in the countries through which they passed, and having carried robbery and desolation through Bulgaria and stormed Belgrade, the inhabitants of those countries rose against them and destroyed nearly the entire band of crusaders. Peter the Hermit and Walter the Penniless had very few followers when they reached Constantinople, where they waited to join the great army of the First Crusade under Godfrey of Bouillon.

Other disorderly and undisciplined bands, which persecuted and even murdered Jews and others who rejected Christ, followed those of Peter the Hermit and Walter the Penniless. However, they were totally destroyed before they reached Constantinople by the people whom they had robbed and plundered. Nearly 300,000 of the crusaders had already perished when the valiant Godfrey of Bouillon led a powerful and disciplined army toward the Holy Land. This great army of crusaders set off for Palestine in six divisions, which took different routes to Constantinople, where all were united before going south. When the crusaders arrived in Asia their army consisted of an estimated 600,000 men, of whom about 100,000 were cavalrymen.

The crusaders captured Nicaea, in Asia Minor, in 1097, after a siege of two months, and defeated the Turks in the Battle of Dorylaeum. Proceeding in their victorious career, the Christians next laid siege to Antioch. That city was finally taken by the strategy of Prince Bohemond and the treachery of one of the Turks, who left a gate open to the besieging crusaders.

The greatest cruelties were perpetrated upon the unfortunate inhabitants of Antioch by the victorious Christians, after taking the city. A few days after the crusaders had taken Antioch, an army of about 300,000 Turks and Persians appeared before that city.

LEADERS OF THE CRUSADE

The principal leaders of the First Crusade were Godfrey of Bouillon, Duke of Lorraine; Count Hugh of Vermandois, brother of King Philip I of France; Duke Robert the Devil of Normandy, son of William the Conqueror of England; and Count Stephen of Blois, father of King Stephen of England; as well as the chivalrous Count Raymond of Toulouse; Earl Robert of Flanders; and Bohemond, brother of Robert Guiscard, the Norman prince of southern Italy.

ABOVE: CRUSADE LEADERS GODFREY, RAYMOND, AND BOHEMOND.

ABOVE: SALADIN, THE WARRIOR SULTAN OF EGYPT.

ABOVE: BRITAIN'S KING RICHARD I (THE LION-HEARTED) FIGHTS SALADIN IN THE BATTLE OF ARSUF.

The finding of a "holy lance" in the Church of St. Peter raised the courage of the Christians, who sallied out of the city, and, after a desperate battle, totally defeated the Moslems and forced them to a precipitate flight. Onward the crusaders proceeded. When they came in sight of Jerusalem, they shouted and wept for joy, and fell down on their knees, offering their thanks to God. However, their joy was succeeded by rage at beholding the Holy City in the possession of the Moslems. The crusaders therefore laid siege to the city, which they finally took by storm, in July 1099, after a standoff of nearly six months.

The streets of the captured city were soon filled with the bodies of an estimated 70,000 slaughtered Moslems. The conquering Christians believed that they were doing God good service by slaughtering all who rejected the Savior. Both Jews and Moslems were massacred. After this most shocking atrocity, the crusaders proceeded to the hill of Calvary with hymns of praise, and kissed the stone which had covered the body of the Savior and then offered thanks to the God of Peace for the signal success of their undertaking. After the capture of the Holy City, the crusaders established the Christian kingdom of Jerusalem.

Their gallant leader, Godfrey of Bouillon, was made ruler of the new state. He was too pious to assume the title of "King," but called himself "Defender of the Holy Sepulcher," and wore a crown of thorns instead of one of gold.

Godfrey defeated the Sultan of Egypt at Ascalon, in August 1099, but he died the following year and was succeeded at the head of the new state by his heroic brother Baldwin. Some time after the First Crusade, two celebrated orders of knighthood arose in Jerusalem. These were the Knights of St. John, or the Hospitallers, and the Knights Templars, or the Red Cross Knights. Both of these orders became famous for their military exploits against the Moslems.

The Second and Third Crusades

The Christian Kingdom of Jerusalem suffered many attacks from the Moslems, and some of the principal Christian fortresses in Palestine were lost. Under these circumstances, Christian Europe undertook a Second Crusade. The speeches of the pious and eloquent St. Bernard, Abbot of Clairvaux, Burgundy, delivered throughout France and Germany in 1147 paved the way, and powerful expeditions to the Holy Land were led by Conrad III, King of Germany, and Louis VII, King of France.

The army under Conrad marched by way of Constantinople into Asia Minor, where it was decoyed by the treacherous Greek generals into a waterless desert. Here the Turkish cavalry suddenly attacked and thoroughly annihilated the army of German crusaders, only a tenth of whom succeeded in escaping to Constantinople.

The French army, led by King Louis VII, marched along the coast, but a large number perished — from famine, fatigue, and by the swords of the Moslems — before they reached Jerusalem.

The shattered remnants of the immense hosts of French and Germans, led by the two sovereigns, after reaching the Holy Land, engaged in an unsuccessful siege of Damascus. This was the end of the Second Crusade.

The situation of the Christian kingdom of Jerusalem became more and more perilous after the Second Crusade. At length, the valiant Saladin, Sultan of Egypt, reduced a part of Palestine under his scepter. The magnanimous Saladin finally granted the Christians of Palestine a truce. However, when a Christian knight interrupted the passage of Saladin's mother, seized her treasures, and slew her attendants, the exasperated Sultan of Egypt recommenced hostilities, defeated the Christians in the Battle of Tiberias, took Joppa, Sidon, Acre, and other towns, and, in 1187, Jerusalem also fell into the possession of the conquering Sultan.

Saladin, who surpassed his Christian foes in virtue, generosity, and nobleness of heart, treated the inhabitants of the Holy City with mildness, but ordered that the crosses be torn down and the furniture of the Christian churches be destroyed.

Upon the arrival of the news of the capture of Jerusalem by Saladin, great alarm prevailed throughout Western Europe. From the shores of the Mediterranean to the coasts of the Baltic, armed bands set off for the Holy Land.

The three leading sovereigns of Europe — Frederick Barbarossa of Germany, Philip Augustus of France, and Richard I (the Lion-Hearted) of England — led powerful armies against the Moslems in 1189.

The Emperor Frederick Barbarossa with the German army marched by land to Asia Minor, and defeated the Sultan of Iconium in a great battle near the walls of his chief city. However, the noble-hearted German emperor lost his life in a stream which he had attempted to cross. His second son, Frederick, proceeded to Palestine with a segment of the expedition, and took part in the siege of Acre.

Meanwhile, Richard the Lion-Hearted and Philip Augustus, with the English and French armies, after reaching the Holy Land by sea, laid siege to Acre for nearly two years before it finally fell into their hands in 1192. During those two years, nine major battles were fought at the city.

Richard the Lion-Hearted was noted for his energy, ability, and valor, as well as for his pride, severity, and cruelty. On the orders of Richard the Lion-Hearted, the German banner, which Duke Leopold VI of Austria had caused to be erected on the battlements of Acre, was torn down and trampled underfoot by the English. When the Moslems failed to fulfill the stipulations for the payment of a ransom for the captives, about 3,500 of them fell victim to the fiery temper of the English king. Richard's courage made him feared and respected by the Moslems. However, despite his military skill and bravery, his efforts for the recapture of Jerusalem were unavailing.

The King of France was jealous of the superior military ability of the King of England. The two monarchs soon quarreled, and Philip Augustus returned to France. After gaining a great victory over Sultan Saladin near Ascalon and concluding a truce with the Sultan, Richard the Lion-Hearted set out on his return, by sea, to his kingdom in 1192. His vessel, having been driven by a storm to the coast of Italy, Richard proceeded on his way to England, by land, through Germany. However, he was seized and imprisoned in the castle of Trifels, by order of the emperor, Henry VI of Germany, in revenge for the insult to the German flag after the capture of Acre. He obtained the payment of a heavy ransom by the English only upon his release.

The Fourth and "Children's" Crusades

In 1202, the Fourth Crusade was undertaken by French and Italian knights under Count Baldwin of Flanders at the instigation of Pope Innocent III. After assembling at Venice for the purpose of being conveyed to Palestine, the crusaders captured Zara, in Dalmatia, for the Venetians. However, instead of sailing to the Holy Land, they proceeded against Constantinople. The purpose of this deviation was to restore Isaac Angelus (who had been dethroned and imprisoned by his own brother) to the throne of the Byzantine Empire.

Headed by the blind Dandolo, Doge of Venice, the crusaders appeared before Constantinople, took the city, and restored Angelus to the Greek throne. However, when the

French crusaders demanded the rewards which had been promised to them, the inhabitants of Constantinople raised an insurrection in which the Emperor Isaac Angelus and his son Alexius perished.

Thereupon, the French crusaders stormed and took the Byzantine capital, plundered the churches, palaces, and dwellings, destroyed many valuable monuments of art, and filled the city with terror and desolation. After plundering Constantinople, the French crusaders subverted the Byzantine, or Greek, Empire, and established instead a new Roman, or Latin, Empire with Constantinople as its capital, and Count Baldwin of Flanders as its sovereign. This Latin kingdom lasted 56 years, after which it was overthrown, and the old Byzantine dynasty was restored to the throne of Constantinople in the person of Michael Palaeologus.

The Fourth Crusade was without results concerning Jerusalem. However, at times after its conclusion, separate bands of crusaders, lacking chiefs and discipline, made journeys to the Holy Land, and ventured upon the hazardous undertaking of restoring the Christian kingdom of Jerusalem and defending the Latin kingdom of Constantinople.

It was in 1212 that 50,000 children left their homes in Europe on a journey to the Holy Sepulcher that was known as the Children's Crusade. They perished from hunger and fatigue, or they were sold into slavery.

The Fifth Crusade

In 1218, King Andrew II of Hungary began the Fifth Crusade. However, his expedition to Egypt had a disastrous result. In 1228, the excommunicated emperor Frederick II of Germany led an expedition into Palestine at a time when the Sultan of Egypt was at war with the governor of Damascus concerning the possession of Syria and Palestine. The pope forbade all Christian warriors to join the expedition until the Emperor Frederick II should be relieved from command.

Nevertheless, in 1229 Frederick II concluded a treaty with Sultan Malek Kamel of Egypt, by which Jerusalem and the greater part of the Holy Land were surrendered to the Christians. However, the pope excommunicated the Holy City, and Frederick II was crowned at Jerusalem without being consecrated by the Church. The abandoned emperor soon returned to Germany.

In 1243, just 14 years after the Fifth Crusade, the Korasmians, a fierce tribe of barbarians from the plains of

Tartary, overran Palestine, carrying slaughter and desolation wherever they appeared, took Jerusalem, massacred its inhabitants, destroyed the Holy Sepulcher, and wasted the flower of the Christian medieval society in a desperate battle in Gaza. They were finally defeated by the Christian and Turkish armies, which, for the moment, had united against the common enemy.

The Sixth and Seventh Crusades

The horrible deeds of the Korasmians in Palestine led to the Sixth Crusade, which was conducted by the French king Louis IX, or St. Louis, who, in 1250, accompanied by many of his nobles, sailed at the head of a powerful expedition to Egypt. After taking the town of Damietta, the French fleet was destroyed in the Nile by means of an incendiary liquid, similar to modern napalm, but known in the Middle Ages as Greek fire (after Callinicus of Heliopolis, who first used it in A.D. 668).

St. Louis was taken prisoner by the Sultan of Egypt, and obtained his freedom only by the payment of a heavy ransom in 1250. At length the Circassians, who had been held as slaves in Egypt, obtained control of the government of that country. In 1270, France's King Louis IX (later St. Louis) undertook the Seventh Crusade — the last of the great expeditions of the Christians against the Moslems. The French fleet, having been driven by a storm upon the coast of Sardinia, St. Louis resolved to attack the piratical Moors of North Africa. The valiant French monarch landed near Tunis and besieged that city. However, an epidemic soon carried St. Louis and the greater number of his followers to their graves. The surviving French leaders concluded a treaty of peace with the Moors and returned to France.

Prince Edward of England (later King Edward I), who participated in the Seventh Crusade, went to the Holy Land, where he performed many gallant exploits, and struck such terror into the hearts of the Moslem Arabs (Saracens) that they hired an assassin to murder him. Prince Edward wrenched a poisoned dagger from the hand of the assassin. However, in the scuffle the prince received a wound in the arm which might have proved fatal had not his affectionate wife, Eleanor, who had accompanied him to Palestine, sucked the poison from it.

The Moslems gradually recovered their lost power in Palestine. In 1291 a Turkish army of 200,000 men appeared before Acre and, after a vigorous siege, took the city by storm. They held it until 1917.

The remaining Christians voluntarily retired from Syria, which for two centuries had been drenched with the blood of millions of Christian and Moslem warriors.

The Failure of the Crusades

If we examine it, the failure of the Crusades and the relinquishment of that chivalrous quest must be found in the gradual extinction of the spirit that animated the medieval society of the Middle Ages. Its very fervor burned out its strength, and as the years advanced its flame grew less and, at last, vanished altogether.

The trading spirit of the great republics of Venice and Genoa and Pisa, which, accompanying the last crusader, did so for their mercantile betterment, infused into the Christian character of a Crusade the base metal of trade and self-interest.

ABOVE: THE ARRIVAL OF FRANCE'S KING LOUIS IX IN EGYPT.

The distance of Palestine from England, France, and Germany — which formed the recruiting ground of the Crusades — meant that the small Christian principalities and the kingdom of Jerusalem possessed numerous logistical difficulties. So Jerusalem became desolate. After years of travail, after an immense expenditure of life and treasure, after countless tears and prayers, thousands of knightly oaths and deeds, it became possible in the decadent ages of medieval society for a knight no longer to say, "If I forget thee, Oh Jerusalem, let my right hand forget its cunning."

The Military Orders

The Crusades ennobled the knightly class by investing their efforts with a higher aim, and gave rise to the establishment of new orders, which presented a model of chivalry and were presumed to possess all the knightly virtues. Among these new orders were the Knights of St. John of Jerusalem, the Knights Templars, and the Teutonic Knights, which combined the spirit of the knight and the monk, their vows being chastity, poverty, obedience, and war against the Moslems.

The Knights Templars acquired great wealth by donations and legacies. After the loss of their possessions in Palestine, the greater number of them returned to France, where they abandoned themselves to infidelity and corruption, the consequence of which was the final dissolution of their order during the reign of King Philip the Fair (1285–1314), the Grand Master, Jacques de Molay, and many others being burned alive, protesting their innocence to the last. Their wealth in gold went into the coffers of the king, while their fortresses and lands were bestowed on the Knights of St. John of Jerusalem.

The Teutonic Knights were celebrated for their services in the civilization of the countries on the shores of the Baltic Sea. They defended

Above: Knights of St. John of Jerusalem (Hospitallers).

Christianity against the heathen Prussians in the region of the Vistula, and converted the inhabitants of the territory between the Vistula and the Niemen to Christianity, establishing there the German language, customs, and civilization. The cities of Culm, Thorn, Elbing, Konigsburg, and others arose; bishoprics and monasteries sprang up. In the German principalities, industry and civilization produced a complete change.

In nearly every kingdom, when knighthood was no longer hampered and held in leash by feudal chains, these secular orders were created to forge new chains to knit together, in their own interests, groups of free knights. Thus, in France, Germany, Italy, Spain, and England, many royal and individual orders arose. The inspiration for such was found in the religious military orders which the First Crusade called into being.

The oldest order of chivalry, whether religious or secular, was that of the Holy Sepulcher, the parent, or incentive, of all the rest, which owed its rise to certain knights grouping themselves together, out of the rest of medieval society, in defense of the Sepulcher and the pilgrims who visited it.

These secular orders existed, therefore, to enlist in their service, and band together, the free knights of different countries in the interest, and for the benefit of, the secular prince who had lost the benefit, that feudal service had given him, of a constraining power over the swords of the knights. They grew up very rapidly in the states of Christendom, and the more brilliant the ornaments of each order in their chains and collars, the greater attraction the prince found in them to lure the knight to strive under his particular banner. The recipient exchanged the feudal chain for the chain of honor or ornament, but it became no less a chain on his actions.

In France, Germany, and Italy, many more collars were invented. The King of Cyprus gave to those he wished to honor or bind to his service a collar with a sword of silver gilt on it. The King of Scotland gave a silver-gilt collar composed of little rings. The King of the Romans gave one of a serpent coiled round — out of whose mouth appeared a cross floree, all worn by those who displayed fealty to the giver, and all militating against the newer and freer knighthood which had recently liberated itself from the chains of feudalism.

However, sometimes it is generous to say that these collars were given as a mark of fraternity, that beautiful virtue which medieval society had nursed and cultivated.

Those sworn to fraternity usually wore the same clothes and arms, mingled their blood in one vessel, received the Holy Sacrament, and kissed the pyx together. They engaged to support each other in all quarrels. Such brotherhood of fraternity in arms overrode all duties, even to ladies, except those owed to the sovereign.

ABOVE: CRUSADERS AND THEIR PRIESTS ON THE MARCH TO JERUSALEM.

The Results of the Crusades

It is highly unlikely that the medieval warriors realized the full extent of the dangers which awaited them. So much ignorance prevailed of geography, and even of the quality and bravery of the foes they would meet. Certainly, the hordes of camp followers, women, and lesser soldiery failed to do so. As early as the end of the Third Crusade no less than a half-million warriors, the flower of knighthood, from Germany, France and Britain, it has been computed, perished, and if we take into consideration the scarcity of population then, in these countries, compared with the present time, it is possible perhaps to realize how much of manhood and chivalry these three Crusades had destroyed and eaten up.

The nobles ceased to wage their perpetual private quarrels, knighthood became emancipated from feudal chains and assumed a regular and solemn character, ordeals by arms decreased, religious orders multiplied, and charitable institutions, first formed for the pilgrims and crusaders, were established on every side. Men's minds became more enlightened, and their manners softened by becoming more cosmopolitan, with a wider knowledge of other lands and people than their own. A new literature sprang forth all at once from the imagination, of troubadours, minstrels, and minnesingers. Meanwhile, the art and technology of war changed, and great strides were made in commerce and navigation.

Partly through contact with the people of the Byzantine Empire, and partly

ABOVE: LADIES OF ST. JOHN OF JERUSALEM (HOSPITALLERS).

ABOVE: RICHARD THE LION-HEARTED SURVEYS THE AFTERMATH OF BATTLE.

After the reconquest of the Holy Land by the Turks, the Knights of St. John established themselves on the island of Rhodes, which was finally wrested from them by the Ottoman Turks. In 1522, they received the island of Malta from the celebrated Charles V, Emperor of Germany and King of Spain.

The Crusades gave rise to a free peasantry and tended to break up the feudal system, as by their means great numbers of serfs received their freedom, and extended the power and influence of the burgher class and of the towns. The rich barons were compelled to sell their possessions for the purpose of raising money to equip troops and to transport them to the Holy Land.

The Crusades promoted the diffusion of knowledge and the advancement of science and literature. Those who engaged in the wars were at first deplorably ignorant and illiterate. However, when they came into contact with the Greek and Arabian civilizations, they acquired a fondness for science and literature. After returning to Europe, they imparted the same spirit to their countrymen.

The Crusades gave great encouragement to commerce, as by their means different countries were brought into communication and more intimate commercial relations with one an other. The advantage of a mutual exchange of products was soon perceived. In consequence, great progress was made in the arts of navigation and shipbuilding. Many flourishing cities, such as Venice, Pisa, and Genoa, acquired immense wealth and attained vast commercial importance. In 1271, the great Venetian traveler Marco Polo went to the Middle East and continued east to China and the Far East.

The Crusades effected a complete revolution in the manners and customs of the European nations, such as the suppression of servitude, the founding of free towns, the alienation and division of the feudal lands, and development of the communal system. These were the immediate consequences of the tremendous emigration of men who went forth to fight and die in the Holy Land.

because of conflict with the Moslems, the Europeans learned new methods building and of attacking fortifications. The concentric castle, with its rings of walls, began to displace the old keep and bailey with a single wall.

The Crusades, on the whole, helped to exalt the prestige of France, until, at the end of the thirteenth century, that kingdom stood as the most powerful — politically and militarily — in Europe, and those connections can still be traced today. The Crusades were also the means of providing for younger sons of the feudal nobility, and, as such, they resulted in a number of colonies, such as the kingdom of Jerusalem, the kingdom of Cyprus, and the Latin Empire of Constantinople.

ABOVE: IN A CLASH OF MEDIEVAL WARRIORS, CRUSADERS FIGHT TURKS IN THE BLOODY BATTLE OF DORYLAEUM.

Epilogue:
The Decline of Medieval Society

 HIVALRY BEGAN TO DAWN at the end of the tenth century. It blazed forth with high vigor during the Crusades, which indeed may be considered as exploits of national knight-errantry on the same principles which actuated the conduct of individual knights-adventurers. But its most brilliant period, though its decline set in rapidly from that period, was during the wars between France and England. It was then that the constant and honorable opposition, not embittered by rancor or personal hatred, gave the fairest opportunity for the exercise of the courtesies required of him whom Chaucer calls "a very perfect knight."

This standard of knightly elegance and courtesy intensified in proportion to the decay of its real powers. In the same way that the civilization and luxury imported into the monastic establishments bestowed a greater pomp and stateliness upon them, but also gradually paved the way for their final dissolution. Yet at this period few could perceive chivalry's coming decline.

A chivalrous king like Edward III gave fresh laurels to its past wreaths. The Battle of Courtrai was fought, and *Amadis of Gaul* written at this time, and the Black Prince embodied the old courtesies of his

Above: Sixteenth century German soldiers.

order, when he waited, after the Battle of Poitiers, upon his captive and overlord, John of France.

The outward courtesies of war were more closely observed. Few knights or those of gentle blood were slain deliberately in a battle. Such encounters were now looked upon as lucrative expeditions where ransoms could fill the pockets of the captors. Defensive armor had been perfected, so this desire could easily be satisfied, for once a horse threw his rider, he lay helpless to rise until assisted to do so by his victor. This commercial value of a noble prisoner more and more penetrated the army of opposing knights. Froissart uses the phrase "many rich prisoners" in describing the after-result of one of these battles. It was now that the self-denial and self-restraint of the medieval knight also became forgotten in the extravagant banquets that followed every tournament and courtly function. The fruits and dainties brought by his crusading fathers from the East all helped to stimulate gluttony. The practice of gambling with dice and other games of chance, despite the Church's warning, became more widespread. While all medieval society outwardly looked prosperous, there was a canker at its roots.

The Crusades over, nothing but idle trifling and licentious

ABOVE: TROUBADOURS SING OF PAST GLORIES AND LOST WARRIORS.

assignations diversified by the hunt or a tournament was left to satisfy the want which the Crusades had supplied to the knights. Religion, too, became less and less the pursuit of chivalry. It was in her churches that her sons had received the accolade. It was for her, and the fatherless, and the widowed, that they had sworn to do battle. Yet with the Crusades over, a coldness to religion swept over Europe, and the very vows in her name the knight now took in this time of decline, he either forgot or willfully neglected.

Eustache Deschamps, calling to mind the good old days and seeing the evil around him, thus wrote: "Knights of the medieval days and their children went to Mass in the fear of God, each subsisted on his own [property] their worth and prowess they realized — and the lower classes led the simple life, everyone was content with his station in life, and religion was placed of all things first but nowadays one sees vice only rule.

"The young lads have become ruffians, players at dice, gluttons, inebriates, proud of heart and fired with no spark of honor, goodness or gentle breeding. There is nothing except lying, pride, and laziness. Everyone does as he likes. The time has gone by for virtue and high-mindedness, but nowadays one sees only vice rule. For a brief while these things last. Chivalry ceases because its virtues can offer only a frail resistance; work fails; religion is wounded. And valiancy dissolves itself into robbery, so it comes to pass all honor perishes. The world also, unless God should redress it all. But today one sees nothing but vice rule."

Appeals to arms by two knights falling out, when they took place, were no longer fought in the lists, or in the presence of the marshals of the field, but in lonely and sequestered places. Inequality of arms was no longer regarded, however great the superiority of one side might be. "Thou hast both a sword and dagger," said Quelus to Antregust as they were about to fight, "and I have only a sword."

The answer was, "The more thy folly to leave thy dagger. We came to fight not to adjust weapons." The combat went forward and, indeed, Quelus was slain.

Above: Sixteenth century soldiers with guns.

The Evolution of Late-Medieval Armies

If there were moral reasons for chivalry's weakening influence owing to the decline of that high standard attained by the medieval knights, this decay must be attributed also to outside changes then developing.

The first of these was the rapid change in the constitution of the medieval armies. Foot soldiers at that time, nearly exclusively archers, were supplanting the mailed knight after the Battle of Poitiers, where the greater part of the French chevaliers were slain and routed by the English bowmen — and so, too, by the use of the crossbowmen at the Battle of Bouvines.

It began to dawn more and more, and at first much against the aspirations of medieval society, that cavalry charges stood little chance against a strong phalanx of foot soldiers. It is true, that often the medieval warrior, both in a tournament and in a battle, would fight on foot. However, his own peculiar place was on horseback, making impetuous charges. By the fifteenth century, the now better armed, better trained, and disciplined foot soldiers began to prove their superiority in the actual battles.

Though the longbow continued, after proving its usefulness, long to be the favorite weapon as far as the English armies were concerned, field pieces gradually became more perfect and more decisive in the fate of battles — owing to successive improvements in them.

Not only did the use of such begin to take the place of the impetuous charges of the knights, or their antiquated measures to reduce a walled town, but they affected the mail of the knight himself. It was found that however much heavy armor might be efficient against lances, swords, and arrows, it afforded little protection against cannons. The armor of the knight was gradually curtailed to a light headpiece, a cuirass, and the usual defenses of the men-at-arms.

In France, the young nobility especially became weary of the unwieldy steel in which their knightly ancestors sheathed themselves, and adopted the light armor of the German Reiters, or mercenary cavalry. They also discontinued the use of the lance, since these light-armed cavaliers no longer carried the weapons or practiced the exercises of knighthood.

French Standing Armies

In France, perhaps the greatest factor in the decay of chivalry arose from the institution of bands of *gens d'armes* (gendarmes), or men-at-arms, constituted expressly as a sort of standing army, to supply the place of bannerets, knights-bachelors and squires, and other militia of early times. It was in 1445 that Charles VII selected from the numerous chivalry of France 15 companies of men-at-arms called *Les Compagnies d'ordonnance,* which were to remain perpetually on the payroll to enable the king to dispense with the medieval model.

He saw the forces of chivalry, which, arriving and departing from the host — after serving 40 days, often collecting their subsistence by ravaging the country and engaging in frequent brawls with each other — rather weakened than aided the cause they were professed to support.

The regulated companies, which were substituted for these desultory feudal levies, were of a more permanent and manageable description. Each company contained about 100 men-at-arms, and each man-at-arms was to be what was identified as a *lance garnie;* that is, a mounted spearman with his proper attendants, four archers, and a page called a *coustillier,* from the knife or dagger with which he was armed. Thus, each company consisted of nearly 600 horses and a vast number of cavalrymen.

The charge of national defense was thus transferred from the cavalrymen of France, whose bold and desperate valor was sometimes rendered useless by their independent willfulness.

At first the officers and often the men were of noble birth, and no doubt some of the knights-bannerets headed them, and the officers were men of the highest rank, while the archers and even the pages were often of honorable birth. However, during the reign of Charles IX (1560–1574), there was a further change. The king was content to seek men whatever their rank, if they were possessed of personal bravery and strength — and were adept in the use of weapons.

The old knights and nobles complained that valets and lackeys were recruited in companies which were put on the same footing as the old men-at-arms, who had been of gentle birth. These complaints — coupled with the charge against Catherine de' Medici that she had, by the creation of 25 new members of the Order of St. Michael, rendered its honors as common as the cockleshells on the seashore — stated that the attempt to establish a standing army operated to the subversion of all the ideas and privileges of knighthood.

In England, knighthood's titles remained, and remain to the present day — but as decorations carrying with them little of the old knights' characteristic services in arms. Nevertheless, the spirit of chivalry would live on in England, even through the great wars of the twentieth century.

Nostalgia for the Old Days

The medieval warriors had laid aside, at the same time, the habits and sentiments peculiar to the old order. As early as 1448, we find complaints made at the Court of France, to Charles VII, of the discontinuance of tournaments. Instead of jousting, the knights diced, followed the hunt, or danced.

So much had a discontinuance in such taken place in the few years between the reign of Charles VII (1422–1461) and that of Henri II (1547–1559), who had been mortally wounded at a tournament by Montmorency, that when the Queen Mother was prevailed upon to allow the lists to be set up for a tournament, it was with difficulty that anyone present knew, or was adept in, the medieval rules for such.

Later still, in 1589, the then Archbishop of Bourges made a speech at the Assembly of the States, pleading as a remedy for the grievances that were affecting the country, for a revival of chivalry such as it was under Francis I "and composed of the nobility."

But the times had passed, for the prelate's impassioned appeal to bear any of the medieval spirit. The watch-fires of chivalry, which had burned so brightly in martial Europe and the Crusades, had left behind only dead or dying embers.

Above: Seventeenth-century armor.

Index

Aachen 23
Abbe Michel 136
Adrian I 12
Advent 11, 16
Africa 78, 81, 149
Agincourt 26-27, 90-91, 128, 137
Aigues-Mortes 18
Ailettes 69
Aix-la-Chapelle 23
Alaric 86
Albert IV 44
Albert of Goritz 47
Albigenses 61
Albigeois 95, 97
Albofledis 11
Alemanni 11
Alexander II of Scotland 72
Alexius 148
Alfonso 123
Alfred 64, 122
Alianora 31
Alice of Lethegrew 32
Alphonso X 10
Alps 19, 26-27
Alsace 69
Amadis of Gaul 154
Amauri 47-48
Amiens 18, 142
Amiloun 38
Andre of Laval 44
Andrew II of Hungary 148
Angelus, Isaac 148
Anglo-Saxons 21, 85, 88, 122
Anjou 40, 42, 45-46, 69, 111, 128
Anne of Brittany 127-128
Anne of Caux 32
Antioch 44, 111, 144
Antoine 45
Anturs of Arthur 83
Apulia 100
Aquilea 47
Aquitaine 32, 126, 133
Arabia 10, 15, 52, 78, 86, 88, 111, 125, 137, 140, 142, 149
Aragon 78, 132
Archers 27, 30, 40, 73-74, 76, 89-90, 94-95, 156-157
Arles 15, 18, 86
Armand of Cervoles 90
Armor 7, 10, 23, 35, 37, 39-40, 43, 47, 50-52, 55-56, 63-83, 86, 104, 106, 108, 110-111, 116-117, 126, 128-129, 133-134, 154, 156-157
Arnoul 46
Arras 134
Arsen 51
Arsuf 146
Arthur 12, 30, 47, 49, 51, 55, 64, 67, 83, 110
Arthur of Cornwall 51
Ascalon 147-148
Ashdown 72
Asia 87, 144, 147
Asinelli, Albert Degli 40
Assyrians 70, 77, 83
Athelstan 64, 122
Attila 87-88
Augsburg 23
Auray 90
Auxerre 47
Avignon 86
Axes 7, 64, 69, 72, 76-78, 93, 105
Baier, Ulrich 60
Baldwin 46, 113, 147-148
Baldwin II 46
Baldwin of Flanders 148
Baltic Sea 147, 150
Banners 7, 20, 30, 36, 39, 45, 63, 73-74, 87, 93-94,

102, 105, 112, 148, 150
Bannockburn 111
Barbarossa 41, 147
Barbour 77
Barcelona 97
Bathing 134
Bavaria 23
Bayard 64, 67, 82, 117
Bayeux Tapestry 64, 67, 73, 130
Beatrix 138
Beaucaire 133
Beaulieu 78
Beauvais 18
Becket 33
Bede 62
Belgrade 91, 144
Bénéton of Peyrins 81
Beowulf 118
Berengar 13
Bermondsey 138
Bernard of Cahuzac 22
Bernard of Naisil 113
Bernier 138
Bertram 17, 133
Bertrand 90
Bethlehem 140
Biblical 135
Bishop Arculf 142
Black Death 120
Black Monks of Sarlat 22
Black Prince 61, 63, 93, 154
Blanceflor 81
Blanche 26, 44, 61
Blois 32, 45, 90, 93, 117, 144
Boars 136-138
Bohemia 46, 87, 134
Bohemond 144
Bohun 31, 111
Bolingbroke 113
Bologna 24, 40
Bonn 23
Bordeaux 18, 33, 52, 77, 139, 142
Boucicaut 37, 109
Bourges 18, 157
Bouvines 19, 156
Brabant 49, 55, 134
Brandenburg 111
Bremen 23
Brescia 24
Breton 31, 98, 111, 129
Britain 8, 12, 55, 85, 112, 121, 136, 142, 146, 151
Brittany 78, 105, 108, 111, 117, 127-128, 136
Bruce, Robert 111
Brugeois 77
Brugge 20
Bulgaria 88, 144
Bureau, Jean 92
Burgos 97, 124
Burgundy 11, 25, 27, 31, 35, 51, 55, 83, 88, 90, 112, 128-129, 147
Burial rituals 62
Byzantine 12, 88, 140, 148, 151
Caesar, Julius 84
Cahors 18
Calabria 100, 132
Calais 109
Calatrava 128
Calendar of Investiture 42
Callinicus of Heliopolis 149
Calvary 147 (see Horses)
Cambrai 18-19, 138
Camelot 12
Cameron, Evan of Lochiel 136
Candlemas 130
Canons 24, 91, 135
Canterbury 21, 63
Canute 111
Caravalla 60
Carcassonne 18, 86

Carolingian 16, 24, 62, 122
Carriages 83
Carver 39
Cassel 26, 63, 90
Castelnaudary 47
Castile 10, 26, 78, 124, 128
Castle 7, 17, 32-33, 35-37, 40, 44, 49, 51, 53, 73, 83, 94, 102, 104, 111, 121, 128, 133-135, 142, 148, 152
Catherine de 'Medici 157
Caucasus 84
Cecile 44
Celtic culture 8, 11, 45, 50, 137
Chace 136-137
Châlons 91, 113
Châlons-sur-Marne 88
Chamberlain 37, 39
Champagne 28, 88, 134
Chandos 93-94
Chanson de Geste 62
Chansons 30, 128
Chapeau Rouge 18
Charlemagne 6, 12-13, 15, 30, 52, 87, 98, 116, 120, 122, 140, 142
Charles 12, 15, 25, 31, 37, 40, 42, 44, 60, 62, 76, 86, 90, 92-94, 98, 105, 108, 111, 118, 124, 132, 152, 157
Charles II of France 124
Charles IX 157
Charles of Blois 90
Charles of Valois 40
Charles V 31, 60, 62, 92-93, 111, 152
Charles V 60, 152
Charles VI 37, 90, 111
Charles VII 90, 94, 108, 132, 157
Charles VIII 76, 92
Charles, Philarete 118
Chartley Park 136
Chartres 94, 102
Chatelaines 53
Chaucer, Geoffrey 50, 83, 154
Cherbourg 111
Chess 32, 138-139
Childeric 11
Children 11-12, 31-33, 35, 40, 50-51, 61, 78, 129-130, 142, 148, 156
China 152
Chivalry 6-8, 10, 27, 30-33, 35-36, 38-39, 42, 45-46, 48, 50-53, 55, 60, 64, 74, 93, 98, 102, 104-106, 108, 111, 115-125, 128-129, 135-136, 150-151, 154, 156-157
Chlodowech (Chlodwig) 11
Christianity 6, 8, 10-13, 31-32, 42, 46-48, 51-52, 55-56, 60, 62-63, 86, 88-89, 106, 111, 118, 120-121, 124, 135-136, 140, 142, 144, 147-150
Christmas 11-12, 42, 132-133
Church Militant 121
Church of St. Peter 147
Cimbrians 84
Circassians 149
Citeaux 61
Clef 138
Clercs 117
Clermont 77, 142, 144
Clotilda 11
Clovis 8-9, 11-12, 32, 86
Cluny 132
Coblenz 23
Cockerel 111
Coffins 65
Colchester Castle 135
Coleyne 67

Coligny 93
Cologne 11, 23, 67
Conrad 24, 26, 147
Conrad III 147
Conrad of Hohenstaufen 24
Constable 31, 44
Constance 26, 132
Constantinople 47, 140, 142, 144, 147-148, 152
Cornish Well 111
Council of Salisbury 31
Council of Trent 31
Countess Matilda 24, 26
Countess of Die 128
Countess of Savoy 19
Courtrai 23, 72, 154
Courts of Love 126
Covenans Vivien 44
Coventry 113
Crécy 26, 73-74, 77, 90
Crossbow 73-74, 83, 93
Crown of Thorns 60, 147
Crucifixion 10, 48
Crusades 6-7, 22, 26, 31, 47, 52, 61-62, 67, 72-74, 88-89, 91-92, 105, 118, 123-125, 128, 140-153, 156-157
Culm 150
Cyprus 133, 150, 152
Czech Republic 13
Dacre of Fynnys 137
Dalmatia 148
Damascus 77, 147-148
Damietta 149, 159
Damsels 30, 102, 128-130
Dandolo 148
Danes 15, 32, 55, 83
Dano-Anglo-Saxon 118
Danos 32
Dante 120
Dauphin Louis 72
Day of Magdalene 113
Denmark 12, 128
Denys 32
Derbyshire 136
Deschamps, Eustache 35, 52, 77, 113, 156
Desiderius 12
Devil of Normandy 144
Dice 138-139, 154, 156
Dictionaire de Ménage 81
Doge of Venice 148
Dogs 33, 97, 136-137
Don Ignatio 10
Doon 35
Dorylaeum 144, 153
Dove 136
Draft horses 83
Dragon 56
Droon 51
Du Champ of Bataille 39
Du Guesclin 44
Du Gueslin 39
Duchess Parise 31
Duchy of Spoleto 24
Duels 35, 51, 115-117, 121
Duke of Alba 92
Duke of Aquitaine 133
Duke of Austria 44
Duke of Bourbon 60, 108
Duke of Brabant 134
Duke of Brittany 108
Duke of Burgundy 25, 27, 35, 90, 128
Duke of Calabria 132
Duke of Exeter 134
Duke of Lorraine 141, 144
Duke of Nevers 35
Duke of Normandy 88
Duke of York 137
Duke Pierre 44
Duke Robert 144
Dukes of Swabia 23
Dun, William 32
Dunois 40

Durandus 62
Dürer, Albrecht 59
Earl of Essex 42, 62
Earl of Exeter 134
Earl of Gloucester 78
Earl of Huntingdon 109-110
Earl of Northumberland 134-135
Earl of Suffolk 44
Earl of Warwick 112
Earl Richard 112
Easter 42, 82, 97
Eastern Empire 142
Eastern Goths 88
Eastern Roman Empire 12, 140
Ecclesiastical knighting 47
Ector 55
Eddas 118
Edward 31-32, 55, 61, 64, 73-74, 77, 82-83, 98, 111-113, 123, 132-133, 136-138, 149, 154
Edward I 31, 64, 73-74, 82, 112-113, 133, 149
Edward II 31-32, 83, 98, 136-137
Edward III 32, 74, 77, 82-83, 111, 138, 154
Edward IV 32, 132
Egerton Collection 112
Egypt 62, 137, 145, 147-149
Elbing 150
Eleanor 126, 149
Eleanor of Aquitaine 126
Eleanora of Guzman 128
Elizabeth 32, 109, 134
Elizabeth of France 109
Enfance Vivien 33
England 6, 13, 16, 21-24, 26-28, 30-32, 35, 42, 44-45, 47-49, 56, 58, 61-64, 70, 72-74, 76, 78-79, 81, 83, 88-94, 98, 100, 102, 105, 109, 110-112, 117, 122-123, 128, 132-133, 135-136, 138, 142, 144, 147-150, 154, 156-157
Enlistment 90, 92, 144
Equestrian 55, 72, 120
Ernest of Austria 44
Espaphus 77
Espringales 77, 97
Esquires 30, 35-40, 42, 45-46, 50, 78, 130
Este Lord of Modena 44
Ethelwulf 64
Eugaine, William 137
Evangels 52
Excalibur 64
Exmoor 136
Falaise 28
Falconry 30, 33, 137-138
Favelle 82
Feast of Pentecost 45
Feast of St. John 42, 47
Ferdinand 60
Ferrand 82
Ferrante of Naples 132
Festivals 16, 42, 47, 102, 105, 108, 113, 115, 125, 135
Feudalism 6, 8, 10, 11, 13-24, 26-27, 47, 74, 77, 86-93, 108, 117, 120-125, 130, 134, 150-152, 157
First Crusade 22, 47, 52, 105, 124-125, 142, 144, 147, 150
Fitz-Richard, Geoffrey 78
Fitzosbert 83
Flanders and the Flemish 19-21, 23, 27, 69, 77, 89, 92, 112-113, 128, 142,

144, 148
Florence 19, 77, 91
Florine 128-129
Foix 133-134
Foucaud 22
Forest Charter 26
Forest of Conscience 136
Forms of Investiture 46, 48
Fornoue 76
France 6, 8, 10, 12-13, 15-24, 26-28, 30-33, 35, 37, 42, 44, 49-50, 53, 55-56, 58, 60-64, 67, 70, 72, 74, 76, 78, 82-83, 87, 89-90, 92-94, 98-99, 102, 105, 107, 109-110, 112, 113, 115, 117-118, 123-124, 126, 128, 129, 132, 134, 136-139, 142, 144, 147-152, 154, 156-157
Francis Bentivogli 40
Francis I 74, 76, 92, 108, 111, 136, 157
Franconia 23-24
Frankfurt-on-Main 23
Franks 8-9, 11-12, 18, 21, 86-88, 92, 133
Frederic 124
Frederick 10, 26, 41, 147-148
Frederick Barbarossa 41, 147
Frederick II 26, 148
Friedrich of Brandenburg 44
Friuli 47
Froissart 27, 40, 74, 111, 120, 133-134, 154
Fromondin 113
Fromont 31
Fulk 42, 44, 51
Funerals 61
Fuseaulx 77
Gages of Bataille 116
Gallo-Romanic 11
Gambling 154
Garin 102, 134
Gascony 56, 78
Gaston 60, 134, 137
Gauerbinate 27
Gauerbschaften 27
Gaul 8, 11, 17, 84, 86, 88, 154
Gautier of Coincy 139
Gaza 149
Genoa 19, 149, 152
Gent 20, 77
Geoffrey 32, 40, 42, 45-46, 69, 78, 98, 105, 111, 133
Geoffrey of Anjou 40, 69, 111
Geoffrey of Preuilli 98
Geoffrey of Scotland 32
Gerald 17
Gerard of Nevers 121
Gerard of Saint-Amand 15
Germany 6, 8, 11-13, 15-16, 18, 20, 23-24, 27, 34-35, 43, 51, 56, 64-65, 67, 76, 84, 87, 89, 98, 100, 105, 108, 117, 122, 129, 142, 144, 147-148, 150-152, 154, 156
Gerson, John 135
Gervais 44
Gherardacci 40
Ghibellines 26
Gilbert of Mons 102
Gilbert of Nogent 20-21
Girart 44, 51, 128
Giraud 23
Gisors 83
Godfrey of Bouillon 33, 52, 141, 144, 147
Golgotha 44
Gondebaud 11, 86
Gonzalvez of Cordoba 92
Goths 10, 84, 86-88
Graelent 82
Grand falconer 138

Grand Master 92, 150
Greece 13, 78, 87, 92, 140, 147-149, 152
Gregory of Tours 11
Gros 30, 58
Guelphs 26
Guesclin 31, 44, 90
Guillaume 78, 102, 133
Guinevere 47, 138
Guiscard, Robert 100, 144
Guisnes 46
Haddon Hall 135
Hainaut 19, 49, 133
Hamburg 23
Hanseatic 23, 27, 64
Hardouin 39, 45
Harold 88, 111
Haroun 140
Hastings 73
Hawise 32
Hawkwood, John 90
Helen of Winchester 32
Helmets 63, 67, 69, 90, 93-94, 108, 110, 121
Hemericourt 129
Hennolu-Bertin 17
Henri II 113, 157
Henri II of France 113
Henri IV 108
Henry 13, 20-21, 26-27, 32, 40, 42, 45-47, 58, 60-61, 73-74, 76, 83, 92, 109, 112, 117, 123, 133-134, 136-137, 148
Henry I 13, 21, 83
Henry II 21, 83, 92, 109, 112, 133, 136
Henry III 32, 58, 73-74, 134, 137
Henry IV 32, 92, 117
Henry V 20, 83
Henry VI 26, 148
Henry VII 61, 136
Henry VIII 27, 76
Herbert of Mesnil 78
Herulians 88
Hervis of Metz 44
Hesse 87
Hirschau 132
Hohenstaufen 23-24
Holland, Sir John 109-110
Holy City 42, 47, 123, 140, 142, 147-148
Holy Grail 125
Holy Land 47, 58, 62, 105, 113, 140, 142, 144, 147-149, 152
Holy orders 53
Holy Roman Empire 12-13, 24, 41, 142
Holy Sepulcher 42, 44-45, 140, 147-150
Honoré of St. Marie 129
Horse armor 75, 80, 83
Horses 7, 15, 33, 37-40, 44, 48-51, 55-56, 62, 73-74, 76, 78-83, 90, 97, 103-104, 107, 109-110, 112-114, 118, 120-122, 128, 133, 139, 154, 157
Hospital 52, 89
Hospitallers 147, 150-151
Hounds 31, 135-137
Hugh of Vermandois 144
Hugo of Bordeaux 52
Hugues 48
Humphrey of Monte 137
Hungary 15, 32, 120, 144, 148
Huns 87-88
Hunting 33, 35, 129, 135-138, 156-157
Huon of Bordeaux 33, 139
Iberians 10, 84
Ignatius 10
Igtham Moat 135

Index

Infantry arms 76
Infidels 33, 47, 60
Innocent II 24, 74, 91
Ireland 8, 21, 27, 32
Ironside, Edmund 111
Isaac Angelus 148
Islam 12, 86, 140
Italy 6, 8, 12-13, 19-20, 24, 26-27, 29, 35, 46, 54, 56, 67-68, 75-76, 84, 86, 88-89, 90-92, 100, 114, 128-129, 132, 144, 148, 150
Jacquelin of Maille 45
Jacques of Molay 150
Jaille 39
Jean 27, 40, 55, 92
Jean of Pepoli 40
Jeanne of Laval 44
Jerusalem 47, 111, 123, 128, 140-142, 147-152
Jesuits 10
Jews 144, 147
Joan 19, 44, 61, 90, 128
Joan of Arc 128
John II of France 55
John of Charvans 45
John of France 35, 55, 154
John of Montford 90
John of Salisbury 122
John X 91
Joinville 72
Joppa 147
Joseph of Arimathea 49
Josselin 111
Jousts 39-40, 52, 92, 98-100, 105, 109-113, 117, 125, 138
Julian 32
Julien 91
Julius II 91
Juste of Saint-Inglebert 109
Justinian 12
Kenilworth 111
Kent 135
Kirkstead Chapel 69
Knights and knighthood 6-7, 10-11, 21-23, 28-63, 65, 67, 70, 72, 74, 76, 78-79, 81-83, 88, 90, 93-94, 98, 102-108, 110-114, 116-118, 120-123, 125-126, 128-130, 132-139, 142, 144, 147, 150-151, 154, 156-157
Knights of St. John 147, 150, 152
Knights Templars 89, 140, 147, 150
Koln 23
Konigsburg 150
Korasmians 148-149
Lackland, John 21, 26
Lagny 112
Lagny-sur-Marne 112
Laissez-les 116
Lake Constance 132
Lambert 46
Lambeth 61
Lancelot 47, 55, 125, 138
Lances 35, 39-40, 48, 50-51, 64, 76-77, 90, 92-93, 98, 100, 104-106, 108-113, 147, 156-157
Laon 16, 18
Largesse 49, 52-53, 106, 108, 132-133
Last Judgment 136
Launge, John 31
Laura 128
Lauretta of Sade 128
Law of Arms 50
Laxton 137
Le Livre 137
Le Mans 17
Le Taverne 18

Leber 50
Leisure 108, 130
Lent 16, 113
Leo IX 91
Leopold VI of Austria 148
Leparito, James 44
Les Compagnies 157
Les Echez Armoreux 138
Lever 94
Levite 10
Liege 20
Lincolnshire 69
Little Saintry 53
Liturgy 53
Livery 56, 78, 103, 130, 133
Loherains 31
Loire 11, 86
Lombardy 19, 23, 56, 86-87
London 21-22, 61, 83, 112
Lord Scales 83
Lorenzetti 46
Lorraine 102, 134, 141, 144
Lothair 24
Lothair II 24
Lotharingian 23
Louis 10, 12, 19, 22, 26-27, 44, 58, 67, 72, 74, 76, 89-90, 92, 98, 108, 111, 117, 134, 136-139, 147, 149, 159
Louis IX 26, 74, 138, 149, 159
Louis V 26
Louis VII 19, 111, 147
Louis XI 27, 74, 90, 108, 136
Louis XII 76, 92
Louis XIII 92, 117
Louis XIV 108, 134
Louvre 16, 19
Loyola 10
Lubeck 23
Luke of Tourayne 133
Lyard 82
Lydgate 138
Lymer 137
Lyons 18
Macagrano 40
Madame 56
Magdalene 113, 115
Magdeburg 23
Magna Carta 21-22, 26
Magnum Belgii Chronicon 46
Mainz 23
Malplaquet 58
Malta 157
Manor of Whitfield 137
Marches of Ancona 24
Marechal 102
Margaret of Bohun 31
Margaret of Daventie 32
Margaret Taaf of Dublin 32
Marriage 10-11, 26, 42, 45, 51, 53, 102, 105, 109, 123, 129
Marseilles 18
Marshal of France 37
Marshal Trivulce 92
Marshall, William 112
Martel, Charles 42, 44, 86
Martin V 47
Mary of Bethune 129
Mason of London 61
Mass 12, 32, 35, 45-48, 56, 60, 92, 135, 156
Master of France 13
Master of Game 137
Maud 45
Maximilian 27
Meaux 19
Mediterranean 140, 147
Melior 32
Meller 6-7
Melun 91
Menestrier 55
Merchants 28, 132, 139
Merovius 88

Mersen 87
Messer 56
Metz 17-18, 23, 44, 87
Meuse 20, 87
Michael, Venerable Father 61
Michaelmas 61
Middle East 72, 81, 142, 144, 152
Milan 19, 67, 77
Millon 17
Mons-en-Puelle 26, 90
Monseigneur 45, 56
Monstrelet 83
Montfort 44, 93
Montgomery 109, 113
Monthermer, Edward 31
Montmorency 157
Moors 12, 28, 53, 81, 86, 125, 149
Moravia 87
Morel 82
Moselle 20, 24, 87
Moslems 6, 15, 52, 78, 86, 88, 111, 125, 137, 139-140, 142, 144, 147-150, 152
Mossen 56
Moulin 18
Mowbray 113
Muhammad 140
Mundina Danes 32
Nancy 90
Nantes Parisiennes 19
Naples 44, 124, 132
Narbonne 18
Navaret 93
Nef 130
Nemours 134
Neville, George 132
Nicaea 144
Nicholas 47
Nicolas III 44
Nicolas of Cividale 47
Nicopolis 90
Niemen 150
Nibelungenied 8, 108
Nithard 98
Nile 149
Nîmes 18
Nineveh 97
Norman Conquest 21, 64, 73, 88
Normandy 15, 17, 21, 35, 53, 64, 73, 83, 85, 88, 100, 102, 111-112, 117, 122-123, 129, 134, 144
Norsemen 70
Northampton Castle 134
Norway 8
Nottingham Castle 73, 134
Noyon 18, 70
Nuremberg 23, 100
Odin 64
Odoacer 88
Offa 142
Oliver 33
Olympus 126
Ordene de Chevalerie 10, 36, 48
Order of Calatrava 128
Order of Cordeliers 127-128
Order of St. Michael 157
Order of St. John 128
Ordinances of Florence 77
Orkney Islands 78
Orléans 19, 40, 47-48, 88
Ormsbro Castle 135
Ostrogoths 12, 86
Otterburn 67
Otto 13
Ottoman Turks 152
Oxford 21
Painted Chamber 83
Palaeologus, Michael 148
Palestine 89, 140, 142, 144, 147-150
Paraclete 136

Paris 19, 28, 36, 56, 74, 98, 113, 116-117
Paris, Matthew 74, 98
Parliament 22, 24, 56, 117
Parma 24
Patriarch of Aquilea 47
Pavia 19, 76, 92
Pax Romana 12
Penance by Proxy 60
Pentecost 42, 45, 113
Perche 102
Perigeux 18
Perigord 22
Perseigne 139
Persians 70, 140, 144
Peter 13, 18, 22, 26, 48, 60, 70, 93, 111, 142, 144, 147
Petrarch 128
Peur 27, 55
Pfahlburger 23
Philip 22, 26, 35, 40, 44, 69, 89, 91, 98, 109, 111, 144, 147-148, 150
Philip Augustus 26, 89, 147-148
Philip I of France 44, 144
Philip II of Spain 109
Philip III 22
Philip IV 26, 98
Philip of Savoy 91
Philip of Valois 26, 40, 111
Philip-Augustus 19, 22
Philippe 89-90, 108
Philippe of Valois 89-90
Picardy 142
Pierrefonds 17
Piers Gaveston 69
Piers Plowman 48
Pightesley 137
Pilgrimages 140, 142
Pisa 149, 152
Plaisance 91, 111-112
Plantagenet, Geoffrey 42, 45-46
Ploermel 111
Plommées 77
Poitiers 26, 73, 86, 90-91, 93, 154, 156
Polo, Marco 152
Pompeii 31
Pont-de-Comines 77
Pont-sur-Seine 21
Pontefract 83
Pontificate Romanum 55
Pope Adrian 12-13
Pope Adrian I 12
Pope Innocent II 74
Pope Innocent III 26, 148
Pope John XII 13
Pope Leo III 12-13
Pope Urban II 142, 144
Porter 94
Portinari, Beatrice 120
Potentia Demonum 62
Pré-aux-Cleres 18
Prelates 48, 91, 138
Près 16, 18
Presenting arms 56
Prince Bohemond 144
Prince Edward 111, 149
Prince Louis 22
Prince of Antioch 44
Priors Gonfalionieri 77
Prohibitions 92, 98
Prosper Mérimée 94
Provençal 18
Provence 8, 10, 21, 35, 53, 126
Prussia 60, 150
Psalter 16, 113
Ptolemais 140
Pugny 21
Queen Marguerite 82
Queen Mother 157
Queen of France 82, 126
Queen of Naples 44

Queen Phillipa 61, 133
Queen-Regent 26
Quelus 156
Quicherat 31
Raimond of Montdragon 15
Raimond of Venous 133
Ralph of Courci 70
Rambaut, Bertram 133
Raoul of Cambrai 138
Ratisbon 23
Ravenna 84
Raymond 78, 81, 144
Raymond of Toulouse 144
Red Count 56
Red Cross Knights 147
Red Hat Inn 18
Redeemer 136
Regnault 44
Relever 94
Religion 35-37, 46, 52, 88, 118, 121, 124, 136, 140, 156
Renaissance 6, 91-92, 97, 142
Renaud of Montauban 42
René 108
Rennes 97, 134
Republic 13, 23, 77, 122
Reynold of Ruy 109
Rheims 11, 18, 91
Rhine 20, 24, 26-27, 87
Rhineland 11, 23
Rhodes 152
Richard 8, 32, 35, 61, 64, 67, 69, 72-74, 81-83, 98, 111-112, 132-133, 146-148, 152
Richard Coeur de Lion (Richard I) 64, 67, 69, 72-74, 82-83, 98, 133, 146-147
Richard II 32, 35, 61, 111, 132
Richard III 32
Richard of Devizes 73
Richard Wagner 8
Rigaud 134
River Seine 18
Robert of Blois 45
Robert of Flanders 144
Robert of Lemblancai 45
Robert of Normandy 111
Robert of Severino 42
Robert of Shirland 83
Roger of Gaugi 113
Roger of Hoveden 98
Roger of Trumpington 69
Rohan 31
Roland 33, 62, 111
Romains 18
Roman Empire 6, 11-13, 94, 140, 142
Roman Equites 122
Roman of Rou 83
Romanus Diogenes 140
Rome 6, 8, 11-13, 15, 19-20, 24, 27, 31, 41, 45, 48, 53, 55, 70, 72, 77, 83-84, 86-88, 94, 120, 122, 132, 140, 142, 148, 151
Roncevaux 87
Rosebecque 27
Rouen 45, 62
Round Table 49, 125
Rovere 91
Rowland 111
Roy of Harrarunz 133
Rudolf of Hapsburg 27
Rudolf of Montfort 44
Saint-Inglebert 109-110
Saint-Denis 16, 113
Saint-Germain 16, 18
Saint-Gilles 78, 81
Saint-Martin 16
Saint-Quentin 18
Sainte Vierge 139
Saladin 48, 145-148

Salic Franks 11
Salutati, Benedetti 132
Sampi 109-110
San Romano 91
Sancho III of Castile 128
Sappho of France 128
Saracens 15, 52, 78, 137, 140, 149
Sardinia 149
Sarmatians 84
Saxon 8, 17, 23, 55-56, 64, 73, 87-88, 111, 142
Scandinavia 117
Schaffro 83
Scheldt 87
Scotland 21, 27, 32, 72-74, 77, 90, 105, 136, 151
Scourge of God 88
Scouts 74
Scythians 84
Seals 15, 72
See of York 132
Seigneune of Ardes 46
Seigneur of Saint Yen 44
Seljuk Turks 140, 142
Senlac 83, 111
Senlis 19
Sens 18, 91
Serbia 88
Servatus 84
Sheppey 83
Shields 21, 35, 37, 39-40, 44, 48, 50-51, 55-56, 63, 69, 72, 81, 84, 102, 104, 106, 108-110, 112-113, 116, 121-122, 128
Sibyl of Anjou 128
Sicily 8, 56, 64, 73, 88, 100, 108, 132
Sidon 147
Sienna 91
Silk 48, 56, 69, 132-134
Simnel 132
Simon of Montfort 22, 47-48, 95
Simon of Namur 60
Sire 48, 105, 117
Sire of Beaumanoir 117
Sire of Preuilli 105
Slavonian 11
Soissons 18
Song of Roland 111
Spain 8, 10, 12-13, 35, 56, 60, 76, 78, 84, 86, 92-93, 109, 117, 128-129, 140, 150, 152
Spiers 23
Splendor 108, 125, 134
Spurs 15, 28, 30, 42, 44, 46, 48, 51, 72-73, 121, 123
Squires (see also Esquires) 7, 30, 32, 36, 39-40, 42, 45, 47, 49-51, 53, 56, 69, 72, 81-82, 88, 104, 109-110, 112, 115, 118, 130, 133, 138
Squire of Honor 39
St. Albans 83
St. Basil 62
St. Bernard 147
St. Edmundsbury 83
St. Elizabeth of Hungary 32
St. Evroul 78
St. Francis 128
St. James of Compostella 49, 128
St. Jerome 142
St. John 42, 47, 111, 128, 147, 150-152
St. Julian 63
St. Just 60
St. Katherine 45
St. Laurence 52
St. Louis 10, 22, 26, 44, 67, 72, 117, 137, 139, 149
St. Palaye 137

St. Paul 61
St. Paula 142
St. Peter 13, 18, 26, 147
St. Remigius 11
St. Thomas 62, 111
St. Thomas Aquinas 62
Staffordshire 136
States-General 27, 89
Statute of Arms 133
Ville-neuve-le-Roi 19
Ville-neuve-les-Avignon 19
Villiers 60
Vincennes 56
Violence of tournaments 112
Virgil 139
Virgin Mary 10, 18, 53, 90
Visigoths 86, 88
Vistula 150
Vitoy 140
Vivien 33, 44
Wace 83
Wales 73, 132
Walsingham 124
Walter 53, 144
Walter of Birklede 53
Warwick Castle 83
Welsh 137
Wenceslaus of Bohemia 134
Westminster 47, 61
White Knight 56
Whittlebury 137
Wiericx Brothers 59
Willebad 142
William of Holland 46
William of Montagu 91
William of Newburgh 136
William of Normandy 21, 85, 88, 111, 144
William of Orange 44
William of Toulouse 63
Windsor 69, 112, 135
Wines 39, 132
Women 7, 22, 32, 36, 49, 51, 53, 111, 115-116, 125-129, 132, 151
Worcester 31
Wurttemberg 87
Wycliff 139
Yeuley, Henry 61
York 21, 132, 137
Yseult 138
Yvain Charnelz 111
Yvaroux 129
Zara 148
Zeno 88
Zulpich 11